EAT
RIGHT

EAT RIGHT

Nick Barnard

Photography by Jenny Zarins

KYLE BOOKS

This book is for my wife, Camilla, and our children, Max and Emily.

First published in Great Britain in 2016 by

Kyle Books, an imprint of Kyle Cathie Ltd
192–198 Vauxhall Bridge Road,
London SW1V 1DX
general.enquiries@kylebooks.com
www.kylebooks.com

10 9 8 7 6 5 4 3 2 1

ISBN 978 0 85783 293 1

Designer: Julian Roberts
Photographer: Jenny Zarins
Food Stylists: Linda Tubby and Annie Nichols
Props Stylist: Alison Roberts
Project Editor: Sophie Allen
Copy Editor: Stephanie Evans
Editorial Assistant: Hannah Coughlin
Production: Nic Jones, Gemma John and Lisa Pinnell

A Cataloguing in Publication record for this title is available from the British Library.

Colour reproduction by ALTA Printed and bound in China by C&C Offset Printing Co., Ltd.

CONTENTS

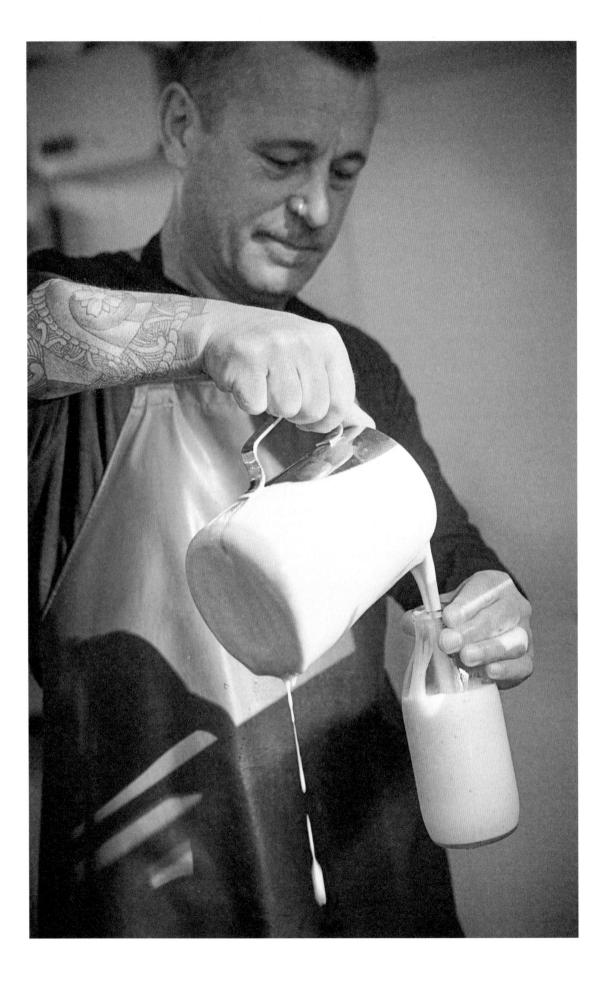

EAT RIGHT

A modern approach to traditional foods

GOOD FOOD SOURCING, STORING AND PREPARATION, combined with an inherited understanding of nutrition, are what our ancestors knew all about. Thousands of generations of pre-industrial societies, whether hunter-gatherers, farmers or urban dwellers, created a legacy of traditional food knowledge that we have spent the past few decades ignoring, rejecting and inevitably forgetting.

Our ancestors were not anxious or fearful about the nature of foods and whether they were healthy or not; their primary focus was on finding enough food for survival. Until very, very recently indeed, the human race has spent its entire existence in a more or less constant state of feast and famine. In much of Asia, the greeting is not 'hello', but 'have you eaten?' or, more accurately, 'have you eaten rice?' such was the overwhelming preoccupation with ensuring you had enough food to live, as well as the great priority placed on food as an integral part of social life and well-being.

Now, in a time of food plenty, we have become disoriented and confused about the nutrient value of food, and dislocated and separated from the origin of foods. There's an obsession with simplistic, brusque and addictive flavours, as well as an expectation for year-round variety and relentless innovation and novelty. We laud and expect convenience and cheapness, and yet, despite all this so-called food sophistication, there's a universal sense of unease, as more and more people realise that modern mass-produced processed foods and drinks are not giving us a healthy relationship with food, or healthy nourishment from it, which our ancestors took for granted.

Over the past 100 years or so we have been engaging in the most destructive food experiments of all time. We have been lured into eating attractive, tasty, cheap and convenient foods and drinks, more often than not made addictive by concoctions of highly refined sugars and fats and, of course, salt, as well as umami flavourings such as monosodium glutamate – MSG. In so many ways we no longer know which foods and drinks to trust.

The signs of disenchantment with, and fatigue from, highly processed nutrient-poor foods are increasing. The thriving interest in sustainably grown foods, in farmers' markets, in truly local provenance and in making seasonal choices reflects an underlying trend towards making better, and more informed, food decisions. Without realising it, we are beginning to reawaken and participate in the wise traditions of our ancestors and to rediscover and appreciate the pleasures and true nutritional values of our ancestral foods.

Don't mess with food

It's crucially important to rediscover ingredients and foods that have not been spoilt or altered out of recognition by overprocessing and refining. Our pre-industrial, largely pre-urban ancestors had a simple diet: it was seasonal, local and organic – regardless of income. They were enjoying truly natural ingredients that they ate raw or cooked, fermented, sprouted or salted, according to regional, local and family customs. They followed time-honoured and proven traditions, which, in Europe, included a diet of unrefined animal fats, carbohydrates from a variety of styles of breads and gruels, fresh protein and fat from the flesh and vital organs of local and very specific breeds of sheep, goats, pigs and cattle, marine creatures and fresh water fish, as well as raw milk and fermented dairy such as yogurt and cheese. Vegetables and fruits were all local and very seasonal, and fermented for storage during the hungry winter months. All of which, when nature was kind, provided an ever-changing variety of sources of nourishment tempered by a healthy respect for the seasonal bounty, and the inevitable paucity that followed, of nature's gifts of food. Nothing was wasted.

Knowledge about origins and a relationship with the farmer

We have really lost our connection with farmers. We have grown accustomed to having our poultry, meat, dairy products and vegetables offered to us by supermarkets in plastic packaging. It's time to create a new relationship of trust, support, enquiry and, hopefully, enthusiasm for their work and produce. Find farmers you can trust, who produce flavoursome, nutrient-dense, high-quality foods sustainably. Visit their farms and, when you see them at the farm shop or farmers' market, thank them.

Let's also bear in mind how we can help farmers make a better and more sustainable connection with nature. For decades, the majority of farmers have pursued what are really industrial production-style goals, using chemical science and reductionist, false and unsustainable accountancy methods, long-distance supply chains and cheap fossil fuels. Government grants have encouraged specialisation, monocultures, and the use of artificial fertilisers and pesticides for short-term commercial success. This goes entirely against nature. Once you know what you are looking for, you'll be able to support not only the enlightened farmers, but by your selective shopping habits, send a clear message to all farmers as to what constitutes nutrient-dense, ancestral and sustainable foods.

Our pre-industrial and largely pre-urban ancestors lived on a diet that was simple: it was seasonal, local and organic – regardless of income.

Nutrient richness, flavour and satiety

Once you select foods and drinks by following the simple but proven values of our ancestors, you not only liberate yourself from a dependency on, and an addiction to, processed foods, but you retrain your taste buds too. Nutrient-dense, well-grown, fresh or properly prepared unprocessed foods have more flavour. It takes a while to wean yourself from the mouthfeel of processed foods designed and formed for mouth pleasure and superficiality with their obvious refined sweetness and saltiness, with added cheap fats; manufacturers really do know how to hook you with unnatural taste cues and false nutrients. In short, they construct addictive foods and drinks that appeal to our base instincts for instant pleasure, rather than nourish our health or well-being.

One of the most significant reactions to switching from refined and processed foods to eating right, other than the sensory pleasure from discovering or rediscovering true flavours, is the need to eat less. Ancestral foods are so much more nutrient dense. Just a small bowl of soaked or sprouted oat porridge with a wedge of melting ghee at breakfast will keep you feeling full until lunchtime. There's only so much pork belly, with a side of kimchi, you can eat before you feel satisfied and replete with living flavours and nourishment. You will eat less, snack less (if at all), waste less, reuse more, and you will look forward to making, preparing and sharing foods and drinks that make you feel energised and alive; in short, if you eat right, you will feel brilliant.

A storecupboard of traditional foods

Choose your foods and drinks like you chose your wine – you like to know the grape, the country, the region and the producer – why not apply the same rigour to all your foods and beverages? When you ask these questions you will be surprised at what you discover, and it's a delight to reclaim a relationship with provenance, nourishment and flavours.

Dairy

Seek out small producers who know their cows personally. Try some raw milk – neither pasteurised nor homogenised, and preferably from cows that are predominantly pasture reared – it tastes infinitely better, which is why cheese made from raw milk is so full of flavour. If not raw, then buy pasteurised milk that's not been homogenised or fat reduced in any way. Spread your butter thick; after all, bread and toast are merely carriers for butter. In Denmark they say you should be able to see the teeth marks in the layer of butter on the bread, which is why it's called tooth butter or, in Danish, *tandsmør*.

Meat

Eat meat from time to time, appreciating the sacrifice made by the animal for our health and well-being. Try to choose from pastured traditional breeds raised in small herds and flocks. Find out more about the nature and qualities of traditional breeds. We can learn from the Inuit who offer respect and love when they catch their food, thanking the creature for finding them. Seek out farmers who understand this, who feed their animals what they are suited to eating, which is predominately grass, and who provide a welfare that is gentle and understanding.

Fats

Follow tradition and select your fats in the style of your ancestors. Mainstream nutritional science is beginning to realise that demonising traditional animal fats such as butter, lard and tallow was appallingly irresponsible. Reject any refined oils and embrace all types of fats from pastured animals, as well as the extra virgin oil from olives and tropical fats, especially raw coconut oil.

Fish

Appreciate and relish the taste and freshness of wild fish, and be mindful of the local fishermen, who forage as hunter-gatherers for our marine foods, rather than farm it (see page 189).

Eggs

An egg is a remarkable package of energy and goodness designed to nourish a chick from conception to cracking open its own shell. So choose the best-quality eggs from sprightly hens that are genuinely living outside, pecking for worms and grubs in pastures and mud.

Fermented, smoked and salted

We have lost our sense of taste for these traditions which are not only embedded in our family histories but locked in our collective consciousness. Before refrigeration, we stored food and drinks for the lean months of winter and early spring using these techniques, which also serve to enhance their nutritional value and to introduce bacterial variety to our microbiome. Try to eat some fermented foods every day – your digestion system will love you for it.

Sprouting

A seed is full of potential energy. When dormant, most seeds protect themselves from being digested; after all they want to survive, grow, flower and produce more offspring. However, a sprouting seed is no longer a seed, it is a plant and through that miraculous transformation locked-up nutrients are released in a most extraordinary way (see page 98–101).

Grains

In all of human history we have never eaten so much refined grain as we do now, or, paradoxically, fed our animals so much

grain – and the same grains, over and over again. For easy digestion, goodness and flavour, look out for traditional breads such as wild fermented sourdoughs or breads made from sprouted grains. Get to know the ancient and traditional grains, such as spelt, buckwheat and rye, for these are grains that have escaped being the focus of plant breeding solely for the unsustainable and nutrient-deprived world of industrial farming and monoculture. Choose flour made from sprouted grains for better digestibility and nourishment, or grains that have been freshly milled at your local mill; these will be less likely to be rancid or lacking in nutrients, which is often the case with grains intended for long-term storage. Or buy a small hand mill and mill your own flour, fresh every time.

Lots of vegetables...

Enjoy your veg, both in variety and quantity – they are surprisingly sweet. Follow the seasons in your region. In spring, your body is craving to wake up from the heaviness of winter with the invigorating sprouting growth of the first salads, wild garlic and chives. Enjoy the energy of the summer's sun, right through to early autumn, in a feast of plenty. Hunker down in winter with the root crops and enjoy fermented vegetables. Select biodynamic or small-scale organic, or truly responsible and sustainable farming

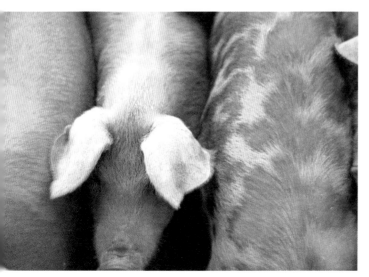

Try some raw milk – it tastes infinitely better, which is why cheese made from raw milk is so full of flavour.

methods. Fresh produce is more nutrient dense and flavoursome when picked and then eaten in as short a time as possible; local produce direct from the farm to you is therefore best. Think variety as well as seasonality; many Asian cuisines propose that every meal should be presented with, or centred on, a medley of vegetables prepared in a myriad of ways – raw, sprouted, cooked and fermented – this is a very wise practice indeed.

...and a little fruit

Like grain, we are eating and drinking more fruits, fruit sugars and fruit juices than ever before, and all year round too. This is very strange, and not ideal. Our bodies, particularly the liver, struggle to handle this onslaught of fructose, particularly when it is derived from refined fruit sugars and highly processed fruit juices. Traditionally, we are hardwired to enjoy a glut of fresh seasonal fruits, and a year-round appreciation for fermented and dried fruits, sparingly. In very recent times we have grown accustomed to finding tropical

and Mediterranean fruits, such as bananas, pineapples and oranges, throughout the year and even in the winter months. Fresh fruits such as these, if they come from a sustainable source and are grown for flavour and nutrient density, are a wonderful treat, rather than something we consume every day. Try this ancestral way and you will appreciate fruit for what it is, a sweet gift of the summer's sun.

Wild sweetness

Natural sweeteners are needed only sparingly, so buy the best, either wild or unrefined, and enjoy their exquisite flavours and nutrient complexity. Wild sources of sweetness, such as raw honey or maple syrup, are ideal. Or choose from a selection of unrefined sugars such as blackstrap molasses or date syrup, rapadura, date palm, maple or coconut palm sugars.

Drinks

The popular drinks today, most of which are free from nourishment, would be completely alien to our ancestors, who revelled in making their local, or family, often mildly alcoholic fermented brews, including very real ales and cider. Some have become fashionable of late, such as kombucha (fermented tea) and kvass (fermented grains and fruits), dairy kefir (fermented milk) and water kefir (fermented sweet water). All of these traditional beverages are included in this book (see Drinks, pages 194–325). They have complex, sweet-sour flavours, and they are always lightly effervescent. It seems that yet again we are hardwired to foods and drinks that are part of our ancestral culinary tradition, because the universal appeal of sparkling industrial soft drinks taps into our innate recognition and trust that a fizzy beverage is a nourishing one. And remember to filter all your tap water and use it fresh.

It really is easy to eat right by reacquiring some of the lost skills, attitudes and techniques that have sustained and properly nourished people throughout human history. None is complicated or costly, or technologically dependent. Inevitably, we are moving to a post-industrial age in terms of the food we prepare and consume. This is because we are beginning to doubt and challenge the industrial processes and techniques that produce so much convenience food at such a low cost. Take a look at the labelling on any packaged food or drink: if it lists processes or ingredients you do not recognise or cannot pronounce, would not understand or keep in your kitchen, then why on earth would you eat it? What we eat and drink makes us what we are. Without doubt we will be fitter, happier and healthier once we are fully responsible for, and aware of, what we eat. Welcome to a new relationship of love and respect for nature's gift of food and drink.

The true value of food

THESE ARE STRANGE TIMES INDEED for our relationship with food. We have become disconnected with not only the nutritional value of food and the central importance of food as a life-giving gift of nature, but we have also become horribly demanding, as well as downright mean, when it comes to the true value and cost of food.

It's worth remembering that we are spending less of our wealth, proportionately, than ever before on food. In recent times we were spending up to a third of our income on food. Now it's less than ten per cent. We are also spending less time seeking out and selecting our foods, and less time cooking and sharing food with family and friends. We are also eating more and more processed foods. In the USA, for example, about 90 per cent of all foods purchased are processed.

Since the Second World War, we have been led to believe that cheap, readily available sources of food are our right, and in more recent decades, that food should not cost more but, increasingly, less. So now we have year-round ready access to cheap chicken, bread and milk, and a veritable orgy of choice in ready meals and convenience foods, shouldn't we be happy, healthy and thankful? Not a bit of it. In fact, it's just the opposite.

All around us there is a growing sense of fear, frustration, dismay and anger about food and the world of food. Let's take one at a time.

Fear
As we become more aware of the crucial relationship between the quality and nutrient density of what we eat and our health, we're not equipped or experienced enough to be able to make decisions based on a foundation of proven traditional food knowledge. So we become anxious, usually about what constitutes healthy food; about food combining, about the healthfulness of staples such as grains and dairy produce, about how much water to drink, about eating meat and about the real value of organic food.

Frustration
It's chaos out there in the food description world as national and regional authorities attempt to pursue clarification and control over claims, just as food corporations become more and more glib and cunning over the use of such reassuring but meaningless descriptions as: natural, real, healthy, goodness, wellness, energy, sustaining, vital, original, simple and nourishing.

Dismay
Many find themselves dismayed by the lack of clarity and independent thinking on the part of governments and their health advisers in their efforts to provide a consistent framework for advice on food and how it inextricably affects our health, and the inability to control powerful food

corporations and their lobby groups. The heart sinks on learning just how poor the provision of truly nourishing food is in places where it is most needed, such as schools, hospitals, homes for the elderly and prisons.

Anger

There are perhaps two key forms of emotion at play here: anger at a personal and selfish level, and on a bigger, more meaningful scale, when we consider the harm done to nature and the land.

We feel anger, selfishly, on discovering that we have been misled, misinformed and misguided; for example when we belatedly realise that pastured butter and eggs are fundamental building blocks in our diet, and not occasional, fat-rich foods to be anxious about. Or when we realise that the food that we willingly place in our bodies is an act of intimate trust, one that has a direct relationship with, and impact on, our wellness. How obvious is that? Think about it; only sex is as intimate a relationship.

At a less personal level, but fundamental to our wellness and survival, is the rage we feel when we become aware of the dramatic and destructive impact of our pursuit of cheap, convenient and tasty foods on our environment – particularly on our soils, our farms and their farmers. What price is cheap enough for milk? Milk is often less expensive than bottled water. How can this be justified, let alone sustained? The solutions on offer are grotesque for the natural world and our health; mega dairy farms and highly processed milk. Easy access to raw milk is a fundamental building block for rebuilding our world of traditional, nourishing foods: fight for it.

In short, we have become dependent on others to guide us, serve us, cure us and please us, and so we have lost our independence, as the memories of our ancestral and traditional foods have been put to one side, in the pursuit of convenience, pleasure and personal gain. For too long we have unwittingly but inexorably allowed ourselves to be duped; in many ways we have been sleepwalking down the supermarket aisles, all the while being encouraged to shop as creatures of habit.

It's time to regain a relationship with, and a respect for, food. It's time to break the shackles of dependence and weakness, and to regain our independence and freedom. Once you do this, you will feel free, alive and thankful. The process is simple. It comes through a combination of enquiry and learning, of challenging and speaking out in order to know more and therefore to be able to make better, informed decisions about what we put in our bodies that will nourish us and make us well and strong. We'll also be reawakening our simple preparation and cooking skills, and in doing so reclaim the timeless enjoyment that goes with preparing and sharing meals with family and friends.

As well as acquiring knowledge, skills and control, it's also time to reject and ignore those foods that have led us astray. When we stop purchasing nutrient-poor processed foods, we send a simple commercial message to producers and their suppliers, and their retail customers. Their model for corporate survival is relentless growth. Turn off their income and they are in disarray. You cannot suddenly repurpose a massive corporation that sells cynically addictive, great-tasting, but nutrient-deprived foods and drinks into a wellness company with values that can be trusted. Instead, we need to kick away their financial support. It's time to end the cosy relationship that the food giants thought they had control of.

So next time you make a value judgement about the food you buy, consider the following:

· What is the value of one's health and the well-being of our family and friends?

· What is expensive? Is it expensive to us, but a poor reward to nature, to the planet?

· What is the calculation of food costs based on? Sadly, they are based on a set of reductionist economics that does not represent the true cost of food in relation to a sustainable and symbiotic relationship with nature. Very little of the profit in food production cascades back down to replenish nature, and in particular to the disappearing and increasingly impoverished soils that we have abused for centuries and that we naively consider to be an everlasting resource.

· What is the value of the processed food that many of us eat a lot of the time? It has poor nutrient and well-being value, and is entirely destructive to the value chain between soil and plate. Farmers receive a fraction of the retail food prices when sold as a commodity or through the modern and completely unsustainable supply chains.

· When you witness a member of the public whingeing to a farmer at a farmers' market, comparing prices between the very fresh pastured eggs and the industrial farmed eggs in the supermarket, feel the farmer's pain at how to explain this differential.

· Waste? In the UK we throw away at least 30 per cent of all food, but at least, hopefully, it's mostly processed food.

· Value? A pastured chicken will nourish and sustain a family of four for at least four meals, such as a roast, cold cuts, stock, soup and risotto. Compare that with packaged, prepared, marinated chicken breast fillets. What is the price of true nourishment?

· Energy and nutrient density in food – you have to eat more of a processed food to match the nutrient profile, density and nourishment of foods that have not been messed with.

Food is not a consumer durable, it is nature's precious and fragile gift to us. Embrace and celebrate that gift.

TECHNIQUES

Dairy kefir

500ml fresh raw milk from pastured cows or, at worst, organic pasteurised milk from pastured cows that has not been homogenised and is not fat reduced in any way

Approx. 3–5g dairy kefir grains (SCOBY) from a friend or purchased online

Equipment

750ml jar with lid

Storage jar, medium-sized

Muslin and cooking twine if you're keeping your grains in a little sack

THERE'S A LOT OF CONTROVERSY surrounding the nutritional and health benefits of cow's milk. One fact is certain: most people the world over are intolerant of the milk sugar, lactose. Go west of Budapest, and most people can digest lactose and do drink milk; go east, and there's no history of drinking fresh milk, but there's often, when there are dairy herds about, a thriving appreciation for fermented and cultured milks, such as kefir and yogurt. How come? It's because the lactose in fermented milks has mostly been broken down to lactic acid, creating that classic sour taste and aiding digestion. Fermented milk also has better keeping qualities than fresh milk.

Kefir is a fermented drink, traditionally made with cow's, goat's or sheep's milk, which relies on the action of a SCOBY (symbiotic combination of bacteria and yeast). Well-made kefir is refreshing, slightly tart and bubbly (it's very mildly alcoholic). Originating in the Caucasus, the rubbery kefir grains (the SCOBY) resemble clusters of cauliflower florets. When well nourished with a regular diet of fresh milk, the grains multiply quite rapidly, and as dairy kefir is best made with only 5–10 per cent of SCOBY, there's every opportunity to share a growing colony of grains with friends. Otherwise it's possible to buy milk kefir grains online. (Note that there are two varieties of kefir and the other, water kefir (see pages 308–311), is made with a different variety of grain, which cannot be used in milk.)

The microbiological life of kefir grains is particularly wonderful. In theory, when well nourished, they are immortal. Kefir grains grow spontaneously, as a symbiotic combination of bacteria and yeast, of which there are about 30 different varieties in the grains, many of which are not at all understood, known or named. What is completely clear is that making kefir is a small-scale pastime. There is just too much variety and randomness in the kefir SCOBY, resulting in very changeable and unpredictable flavours, textures and effervescence. That's the beauty of fermentation at its best. It's alive, and it's unique at that moment. Try to mass-produce kefir? Forget it. Any widely distributed kefir you see on sale is made from a kefir-like culture in powdered form, in an attempt to replicate the taste of kefir but with a consistency that's unknown in the real thing. It should be called a kefir-like drink.

What, then, are the health benefits of kefir? Well, it retains so much of the goodness of milk, especially if you make it with raw milk, plus the added beneficial probiotic elements from the good bacteria and yeasts present. The grains thrive on the lactose (the milk sugar) and in doing so also increase the vitamin content. It's milk with super powers. When cooking, it's often appropriate to replace buttermilk with kefir (in ice creams, rice pudding, scones, soda bread and milkshakes).

One fact is certain: most people the world over are intolerant of the milk sugar, lactose.

Rhythm

Making kefir is easy. Keeping the grains alive and thriving is all about establishing a rhythm, and fully realising that you're the mother of a set of unique living creatures, a family of micro-pets, in essence. You can make kefir on about a two day rotation, so that, assuming you drink a couple of glasses a day, you will be always enjoying fresh kefir.

Loose grains or grains in a little sack?

The grains can float in the milk as they are, or you can tie them up into a little sack of muslin and drop this into the milk. From time to time you will need to open and remove some of the growing population of grains so that the proportion of grains to milk doesn't exceed 5–10 per cent. When you do this, it will also be time to replace the muslin and string tie. Do give away your surplus or you can pat them dry and freeze them, for future use.

Ferment the kefir

Pour the milk into the jar and add the grains. If you want a faster ferment, let cold milk stand in the jar and come to room temperature before you add the grains.

Close the lid or cover with muslin. Leave out at room temperature, not in direct sunlight. The warmer the ambient temperature, the faster the ferment. Stir from time to time as the grains will sit on the surface, or if sealed, shake the jar. After about 24 hours, the milk will have thickened. If you like your kefir more sour, leave it for longer, until it tastes just right.

Spoon out, or collect the grains in a coarse sieve. Or if you are wise and used a little muslin bag, just lift it out. Transfer the fermented milk to another jar, seal and refrigerate. If you like a fizz, keep it sealed and leave out at room temperature for a few hours, then refrigerate.

Kefir will keep for more than 10 days in the fridge. It will tend to separate after a few days into curds and whey, but will reintegrate readily if you shake or stir it before drinking. Kefir whey is very useful indeed: it's an extremely vigorous starter for fermenting foods, such as sauerkraut and beetroot, and will readily carbonate fermented beverages like kvass (see page 314).

Make more kefir
Rinse your grains or mini sack of grains in fresh filtered water, and you're ready to start again... everlastingly.

Kefir-making time off?
Your grains will thrive and multiply if you make kefir continuously as they are feeding on the nourishment provided by fresh milk.

Longer term – no feeding
Rinse and dry the grains carefully and thoroughly, and freeze them.

Medium to longer term – feeding every 7–10 days
Rinse the grains in filtered water and pop them into a sealed jar of milk. Store in the fridge. Every 7–10 days remove and rinse the grains, feed the fermented milk to a houseplant or garden plant and then return the grains to the fridge in a fresh sealed jar of milk.

Short term – 2–3 days max
Rinse the grains in filtered water and keep them in a sealed jar of water in the fridge.

Coconut kefir

You can ferment coconut milk with your kefir grains. Use tinned or homemade coconut milk (see page 318), or coconut drinks without added sweeteners – in fact without anything added that's unpronounceable or that you wouldn't use in your kitchen.

Make coconut kefir as for dairy. You may find that the kefir grains take a batch to adjust from dairy to coconut. Persevere. However, your kefir grains will require regular feeding with their natural dairy nourishment; revert to dairy milk at least once for every three or four batches of coconut kefir you make.

1. *The kefir grains look like cauliflower florets*

2. *Cut the muslin into a circle*

3. *Drop the kefir grains onto the muslin*

4. *Tie the muslin into a little bag with cooking twine*

5. *Two-thirds fill your jar with milk*

6. *Drop the muslin bag into the milk*

7. *The bag will tend to sink at first*

8. *Seal the jar and leave out at room temperature*

Yogurt

Starter culture – use some unsweetened organic plain yogurt, or acquire an heirloom yogurt culture online or when you next visit your distant relatives in very rural Bulgaria

Fresh raw milk from pastured cows or, at worst, pasteurised organic milk from pastured cows that has not been homogenised and is not fat reduced in any way, or gold top milk that has not been homogenised

THE MAJORITY OF OUR ANCESTORS, certainly until recently, did not possess the luxury of reliable refrigeration in the home. To maintain a year-round supply of nourishing milk-based foods for the times when the cows were dry and for the warmer seasons, they became experts in fermenting and culturing. From this knowledge comes cheese, butter, buttermilk, dairy kefir and, most recent in global popularity, yogurt.

Yogurt is milk fermented by bacteria, and it can vary from semi-solid creaminess to a more solid, set style with some accompanying whey. All versions are slightly sour, or more or less tart. Yogurt is a Turkish word, and its origins reside in the Middle East – indeed, until about a century ago, yogurt was unknown outside the region and all yogurt was made in a family environment, from handed-down, slowly evolving and complex collections of local bacteria. These bacteria are, for the most part, thermophilic, or heat-loving, being active at temperatures typically in the region of 43-46°C.

One of the unexpected commercial benefits of Louis Pasteur's war against all bacteria was the isolation and cultivation of some of the strains of bacteria found in Bulgarian yogurt. These particular strains, usually only two or three, are now used the world over to make yogurt. Such unnaturally simplistic methodology suits standardisation and the profit motive at the expense of variety. It's almost impossible to nurture and recreate yogurt from a previous batch of commercially produced yogurt after a while – it simply doesn't contain the necessary variety, vitality, complexity and ever-evolving combinations of bacteria.

Therefore, each and every batch of most commercially produced yogurt requires a fresh new starter made using a few strains of freeze-dried bacteria. Although a lot of such yogurt may be delicious with a moreish and reliable consistency, it is very much at the expense of natural variety and local adaptation. This is dependency at its worst, reminiscent of the unsustainable and irresponsible international attitude to vegetable seeds and seed grain in the world today. In the pursuit of commercially improved varieties of seeds that will only really thrive if artificial fertilisers and pesticides are applied, we have lost the varieties well adapted, over thousands of years by local breeding and use, to the soils and climate of their locality. Our ancestral heirloom seeds are essential to the security, variety and vitality of our food supplies.

Rant over. Back to yogurt. Once you realise how simple it is to make yogurt successfully you will wonder why you have never made it before, and, hopefully, be inspired to acquire a truly ancestral yogurt culture, an heirloom culture, no less. As with dairy kefir (see pages 22–25), once you begin to nurture a unique and evolving collection of micro-organisms, you're looking after a very special pet, the reward for which is delicious and ever-changing quantities of yogurt, for your lifetime, and that of your children too. There are plenty of thermophilic heirloom cultures readily available online, usually named Bulgarian or Greek. You can also make yogurt with mesophilic bacteria (those active at a warm room temperature), of which the best-known varieties originate from Georgia and the Nordic region. These too are available as heirloom cultures.

You can make yogurt very successfully with raw milk not heated beyond 46°C, but it will never be as thick as a batch made from milk preheated to at least 82°C. One of the most sought-after styles of yogurt is thick and smooth, rather than set, and it's easy to achieve this if you heat the milk first, which alters the structure of the casein, the milk protein. Take a look at the ingredients listed on commercially made yogurt, and often you will find that powdered milk and other thickeners are sneaked in to create a consistent, smooth and thick style. While you're there, check to see whether there are any other unnecessary ingredients. Genuine yogurt, like good bread, has a minimum of ingredients. Milk and some bacteria. That's all you need. And if it's a fruity or fruit-flavoured yogurt, watch out for added refined sugars.

While we are on the subject of ingredients and processing, how is it that there's no cream sitting on top of full-fat yogurt? I'll tell you why. It's because the yogurt has been made with homogenised milk. The homogenisation is a destructive process, where the milk is either forced through a fine mesh at high pressure or smashed between two plates

to break up the fat into smaller, unnatural particles, which will then disperse through the milk, rather than rise to the top as a layer of lovely rich cream. Avoid homogenised milk. There's never been any testing undertaken or consultation with consumers as to the digestibility and true nourishment of the fats created. It is done for commercial gain; there's an improvement in shelf life and of course the milk is a very unnatural optical white from top to bottom in the bottle. How strange is that?

Yogurt is universally touted as a health food, which can be true when it is made with few ingredients and from quality milk. As with other fermented milk products, it's much more easily digested than fresh milk. Firstly, the bacteria digest much of the milk sugar (the lactose) and convert it to glucose and in doing so not only create a sourness, but also make the yogurt available to the majority of people worldwide who cannot digest lactose. Secondly, the presence of enzymes, such as lactase, in the yogurt help to break down the lactose further in the gut and, finally, some of the milk proteins (casein), making the proteins much easier for our digestion systems to assimilate. Yogurt gives us all the benefits of milk, such as calcium, and (if well made) good fats, as well as enhanced access to its protein and vitamins.

Incubating your yogurt

It's worth investing in an electric yogurt incubator, particularly one that allows you to make yogurt in individual pots or jars, complete with a lid. This type of yogurt maker will make what is known as pot-set yogurt. The domestic models are not costly and you don't need anything sophisticated, but it's important that the heating element is reliable, and keeps the yogurt at a steady temperature, no higher than 46°C. Test its accuracy with a jar of milk and a jam thermometer if you have any doubts.

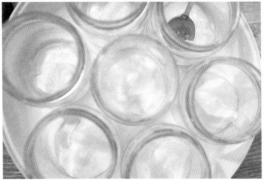

Once you realise how simple it is to make yogurt successfully, you will wonder why you have never made it before.

1. Raw milk method

Let the milk, yogurt (if you're using it as a starter culture) and jars warm to room temperature.

Fill the jars with raw milk and stir into each jar a teaspoon of the yogurt, or activate your freeze-dried starter culture and use as specified.

Combine the starter and the milk thoroughly – some like to whisk them together; a good stir will do.

Turn on your incubator and fill it with your jars. Do not screw on or fit the jar lids; leave the jars open and merely close the incubator lid. This should keep the yogurt at about 42–43°C, and at this temperature your yogurt will have coagulated and be ready in about 4–8 hours – do not stir or disturb the yogurt in the incubator during this time.

When you use unhomogenised milk you will see a layer of cream forming on the top of yogurt. Good. This is particularly delicious and one of the great treats of making your own.

Your yogurt will be ready when, if you lift up one jar and tilt it, the yogurt pulls away slightly from the side of the jar. At this stage it does not look firm or set, but it will thicken once chilled. Switch off the incubator, remove the lid, let the yogurt cool down for an hour or so and then screw on the jar lids and refrigerate. The yogurt will keep for about a month.

If you are using an heirloom culture, reserve some of your yogurt to serve as the culture for your next batch, and the next, and the next...

2. Preheating method

Bring your culture and jars to room temperature as before, but this time slowly and gently heat the milk to at least 82°C, stirring frequently to avoid scalding. The faster you heat the milk the more grainy the result.

Let the milk cool to 46°C or below and then proceed to fill the jars and add the culture, following the instructions above.

Make mine raw – an introduction to milk

Milk is a simple, convenient food. Not many generations ago it was common for all farms, homesteads or smallholders to have a milk cow for their own needs. More recently, one bought milk from a local dairy, and, until about 25 years ago, most milk was sold in glass bottles, and it had an off-white hue with a head of delicious cream.

Today milk comes in a multitude of choices and varieties, promoting the wonders of lower fat, filtering for purity or delivering standards you can trust, yet almost all of it, organic or not, is now a highly refined, blended commodity. As local dairies have closed, milk is now sold regionally and often nationally, from a small number of mega dairies. It's also become unnaturally white. Look again at the shelf when you shop. Row upon row of containers of optical white cow's milk. This is not natural. Cow's milk is never brilliant white.

Study the label. Often your only choice is milk that has been pasteurised and most likely homogenised too – which involves smashing up the milk fat, unnaturally, so that it does not separate from the milk. Pasteurisation was introduced widely a century back, to combat poor or inadequate hygiene on farms and in the dairy trade. It was considered a necessary compromise to improve milk's overall safety; there was, after all, less effective regulatory control, inadequate public sanitation and no refrigeration at the time. The process is simple: the milk is scalded to kill bacteria and other pathogens, then cooled rapidly. Inevitably, and tragically, pasteurisation is indiscriminate – the good as well as any bad bacteria are killed. Is this wise and beneficial? Well, we're beginning to realise, somewhat lamely, but increasingly, that our bodies work best when we coexist in harmony with our own bacteria. Each of us has as many as ten times more bacteria than the total number of cells in the human body and, to be healthy, we have to top up this microbiome with as much bacterial variety as possible, rather than destroy all bacteria in pursuit of so-called food safety. Raw milk is straight from the cow and is not pasteurised or treated in any way, except for refrigeration. When produced to exacting and closely regulated standards, raw milk is an excellent source of the bacterial variety we so badly need.

The right of the citizen to choose to drink raw milk does, however, polarise opinion in a most surprising and unnatural way. It's important to realise that the production and consumption of raw milk is very much a conscious act by both the farmer and the consumer. The controls and standards at the farmgate and the dairy are far more rigorous for raw milk (and its products such as cheese and yogurt) than for pasteurised milk. No dairy farmer would agree to such intervention and rigorous hygiene without having complete faith in the life-giving quality of the raw milk from their herd. This is a wholly responsible, intimate and serious relationship; it's really an old-fashioned handshake, so that from cow to consumer, the raw milk producer is traceable and accountable. Contrast this to the mass-production of pasteurised milk, where, typically, the bulk tanker calls at many farms, collecting and mixing milk, which is then pasteurised in a regional dairy and sold incognito as standardised milk.

At the end of it all, the purchase and consumption of raw milk is a particularly conscious individual decision; no one drinks raw milk unwittingly. Try it. It's a revelation in taste and nourishment. You'll never go back.

Raw milk is straight from the cow and is not pasteurised or treated in any way.

Cream, butter and buttermilk

500ml fresh raw cream, ideally from pastured cows or, at worst, pasteurised cream from pastured cows that has not been meddled with in any way, other than pasteurised

Sea salt to taste, or 5g sea salt, finely ground, or as flakes or grey sea salt crystals (optional)

THE JOY OF COW'S MILK is the bounty of the cream. The cream, being lighter, separates naturally from the milk, and it can be skimmed off, or in a commercial dairy, spun off in a centrifuge, leaving behind the skimmed milk. The cream can then be enjoyed as it comes, or soured, making crème fraîche and also soured cream, or churned into butter, separating the butterfat from the buttermilk. Raw butter is the finest and healthiest of nature's animal fats, and the most benign, as it is produced without any harm to the animal.

Cream, especially that from raw milk, is quick and easy to ferment and churn into butter. Before the invention of the centrifugal separation process, cream would be skimmed from milk, a slow process, and usually collected from two or three days' milking, ensuring that most of the cream waiting to be churned would have soured or lightly fermented, giving the butter its correspondingly sour taste. Today there's a clear divide in tastes for butter; most of the butter of mainland Europe is soured, whereas the butters of England, Ireland and America are not, and indeed, butter in America is known as sweet (cream) butter. Also, European butter typically has a higher butterfat content, up to 86 per cent, whereas butter from America has around 80 per cent. The rest is predominantly water and milk proteins, including milk solids, which burn when hot. For more effective frying at higher temperatures, make and use either clarified butter or ghee, both of which are almost entirely butterfat (see pages 36–38).

Some of the most famous soured butters, with protected producer status, come from France. It's somewhat ironic, therefore, that due to a shortage of butter in the Franco-Prussian wars in the nineteenth century, a Frenchman created the first industrial butter substitute, called oleomargarine. Made from animal fats and offal flavoured with milk, this cheap butter substitute was far more nourishing than its successor, margarine, made from animal fats and hydrogenated vegetable oils, and latterly, from hydrogenated vegetable oils and milk products to produce a spread with a butter taste. Cheap, convenient, possessing a long shelf life and marketed with a religious enthusiasm, it's no wonder that margarine and its fellow butter substitute spreads have been successful in the recent past. Regardless of research showing that margarine is a truly impoverished substitute for butter, you only have to follow the grotesquely complex industrial processes that are required to make the stuff to know never to eat it again. Happily, per capita, consumption of butter is now on the rise again, after decades of decline.

The French have always enjoyed superb dairy produce and top producers in northern France have been justifiably successful in controlling and marketing their AOC butters. That AOC label guarantees the milk comes from pastured cows in designated areas of Normandy, Brittany and

Charentes-Poitou, and the butters are fermented for at least 12 hours. Many producers produce by hand in small batches, some in wooden churns, so that some of the French butter brands have an international gourmet following.

Butter is not pure fat, it is an emulsion of butterfat, milk proteins (including milk solids) and water. It is the milk solids – whether soured or not – that give butter its flavour. Butter is rich in fat, calories and cholesterol, so it's not surprising that butter has been demonised by the anti-fats brigade, despite its happy use for centuries by our ancestors. Most of the saturated fat in butter is metabolised rather than stored as fat, supports our immune system and also helps to balance our levels of bad cholesterol. Crucially, butter, and principally raw butter from pastured cows, contains the fat-soluble vitamins A, D, E and K that we need to maintain good health, as well as the minerals zinc, selenium, iodine, chromium and copper.

Butter is a truly nourishing food and, like eggs, we should eat as much as we want, especially spread as thick as you like on a slice of good bread. Tooth butter for me, please (see page 12). But, like eggs, we should be very selective about the source of this essential food. Fashions in food are truly bizarre; we spend a fortune on boutique, so-called extra virgin olive oils, yet we select butter on price, largely as a commodity. This is crazy. Butter is one of the cornerstones of our health, our pleasure and our cooking, and much of what is on sale provides neither the flavour nor the nutritional qualities that we need. Most butter is mass-produced, made from pasteurised milk collected from a variety of breeds of cows, is often stored frozen for months, and is standardised year round to suit the brand and its flavour profile.

Select and buy butter with the same zeal as you would your natural wine, raw milk cheese and real extra virgin olive oil. Just like olive oil, compare butters and try them on their own. Let a slice melt in your mouth, and taste its rich and varied flavours. Butter is a wonderfully complex animal fat, containing more than 500 fatty acids and 400 volatile compounds, all of which influence its flavours and nutritional quality, and all of which are in turn influenced by the breed of cow, what the animal eats, its welfare, and therefore the quality of its milk and cream. Butter intimately reflects seasonal qualities of the cow's diet; rich grass in the spring makes particularly flavoursome, unctuous and nourishing butter, prized and respected by many of our ancestors as a true superfood, essential for pregnant women and fast-growing babies and children.

It is possible to buy butter that truly reflects the seasons, the breed of cow, and the quality of its food and welfare. Seek out butter from pastured cows that is produced to time-honoured standards and, best of all, raw butter made from raw milk. A farmers' market is a good place to start. Question the farmer, taste the butter, appreciate its individuality and its ever-changing seasonal flavours, and be thankful that small-scale butter production is alive and well. The more you support the producer, the more reliable and sophisticated the product.

Making butter is so easy; if you have access to pastured raw milk, don't hesitate. Not only will you create a truly freshly made seasonal butter, but in doing so, you will also produce raw fresh buttermilk, which is smooth and delicious to drink, quite unlike any store-bought buttermilk. Mass-produced buttermilk is not a by-product from making butter; it is merely pasteurised and homogenised milk that has been inoculated with specific bacteria in an attempt to recreate the real thing. It's viscous and not at all good to drink.

–

Souring cream – more than one method

Straight up Let your cream sit out in a warm place for about 24 hours and up to 48 hours until it thickens and sours. Taste it to be sure. This is, in essence, crème fraîche and you can enjoy it as such.

Yogurt Add 1 tablespoon of live yogurt to the cream and leave in a warm place for 12–24 hours.

Kefir To make the rather glamorous-sounding kefir butter, add 1 tablespoon of dairy kefir (see page 22) to the cream and culture (let it ferment) for 12–24 hours.

Buttermilk Combine 1 tablespoon of fresh buttermilk to the cream and leave in a warm place for 12–24 hours.

Not sour? That's fine. Bring the cream to room temperature before whipping.

Seek out butter from pastured cows that is produced to time-honoured standards and, best of all, raw butter made from raw milk.

Beat

Use a mixer with the whisk attachment: or if you want the exercise, whisk it by hand. This may take up to 15 minutes.

Select a medium speed to whip the cream; within 5–15 minutes, it will thicken, go rather firm, and then in an instant separate into solids and a milky liquid – the buttermilk. You can stop beating now.

Squeeze and press

Collect all the pieces of butter and place them in a sieve, and then pour the buttermilk through the sieve too. Save the buttermilk for drinking, it's so delicious and refreshing, or to enhance so many baking recipes. Refrigerated, it will keep well for at least a week.

If it's a warm day, take a break and put the butter in the fridge to harden a little, it will be easier to handle and press, otherwise continue...

Now alternate between squeezing the butter with your hands to remove as much of the whey and water as you can, and then rinsing it thoroughly under cold fresh filtered water, until the liquid milk protein (the whey) is washed away as much as possible and the water runs clear. Too much whey in the butter will cause it to go rancid within a few days.

Place the butter on a wooden board, or even better a cool slate surface, and knead and press firmly with your hands; a dough scraper is a useful tool here. Keep pressing and kneading vigorously until no more water emerges. If it's too warm, pause, chill the butter and then continue. If you want to add salt, do so now, working it thoroughly into the butter before shaping and wrapping it.

Done. Shape the butter into a roll or slab and wrap tightly in greaseproof paper. Shaping would, traditionally, be done using wooden paddles or a wooden mould, often engraved with elaborate designs, such as beautiful pastoral scenes or the maker's stamp.

Storage

Homemade raw butter will keep for about a week in the coolest part of the fridge if you succeeded in removing most of the whey and water. Butter freezes well, for months.

Salt?

There's no right or wrong when it comes to salted or unsalted butter. It's a matter of preference and tradition: butter from Brittany is renowned for its saltiness, whereas most of the butter from Italy is unsalted. In general, unsalted butter is easier to cook with and means you can control the amount of salt you add to a dish. When you want an exciting salty butter, use unrefined grey sea salt, called 'sel gris'; the blend of rich, smooth fat and crunchy salt crystals is thrilling (it also makes exquisite salty caramel).

1. Beat the cream medium to fast

2. The cream will soon thicken

3. In an instant the cream will separate

4. Strain off the buttermilk

5. Squeeze out the remaining buttermilk and water

6. Wash the butter in cold water

7. Squeeze out the last of the water

8. Press into a container or paper wrapper

Clarified butter and ghee

250g (or more, or less) chilled, unsalted, raw butter from pastured cows, or unsalted pasteurised butter from pastured cows

Chilled butter is much easier to handle. Cut it into small pieces and place them in a small heavy pan – an enamelled cast-iron pan is best.

BUTTER IS MADE UP OF BUTTERFAT, milk proteins and water; namely the milk solids (curds) and the whey. You need to be gentle when you fry with butter or it will burn. Its smoke point is, typically, around 120–160°C, depending on the butter's constituents. The sizzle as the butter hits the hot pan is the water and whey evaporating and bubbling, and what then starts to burn are the milk solids.

When you make clarified butter, you remove pretty much all of the milk proteins, leaving a high percentage of butterfat and some water. Clarified butter has a smoke point between 160–190°C. It's a terrifically versatile animal fat for cooking, with a mild buttery taste. Without the milk proteins, provided it is kept chilled, clarified butter also has a naturally good shelf life of many months.

Ghee is not another name for clarified butter. It is clarified butter that has been heated at a higher temperature and for longer, which not only separates or evaporates the milk proteins but drives off most of the water. Ghee has a higher smoke point, between 200–260°C, making it a very useful animal fat, capable of withstanding high cooking temperatures, and it has a naturally very long shelf life. Chilled ghee easily keeps for a year or more. In India, where ghee originated, you can find aged ghee that is over 100 years old.

Preparing ghee also flavours the butterfat. At higher temperatures the milk solids start to colour and caramelise, infusing the butterfat with the most exquisite caramel fragrance and a caramel nutty flavour. How strong a flavour is up to you, but do not burn the milk solids, otherwise your ghee will taste very nasty. The browning of the milk solids also creates antioxidants, and these contribute to the keeping qualities of ghee.

The stability and keeping qualities of clarified butter and ghee are well understood in warmer regions of the world. Butter is clarified throughout North Africa and the Near and Middle East, and often flavoured with herbs and spices. Throughout the Indian subcontinent the uses and significance of ghee are embedded in the many religions and cuisines; a popular image of the infant deity, Krishna, shows him stuffing his naughty face with ghee balls. Ageing ghee is said to increase its nutritional and healing powers; in the Vedas sacred Hindu texts, ghee is recommended as a source of strength and nourishment for the brain, and it is common practice in India for babies to be given a daily spoonful of ghee; this is much the equivalent of the deeply nourishing habit in the west of a daily spoonful of pure cod liver oil. Why not take both?

To make clarified butter

Warm the pan over a very low heat to melt the butter. Do not stir the butter while you clarify it. Skim off any foam that comes to the surface. This is the whey.

You will see that the white milk solids have separated from the clear golden butterfat and are sitting at the bottom of the pan. Remove the pan from the heat and let it stand to cool a little, about 5–10 minutes.

Either carefully pour off the butterfat into a storage jar, leaving the milk solids in the pan, or, more effectively, line a sieve with a double layer of muslin and pour the clarified butter through the sieve and cloth into a storage jar, leaving behind the milk solids in the muslin (don't throw these out: see left).

Let the clarified butter cool, screw on its lid and store in the fridge. It will solidify when cold.

To make ghee

Warm the pan over a very low heat. Once the butter melts, turn up the heat to medium so that the liquid simmers. Do not let it boil hard or you may burn the milk solids.

The whey will separate out as a layer of rather opaque white foam on the surface. There will be a lot of bubbling and possibly a little spitting; this is the water surfacing and evaporating. Give the ghee a stir while it is actively foaming and bubbling – to help drive off the water and the whey.

After about 5–10 minutes the foaming will disappear and you will be left with some bubbling. Push this gently to one side and you will see the off-white milk solids coalescing on the bottom of the pan.

Don't stir again, and keep an eye on these milk solids. You want them to turn dark yellow (for soft caramel flavours) or medium brown (for nutty caramel flavours), no darker. Remember that when you turn off the heat, the heavy pan and the butterfat retain the heat very effectively, so it's best to remove the pan from the heat just before you achieve the colour you want. Remove the pan from the heat and let it sit for about 5–10 minutes. This gives the butterfat time to absorb the caramel flavours from the cooked milk solids.

Pour off the sweet-smelling and beautifully golden ghee into a glass jar, and take a moment to admire it from the side and to inhale its intoxicating aroma. Allow some of the coloured milk solids to flow into the jar. They will settle to the bottom and will provide you with a caramelised treat to look forward to before you finish the jar. Spoon the rest into a pot and keep in the fridge.

Let the ghee cool, and then screw on the lid and store in the fridge. It will solidify when cold.

Flavoured ghee?

The Indians like to flavour their ghee. Throw in some spices or herbs to cook with the butter, such as chillies, cumin seeds or cloves.

Nothing wasted

Don't discard the milk solids after making clarified butter or ghee. You can flavour cooked vegetables or rice with them, or even smear them on bread. Try the caramel-flavoured solids left from making ghee on rice pudding; they are particularly delicious as a porridge topping.

1. *Let the butter melt over a low heat*

2. *Turn up the heat, the whey will appear on the surface*

3. *Stir to help the water evaporate*

4. *As soon as you see clear bubbles you're nearly done*

5. *Once the milk solids have coloured turn off the heat*

6. *Let the ghee rest, it will absorb the caramel flavours*

7. *Ladle or pour off the ghee, keep the milk solids*

8. *Once cool the ghee will solidify*

Soured milk, or early-stage fermented milk

Fresh raw milk from pastured cows

Let it sour

Raw milk, unless you freeze it, will eventually sour. Even if you keep it chilled in the fridge, it will sour after 7–10 days.

What to use it for

Marinating pork or frozen white fish before cooking

Adding to scrambled eggs or omelettes

Making slightly sour hot chocolate

Kefir or yogurt (see pages 22–25 and 26–29)

Waffles and pancakes, muffins and quick breads

Making a simple soft cheese and whey (see pages 41–43)

MANY RECIPES from traditional European food cultures call for soured or sour milk. Soured milk is exactly what it says: milk that tastes sour as opposed to milk that tastes sweet. If the soured milk originates from raw milk that is clean and safe, then the soured milk is too, it has simply been transformed into a vital and health-giving version of sweet milk. Such a transformation will only take place in raw milk. Fresh raw milk is sweet because of the predominance of lactose, the milk sugar. After a while – the timing depends entirely on the temperature of the milk – the naturally occurring lactic acid bacteria will devour the lactose, creating lactic acid in the process, and hence soured milk.

Soured milk from raw milk that has been well produced is also a deeply nourishing drink one that is commonly enjoyed in Eastern Europe and Scandinavia. So don't discard your raw milk when it sours, consider how you might benefit from its natural evolution.

If you allow raw milk to continue to ferment, the milk will clabber, forming curds (the clabber) and whey, both of which are equally nourishing – the former to make a simple cheese, and the latter, either as a protein-rich drink extremely popular with body builders, or as a baking ingredient or fermenting aid (see left for uses).

What happens if you let pasteurised milk sour? Well, in simple terms, it can't, and therefore won't. When pasteurised milk ages, it does not ferment, it turns bad. Pasteurisation is a heat-treatment process, one that is completely indiscriminate. The heat kills microorganisms, the good, the bad and the indifferent. Therefore, when pasteurised milk develops, there are no natural microorganisms present; no naturally occurring enzymes or bacteria that would ordinarily, in a healthy raw milk environment, co-exist and happily ferment the milk. Soured pasteurised milk is pasteurised milk with added lemon juice or other acid, such as vinegar, and the addition of the acid merely mimics the taste of naturally soured milk. It is putrefying milk that's been soured, or acidified, artificially, and should not be considered fit for consumption by man or beast.

Curds and whey

Makes about 1 litre whey and about 400g simple cream cheese

2 litres fresh raw milk from pastured cows, or 2 litres raw milk yogurt (see pages 26–29)

ONCE YOU DISCOVER the satisfying flavours and health benefits of raw milk you will also be able to create a bountiful selection of foods and drinks because raw milk ferments naturally, or curdles. Raw milk, well produced, is alive with nutrient-dense ingredients evolving in harmony, yet despite the millennia of raw milk consumption, a full assessment of its complex constituents has never been made. What is clear is that, left to itself, the naturally occurring lactic acid bacteria in raw milk digest some of the sugars present and in doing so, create an acidic environment; in this process the liquid milk protein (the whey) separates from the curds (the solid milk proteins and the milk fats).

Curd in its simplest form is cream cheese, and the more whey you remove from the curds, the harder the curds, now called cheese, and the longer you can ferment, develop and preserve the cheese. Whey, by contrast, contains very little milk fat and a lot of milk protein (casein), which in this day and age makes it, especially in powder form, a convenient supplement and tonic for bodybuilders and those wanting a protein-rich diet. Whey is not a modern wonder food – it is another of our ancestral foods that has been put aside in the relentless pursuit of profit, cheap foods, homogeneity, supposed hygiene and the desire for an extended shelf life.

Whey, in its varying stages of sourness, was valued by our ancestors as a food and digestive tonic, and used to soak their grains, enrich their stews and soups, in baking, as a wild ferment culture for preserving vegetables and fruits, and as a starter for fermented drinks. Fresh whey is full of living bacterial cultures that bolster our immune systems by enriching and diversifying the microbiome we all carry in our gut (see page 155); it contains a wealth of beneficial vitamins and minerals, and of course, the protein. Hydrated whey powder is no substitute for fresh whey because it does not contain the live cultures or the heat-sensitive nutrients.

Whey is not only a by-product from making cheese but also yogurt and dairy kefir. Once you have made yogurt (see pages 26–29) you can release the whey by suspending the yogurt solids in a muslin cloth over a bowl and whey will drip slowly into the bowl. The most vigorous and useful whey, ideal as a starter for fermenting drinks, comes from dairy kefir, as it contains lactic acid bacteria as well as yeasts. When you make dairy kefir (see pages 22–25) you will find that after a few days it will curdle and separate, and you can pour off the whey.

Whey was valued by our ancestors as a food and digestive tonic.

Leave out and wait
Leave a jug of raw milk out of the fridge, at room temperature. Dependent on the ambient temperature, the milk will sour and then curdle (separate) within 1–4 days.

Line a large sieve or colander with a clean cotton tea towel or muslin and place it over a large glass or ceramic bowl, such as a mixing bowl.

Pour your curdled milk into the lined sieve; do not stir. The whey will collect in the bowl and the milk solids will remain in the lined sieve. Let it stand for about half a day.

Handle gently and suspend for a while
Now gather up the tea towel or muslin – very gently as you must not squeeze the curds – and tie it as a bag so that you can suspend it either from a hook over the bowl of whey or across a wooden spoon over a jug.

If you squeeze or press the curds they will tend to fall apart, so don't. The whey will continue to drip (for a few hours) from your suspended bag; when it stops, your cream cheese is ready.

Storage
Whey Keep your whey in a glass jar in the fridge; it will keep for a long time, about 4–5 months. Freeze whey in an ice-cube tray and turn out into a freezer bag.

Cream cheese This will keep for about a month in a sealed container in the fridge.

1. Pour off the whey into a colander and bowl lined with a clean tea towel or muslin

2. Let the curds fall into the colander

3. Don't press or stir the curds

4. Let the curds sit in the bowl

5. Gather up the cloth and let the whey drain

6. Suspend the cloth to let the whey slowly drip away

Sauerkraut
Fermented cabbage

The classic German version is plain white cabbage with caraway seeds and juniper berries, but how about:

4 cabbages, white, red or both – red will make the sauerkraut go dark pink

3–4 beetroots, any colours, or all

3–4 carrots

Some chilli peppers

2–3 garlic bulbs

Any of the following also ferments beautifully and tastes wonderful in combination with cabbage:

Celery, celeriac, radishes, sweet peppers, aubergines, pumpkin, winter squash, Jerusalem artichokes, onions, leeks, fresh ginger, fresh turmeric, juniper berries, caraway, mustard, fennel and coriander seeds

Flaked sea salt – about 2 teaspoons per 500g vegetables, but it's not an exact science

Equipment

Some big bowls or, best, 5-litre or bigger plastic food-grade tubs/buckets

Kraut masher or pestle, or a flat-ended rolling pin

Chopping boards

Selection of sharp knives in different sizes

4–6 large (750ml–l litre) pickling or storage jars, with secure lids

SAUERKRAUT (sour cabbage) made as a traditional German recipe, is fermented cabbage with flavourings of juniper berries and caraway seeds. That's one recipe. There are no right or wrong ingredients for sauerkraut, as each family, each maker and each region will have their own recipes, albeit always with a base of cabbage. Let the tradition continue to evolve and thrive, because making sauerkraut is probably, along with mak kimchi (pages 52–55), one of the best ways to discover how simple it is to make your own fermented vegetables, and just how easy it is to become addicted to them. Throughout human history and on all continents, people have been fermenting raw vegetables, and their wisdom and recipes are varied and wonderfully imaginative.

Fermentation is the transformative action of microorganisms on fresh produce, an entirely natural process that our ancestors learned to harness to create nourishing, flavoursome and stable food and beverages. The science behind fermenting vegetables is very simple. All plants harbour a tiny percentage of lactic acid bacteria, which are anaerobic, meaning they do not require oxygen to flourish, alongside aerobic bacteria. Once the plant is harvested and in effect starts to decompose, the anaerobic bacteria thrive and multiply as they feast on the plant sugars, and in doing so produce lactic acid, carbon dioxide (the gas), alcohol and acetic acid.

During the early stages of fermentation, when it's crucial that the vegetables are fully submerged in salted water, there's a lot of fizzing and bubbling, which then rapidly subsides as the environment becomes more acid. It's this lactic acid environment that we're looking for, as it not only makes for great flavours, but it also preserves the vegetables and either enhances or maintains many of their nutrients.

The process of fermenting pre-digests vegetables, breaking down dense and complex nutrients, and making them more bio-available to humans, as well as enhancing levels of B vitamins. Fermentation does not enhance levels of vitamin C, but it does preserve the vitality of this fundamental nutrient for an extended period. Captain James Cook took barrels of sauerkraut on his seafaring voyages as a way of preventing scurvy, known as the scourge of the seas. In his day no one was aware that fermented cabbage was rich in vitamin C, but by including sauerkraut in his crews' daily rations, Cook conquered the disease.

The simple act of preserving vegetables while either enhancing or maintaining nutritional values was a boon to the health of not only mariners, but all communities of temperate regions of the globe, where fresh vegetables were, and remain, largely unavailable during winter and early spring. Before domestic refrigerators, the art of fermenting and

then storing vegetables in the coolest part of the home was fundamental to the health and well-being of people.

Fermenting also enhances the tastiness of foods, by intensifying flavours and aromas; sometimes the result is definitely an acquired taste, such as fermented yak butter in Tibetan tea, or fermented (read: mostly decomposed) fish from the Arctic, or fish sauce used more or less as ketchup in China, but there are many fermented foods, sauerkraut among them, that are internationally popular.

Finally, raw fermented foods are alive, literally, and teeming with a multitude (both in quantity and, often, in variety) of benign lactic acid bacteria. In the modern age when all bacteria are under assault at every turn by antibiotics, antibacterial sprays, wipes and washes, and by the all-destructive forces of pasteurisation and sterilisation, it's fundamentally important that we do all we can to return bacterial variety to what nutrition experts now call our microbiome – the flora in our gut or digestive tract (see page 155). Gradually we are starting to understand that our microbiome is the epicentre of our immune system. We must take positive steps to nurture our microbiome, which we can easily do by including at least one homemade fermented food and drink in our diet every day. Well-made, fermented foods and beverages replenish and renew bacteria and their genetic diversity to our gut cultures.

What about pickling? Well, in the strictest sense of the word, pickling describes the preservation of foods in an acid medium. Until about 70 years ago, all pickles were fermented, but this tradition was broken by the introduction of pasteurisation and the immersion of the heat-treated vegetables in highly acidic vinegar. Modern-day pickles that you can buy, therefore, are not fermented. Far better to make your own.

There's no need to be a purist when it comes to making wild fermented sauerkraut. As long as you start with a base of cabbage you can add other vegetables, spices and herbs to create an ever-changing array of flavours and textures. Whatever your recipe, there are some simple principles and techniques that you should follow to enjoy success.

First, you'll need to chop the vegetables: this breaks them up, increases their surface area to the action of the salt and bacteria, and releases moisture. The next step is to salt and squeeze or pound them. The salt slows down the fermentation and therefore prolongs preservation, and makes the sauerkraut tastier too. Pounding and/or squeezing releases more moisture. Then, you press the chopped and pounded vegetables tightly into a storage jar until there's no air in the jar and the vegetables are covered in the brine. The total immersion of the vegetables in the salty water is essential, because you want only anaerobic bacteria to be at work. Finally, you manage the fermentation; at first the jars need to be kept at room temperature to encourage the fermentation, and then, once they have stopped being so fizzy and gassy, they should be kept chilled to slow down the fermentation.

There's a number of simple tasks involved in making sauerkraut, and if you're making a big batch there's a lot of vegetables to chop. You will be surprised at just how few jars you get from some big heads of cabbage.

Throughout human history, people have been fermenting raw vegetables, and their wisdom and recipes are varied and wonderfully imaginative.

Making sauerkraut is perfect, therefore, for a community or family gathering, especially as the work is so simple that at the same time one can talk, drink beer, munch on some of the fresh vegetables and so on. Historically, sauerkraut making was a big family or community event in the late autumn, filling the storecupboards and cellars for winter. So, how about a sauerkraut party? Everyone gets to go home with a jar full of life and nourishment. Much better than a tea party or a coffee morning.

–

Prepare
For each cabbage, halve and then remove the core, but keep it to one side as it will make a useful plug (see page 48). Remove or peel the skins and outer layers from the other ingredients as necessary. Where required, top and tail and core, removing seeds if you wish.

Shred the cabbage, then chop coarsely. Chop small or finely dice all hard vegetables; there's no exact specification to this, but the harder the vegetable, the smaller the pieces should be.

Salt then pound, squeeze or both
Throw your vegetables and any other herbs, seeds and spices into your bowl or tub, huggermugger, salting as you go. Taste for salt. The mixture should taste salty, no more.

Get your hands into the mess of vegetables, mixing it up and then pressing down with your fists, or mix with your hands to combine and then start pounding with your masher. Keep mashing and pressing; you will see the vegetables start to glisten and sweat. Keep going – you want to see a pool of vegetable-coloured water at the bottom of the vessel.

Jar

Once there's water swimming about, start to jar the mixture. Do this by hand and press down the vegetables in layers; use your masher to help you if it will fit inside the jar. You don't want any air in the jars, so press down hard.

Once the jars are about three-quarters full, you should find that the vegetable water is rising too. This is good. You want to pack each jar with your mixture to about 2.5cm below the top of the jar and the water should submerge the contents. If it does not, pour some of the juice or some filtered water into the jar.

Submerge and seal

You want your mixture to stay submerged but you can't fill the jar to the brim or it might leak or, at worst, explode. This is where the cabbage cores come in useful. Cut them into suitable-sized cubes and lay one in the top of each jar. When you secure the lid the cabbage core plug will press down and submerge the contents. You can discard this plug later.

Label the jars and leave them out at room temperature, on a tray, and in a cardboard box too if you're worried about the volatility of your mixture. You can manage its fizziness by burping the jars.

Burp

For the first few days, release the build-up of carbon dioxide gas by undoing the lids, burping the jars, and then sealing them again. Do this morning and evening. After 3 or 4 days their liveliness will subside and you can cease burping.

Eat and store, or store and eat

You can start eating your sauerkraut when you like, such as when it stops bubbling. If you want to slow down the fermentation and to ensure winter-long keeping, store your sauerkraut in the fridge or a similarly cold place.

Taste and enjoy your kraut as it develops, that way you will be having the benefit of not only different flavours as the sauerkraut ages and ferments, but a constantly evolving selection of lactic acid bacteria too. Long live bacterial diversity in our microbiome.

Salt

We very much take salt for granted and are rarely selective about which type of salt we choose. This is in complete contrast to our ancestors' sentiments. For most of human history, salt has been a life-enhancing substance as well as a preservative, one so highly prized that it was used as a form of currency. The word 'salary' is derived from the Latin salarium and has a connection with the daily preoccupation with the value of salt.

Life enhancing? Our bodies need sodium and chloride, the main constituents of salt, as these are critical for the production of stomach acid (without which we cannot fully digest food) and for the activation of amylases, a group of enzymes that enables the breakdown of starches into simple, easily digestible, sugars. Salt is also fundamentally important for the healthy functioning of the brain and nervous system.

Preservative? Salt, alongside settled agriculture, has allowed for the establishment of civilisations. All traditional peoples discovered ways to extract salt, whether from sea water, rocks or plants. They relied on salt's preservative qualities, which permitted food to be stored during the lean months when fresh produce was scarce or unavailable. Salt is also fundamental for preservation by fermentation; in the early stages of fermentation, salt inhibits the proliferation of putrefying bacteria until there are sufficient lactic acid bacteria at work to create the ideal conditions for preservation.

All salt is derived from the evaporation of a salt water solution. It is extracted either by crushing rock salt derived from the dried-up remains of ancient inland lakes or seas, by pumping pressurised water into underground deposits of rock salt to create a brine, or by evaporating the liquid from the sea or naturally saline inland waters, or pans. Many settlements were founded on, and named after, their local salt works, such as Salzburg in Austria, and in the UK, some place names ending in -wich are linked with a history of salt production, for example Droitwich in Worcestershire and Nantwich in Cheshire.

Unrefined salt contains about 86 per cent sodium chloride and 14 per cent other minerals, and it may well include certain impurities or pollutants from the local sea, air or land. This explains why the purest, most natural sources of salt are prized. Most salt, whether it's described as table salt, or rock or sea salt, is now highly processed and refined to make the salt easier to handle, or whiter, or to remove the other minerals to achieve about 99 per cent sodium chloride – or all three. To remove the other minerals the salt is vacuum evaporated. To make salt whiter, it is bleached. To prevent clumping in the packing machinery, anti-caking agents are added.

In principle, all salt contains the same levels of sodium chloride, or saltiness. What you will be missing when the salt is industrially processed are the other minerals (including sulphate, magnesium, calcium and potassium), and, fundamentally, the extra flavour complexity derived from these trace minerals and any other unique ingredients specific to that source of salt. Sea salt may contain about 70 trace minerals, which are stripped out when salt is processed. It's also worth noting that as well as choosing salt for a specific flavour profile, you can also choose salt by texture too, from very fine and dry, to coarse and wet, to a large flake.

So, select your salt to suit your taste, your cooking needs, your understanding of what constitutes better mineral nourishment, and also what you consider to be a natural substance. You may well find that you'll want to keep a variety; whether exotic coloured rock salts, wet clumping grey sea salt or the finest sun-dried sea salt flakes. Enjoy your salt. You need it.

Tsukemono
Japanese fermented vegetables

1 head of Chinese cabbage

2–3 tablespoons shio-koji (see page 67)

To serve

Tamari, and also try it with some freshly squeezed lemon juice and finely chopped spring onion

Equipment

Large mixing bowl

Kraut masher or pestle (or use the flat end of a rolling pin)

Some glass containers, such as pickling jars with lids, or flip-top jars

THE JAPANESE CULINARY TRADITION is deeply rooted in variety and seasonal availability. Every meal is a medley of cooked, raw and fermented foods, including this dish. Tsukemono means fermented things, and the Japanese lacto-ferment, with enthusiasm and terrific imagination, a great variety of vegetables such as daikon, cucumber, aubergines, Chinese cabbage and plums (umeboshi). Tsukemono is popular as a side dish with rice, as a snack with a glass of beer, and also as a garnish.

Tsukemono can be made in the same way as sauerkraut and mak kimchi, by chopping, pressing and lacto-fermenting in a sealed glass container. The Japanese use a pickle press (tsukemonoki) to make tsukemono, which is a simple arrangement of a vessel with lid and weights, or with a screw-down mechanism to maintain pressure on the fermenting vegetables to ensure there is as little air as possible so that the lactic acid-producing bacteria will thrive.

Chop
Remove the core of the cabbage and trim off any outer leaves that don't look fresh. Chop or shred the rest as finely or as coarsely as you like. Throw all the cabbage into your bowl and add the shio-koji. Work the shio-koji into the cabbage with your hands so that it is as well distributed as possible.

Pound and cram
Mash and press the cabbage with your fists or with a large pestle until the kraut glistens and gives off liquid into the bottom of the bowl.

Cram the cabbage into the jars, pressing down hard to expel as much of the air as possible. Leave about 2.5cm at the top of the jar and make sure that the cabbage is fully covered with its liquid. Top up with some of the liquid left in the bowl or filtered water. Seal and leave out at room temperature for 1–3 days, burping the jars morning and evening.

Enjoy fresh
This fermented cabbage is so delicious when freshly made. It will, though, keep for months in the fridge.

Tsukemono is popular as a side dish with rice, as a snack with a glass of beer, and also as a garnish.

Mak kimchi
Easy kimchi

**Makes approximately
3.75 litres/3–4 good-sized jars**

2 medium Chinese cabbages
(about 3kg), quartered, cored and
cut across into 2.5cm slices

250g coarse sea salt, plus
1 extra tablespoon

Freshly filtered water

1 Asian radish (daikon)

A bunch of spring onions

A bunch of Chinese mustard
(mustard greens)

For the paste

1 garlic bulb, cloves separated
and peeled

5cm piece of fresh ginger, peeled

100g Korean flaked chilli (this
seems a lot, but Korean chilli is
relatively mild)

60ml fish sauce (Vietnamese
or Thai)

60ml shrimp paste (Vietnamese
or Thai)

1 tablespoon rapadura sugar or
coconut palm sugar

Equipment

3 or 4 wide-mouth 1-litre glass
jars with lids

Plastic or rubber food/kitchen
gloves, or 2 serving spoons

MAK MEANS ROUGH in Korean, but here it refers to making kimchi
quickly and conveniently for everyday use. Traditional kimchi, such as
Baechu or Poggi, is made by quartering and salting Chinese cabbage and
then carefully stuffing each leaf with seasoning. This simpler recipe is
more familiar to makers of sauerkraut (see pages 44–49) as the cabbage
is coarsely chopped into small pieces before salting and seasoning.

Well-made kimchi is remarkably addictive, for several reasons. Firstly,
it's spiked with chilli, which is more or less an addictive drug, albeit a
beneficial one. Chilli peppers contain capsaicin, which is a stimulant, as
well as lots of potassium, magnesium and iron. Chillies are also packed
with vitamin C and iron, and that becomes more available when you
eat chillies with beans and grains – yet another time-honoured wise
relationship between ingredients that our ancestors understood and
respected. Secondly, kimchi should have a crunch to the bite, which is
rather unexpected and therefore all the more satisfying. Finally, when
fresh, it should fizz a little from the fermentation, so that it sparkles on
the tongue.

The flavour of freshly made kimchi is very influenced by the raw
fishiness of the shrimp paste and the fish sauce – not surprising,
given the profound pungency of shrimp paste. This fermented, salted
ingredient and condiment is absolutely packed with readily available
nutrients, and used widely in southern Chinese and Southeast Asian
cuisine. Moreover, the combination of saltiness with glutamate provides
a powerfully attractive umami. The taste and health benefits found in
fermented fish paste and sauce were also well known and respected in
Greek, Roman and Byzantine antiquity. Called garum, it was perhaps
more rank smelling than shrimp paste, as it was largely composed
of fermented fish guts and organs. Garum was not only the highly
sought-after umami of ancient times, but also the inspiration behind
Worcestershire sauce, a fermented condiment that contains anchovies.

Brine the cabbage

Place the cabbage pieces in a large bowl. Make up a brine solution of
250g of salt in 1.5 litres of filtered water and pour this over the cabbage.
Toss well so that all the cabbage pieces are thoroughly wetted with brine.
The cabbage should glisten at first, and will then wilt quite quickly and
settle into the brine. Leave to stand for 2–3 hours, turning the cabbage
pieces occasionally, until the white part of the leaves become floppy.

Salt the radish

Peel then cut the Asian radish into thin chunks (about 2.5cm square,
about 0.5cm thick), and as you are doing so, reserve three or four 2.5–3cm
lengths to use as a plug later. Place the chopped radish in a bowl, sprinkle

over a tablespoon of sea salt and toss well. Let the chunks rest for about 30 minutes, then drain but do not wash.

Make the paste

Put the garlic, ginger, chilli, fish sauce, shrimp paste, sugar and 240ml filtered water in a blender. Mince. The shrimp paste is overpoweringly fishy at this stage (the smellier the better, they say) but as the kimchi starts to ferment it will be more than balanced by the other strongly flavoured ingredients.

Bring it all together

Rinse the brined cabbage three times and then drain, gently squeezing out as much water as possible.

Wash, trim and cut the spring onions into 1–1.5cm lengths. Wash carefully and roughly chop the Chinese greens, leaves only.

In a large bowl combine the cabbage, radish, spring onions, Chinese mustard, along with the chilli, garlic and ginger paste. Note: the mix will be very chilli hot – if you mix with your bare hands be prepared for chilli burn. Wear food gloves to protect you or use two serving spoons. Mix and toss thoroughly, so that the cabbage is well coated in the seasoning.

Ferment and burp the kimchi

Cram the cabbage into the jars, pressing everything down with the flat end of a rolling pin or a kraut pestle so that there are no air spaces. Leave about a 2.5cm gap at the top of each jar.

Swill some filtered water into the kimchi mixing bowl, then pour a little into each jar so that when you press the cabbage down the contents remain just covered in water.

To keep the cabbage submerged, use a small glass or jar to press down on the vegetables, and then cover with some muslin. Initially, kimchi is very likely to bubble up and out of the jar, so to contain any spills place your jars on a baking tray or in a suitable container.

Alternatively, use the reserved piece of radish as a plug to keep the kimchi submerged. Place a plug of radish on top of your kimchi, then seal the jar; the plug will push down the kimchi.

Burp the jars by opening them, morning and evening, to release the carbon dioxide. Keep the jars on a tray in case they bubble over when you burp them.

After about 3 days, the kimchi will start to ferment and bubble but become less active within another few days. Once it is calmer, seal the jars and store in the fridge. It will continue to ferment, but more slowly.

Serve fresh – from within 2–3 days of making
Freshly made – and for a week or two – this kimchi is more like an invigorating salad, delicious as a condiment or on its own.

Sprinkle fresh kimchi with sesame oil and some sesame seeds. Even better, garnish with sesame oil and gomashio (see page 72).

Once you have started on a jar of fresh kimchi, refrigerate any leftovers in a sealed jar or non-metallic container.

Fermented kimchi
After a few weeks kimchi is likely to be too strong for most mortals, but is ideally suited for cooking, with plain sprouted brown rice, as an omelette filling or in pork and tofu soup (see page 142–143).

Store older, fermented kimchi in the fridge, tightly sealed. Kimchi is very pungent: you may well want to invest in a small fridge, just for your kimchi (and the fish sauce too, alongside its cousin, the shrimp paste).

Kimchi should have a crunch to the bite, which is rather unexpected and therefore all the more satisfying.

Fermented garlic

Approx. 12–14 garlic bulbs

Freshly filtered water

Flaked sea salt

Whey (optional, see page 41–43)

GARLIC HAS LONG BEEN TOUTED AS A HEALTHY if somewhat full-flavoured cousin of onions, leeks and chives. Originating from central Asia, garlic had very long history of medicinal and culinary uses, before finding it had a natural home in the foods of the Mediterranean, the Middle East and Asia. Interestingly, both onions and garlic are held to have protective powers, as well as being stimulants. Garlic is often hung over an entrance door to ward off evil, and among the Jain people as well as orthodox Hindus, garlic and onions are avoided in order to discourage lusty feelings.

Garlic certainly possesses cleansing and restorative properties, and has long been known for its ability to fight off infections of both the digestive system and the lungs. It is a rich source of sulphur and selenium and, by breaking open garlic by crushing, chopping or mincing it and letting it rest for 5–10 minutes before use, you encourage the creation of allicin, a sulphur compound. This is strong stuff – the source of not only garlic's pungency, but also its antibacterial, antiviral and antifungal properties.

If you want all the powers of garlic without its heat and raw pungency, lacto-ferment it for a more mellow flavour. Preparing the garlic is time-consuming, as you will be peeling many cloves, but worth it: keeping the bulbs raw retains all their enzymes and nutrients.

> **Breaking open garlic by crushing, chopping or mincing it and letting it rest for 5–10 minutes before use encourages the creation of allicin.**

Slow prep but worth it

Separate and peel the garlic cloves by hand and chuck them into a 1-litre glass storage jar. Pour filtered water over the garlic so that the cloves are submerged, leaving about a 2.5cm space at the top of the jar. Pour off and reserve the water – use this to make your brine.

Brine, with or without whey

Make brine by adding 2 tablespoons salt, or a combination of 2 teaspoons salt and 2 tablespoons whey to your reserved water. Pour your brine back over the garlic, and ensure that all the cloves are submerged.

Ferment

Seal the jar and leave it out at room temperature for 3–4 weeks, depending on the ambient temperature, before transferring to the fridge or cool room, for slower fermentation and a longer shelf life.

Herbs and flavours

Garlic pairs wonderfully with fresh rosemary, thyme and also oregano, so add these as desired at the start.

For extra nourishment, add some fresh turmeric root, grated or sliced, to the jar with the garlic cloves; it provides colour, flavour, additional antioxidant and antiviral properties, and also digestive qualities.

Fermented tomato ketchup

Makes about 1 litre

700ml puréed tomatoes (passata)

150ml tomato paste

60ml whey (see pages 41–43)

2 teaspoons shio-koji (see page 67) or 1 teaspoon sea salt

3 garlic cloves, crushed

Pinch of cayenne pepper

110ml maple syrup, or about 150g raw honey

1 teaspoon ground allspice

¼ teaspoon ground cloves

And, for authenticity:

100ml fish sauce

> The word 'ketchup' derives from the Chinese or Malay name for fermented fish sauce.

IF YOU WANT TO INTRODUCE YOUR FAMILY to a lacto-fermented food the easy way, make some real tomato ketchup. It's full of savoury flavour, with the added sweetness of wild sugars, and made mysteriously addictive with just the right amount of fish sauce. Make it more sweet or more savoury, as you prefer.

In history, ketchup has referred to a condiment preserved and nutrient-enriched through lactic acid fermentation; only recently has it become a mostly sweet, subtly savoury sauce, preserved by virtue of its high sugar and vinegar content and made appealing with the same base sugars and their natural affinity with tomatoes. It's a revelation, and not a good one, to discover the amount of sugar in mass-produced ketchup, and the type of sugar too. Often it is high fructose corn syrup and... corn syrup.

The word 'ketchup' derives from the Chinese or Malay name for fermented fish sauce (with spices) that was the addictive umami-rich condiment of the ancient world; in Latin, its name is 'garum'. Worcestershire sauce, in its original form, is a cousin too, as it was fermented and contained anchovies. By the eighteenth century, European ketchup was made with fish sauce and primarily mushrooms, some onions and sometimes walnuts too. Making fermented ketchup with tomatoes originated in nineteenth-century America. It too included anchovies and spices – no sugar at all – and was very much a local farm- and family-produced condiment. In order to make and sell the bottled tomato ketchup nationally by the late nineteenth century, sugar and vinegar replaced lacto-fermentation as the preserving method and of course provided the flavour-rich yet nutrient-poor sauce we know today. It's time to make it at home again. It's so easy.

–

Combine all the ingredients in a bowl and mix very well with a whisk, or process. You may need to warm the honey a little to make it runny.

Taste for savouriness, sweetness and saltiness, and adjust to your preference. You could always try to match shop-bought ketchup to begin with.

Pour into a wide-mouth glass jar, leaving about a 2.5cm space at the top. Seal and leave out at room temperature for 2–3 days to ferment. Burp the jar morning and evening.

Store the sauce to the fridge to slow down the fermentation. It will keep for months.

Fermented beetroot

12–14 medium beetroots (mostly red, with some yellow, white and striped varieties), scrubbed, topped and tailed

Optional

Freshly chopped horseradish, onion, ginger, garlic and dill

Seeds, such as caraway, or fennel are also good – cloves too

Sea salt or shio-koji (see page 67)

Freshly filtered water, or a mix of 80% water and 20% whey (see pages 41–43)

Equipment

Suitable glass containers, such as flip-top jars, or preserving jars and lids

ONCE UPON A TIME, all pickles were made by the process of fermentation using lactic acid bacteria. Now, all commercially made pickles are made and their shelf life extended by a combination of pasteurisation (kills all bacteria) and drowning in a bath of acetic acid, which is of course, vinegar. These pickles are sour, cooked, definitely lacking in subtlety and, importantly, any deep nourishment.

Homemade fermented beetroot pickles are a revelation, with their complex blend of sweet–sour flavours and a wonderful fresh earthiness. Beetroot fermented this way is completely raw and therefore nutritionally complete. It is a relatively recent addition to our vegetable repertoire; in ancient times it was the leaves of wild beetroot that were harvested, and the root was a medicinal ingredient. By the Middle Ages, beetroot had been selectively bred in Germany as a root crop.

Beetroot has attracted much scientific study of late and, consumed as a food or drink, it has proved itself in many ways, for example to boost energy, to lower blood pressure and to play a part in cancer therapies. It is certainly packed with good things, including nitrates, potassium, magnesium, iron, folic acid, fibre, antioxidants and vitamins A, B6 and C.

Enjoy as it comes, or with a dressing of apple cider vinegar and some extra virgin olive oil. Your added bonus when fermenting is the wonderfully alive-tasting juice, which makes a great tonic, and also the final nutrient-packed addition to borscht.

Try to buy your beetroot extra fresh, with its leaves or tops as they are especially rich in antioxidants, and their bitterness combines perfectly with the sweetness of the roots. Wash the leaves, chop coarsely and sauté or stir-fry briefly in lard or coconut oil.

> **Beetroot fermented this way is completely raw and therefore nutritionally complete.**

Clean and chop

Peel the beetroots if you wish, then chop into coarse julienne strips or cubes. Don't be lured into chopping them up in a food processor; this will release too much liquid and make the fermentation too rapid.

Prepare the other vegetables, seeds and herb ingredients (if using) and mix in with the beetroots.

Salt? Add to taste. Try a tablespoon to begin with. Mix it in well and see how it tastes.

Press and seal

Pack the chopped beetroots or mixture into the jars and tamp it down with a suitable masher, such as the flat end of a rolling pin or a kraut pestle so that there are no air spaces. Leave about a 2.5cm gap at the top of each jar.

Top up with enough filtered water or water and whey to cover the vegetables. Press them down again into the liquid and seal. Leave out at room temperature.

Burp and press again

For the first 3 or 4 days, burb the jars by opening them, morning and evening, to release the carbon dioxide. Press down the vegetables again to keep them under the liquid. Initially, you will see a froth form as the fermentation kick-starts, then, after a few days, the liquid will thicken and take on a rich, deep red hue.

Enjoy and chill

Taste the beetroot now – it's ready to eat. Preserve for months by slowing down the wild fermentation in the fridge.

Super borscht

Beetroot soup with added raw beetroot juice power

Serves 4 with plenty left over

50g butter, preferably raw

1 onion, diced

275g beetroots, peeled and diced

1 carrot, peeled and diced

1 leek, trimmed and sliced

1 celery stick, thinly sliced

1.5 litres hot Chicken stock
(see pages 78–80)

2 medium potatoes, peeled
and diced

½ small cabbage, trimmed
and shredded

4 garlic cloves, crushed

Sea salt and freshly ground
black pepper

To serve

Fermented beetroot juice

Soured cream or crème fraîche

Chopped hard-boiled egg
(optional)

Melt the butter in a heavy saucepan – select one big enough to accommodate the ingredients for the entire recipe.

Sauté the onion until it softens, then add all the vegetables except for the potatoes, cabbage and garlic, and cook for about 10 minutes.

Now add the stock and the potatoes, and simmer for 15–20 minutes. Add the cabbage, garlic and a few grindings of black pepper and simmer for 5–10 minutes, until all the vegetables are cooked as you like – tender or slightly crunchy.

Remove from the heat and stir in some of your fermented beetroot juice, say 200ml, but really to taste. Do this off the heat so that the juice remains raw.

Taste for salt and serve with a big dollop of soured cream or crème fraîche, and perhaps some chopped hard-boiled egg.

Quick apple cider vinegar

Makes approx. 4 litres

5 large apples – 3 sweet and
2 sour

Freshly filtered water, at room
temperature

300g raw honey or 175g
rapadura sugar

Equipment

1 wide-mouth 5-litre glass jar

4 wide-mouth 1-litre glass jars
and snap-top glass bottles

Muslin or cheesecloth

Large rubber band and 4 smaller
rubber bands

APPLE CIDER VINEGAR, WHEN RAW and with the mother (see page 64), deserves to be a staple in every home. It is a life-enhancing elixir, full of nutrients and enzymes, which acts both as a cleanser of toxins and a restorer of well-being. It has a host of uses and will fast become indispensable. Diluted with water, it's an invigorating tonic that will also be a balm for the digestive system. (Try it diluted with sparkling water and you have the perfect soft drink replacement.) Added neat to meat stocks it brings out the nutrients in the bones; it can be used as a marinade and works well as a flavour spike in a vinaigrette. Its benefits are far more than culinary: you can soothe a sore throat with a gargle of warm diluted apple cider vinegar, drive off warts, defeat dandruff and use a solution as an all-purpose totally natural household cleaner.

Apples are one of nature's most symbolic and generous of fruits; they are easy to grow, store pretty well, and have been bred and nurtured by people into thousands of flavoursome varieties. They're rich in nutrients, refreshing, often beautifully marked and shaped, and are of course super-convenient to snack on. This is natural fast food at its best.

Commercially produced raw organic apple cider vinegar is made by pressing apples to first make apple juice, and then, by allowing this juice to ferment, cider. This is an anaerobic alcoholic fermentation, in which yeasts convert sugar to ethanol in a controlled environment. To progress to cider vinegar, there's a secondary fermentation, this time aerobic, when acetic acid bacteria take over, converting the alcohol to acid.

The commercial process uses apples only and it's certainly the best way to make strong, full-flavoured apple cider vinegar. But there's a quick method to make your own, which is also the perfect way to introduce you to the simple charms of wild fermentation.

Making this vinegar, as with all wild fermentation, is not an exact science. Every batch is an experiment in its own right, especially when made from different varieties of apples, and will ferment in its own special way and make unique-tasting apple cider vinegar. Try different combinations of sweet and sour apples to vary the overall taste profile.

As for timings, well, they're very much guidelines. It all depends on the ambient temperature, the sweetness of the apples, and the amount and type of sugar added. Experiment – you will love it, and your kitchen will soon look and smell like a fermentation workshop.

–

Stage 1: Make very rough apple cider – the primary fermentation
Wash the apples and coarsely chop into pieces no smaller than 2.5cm. Include the skin, cores, stems and seeds. Let the chopped pieces sit on your chopping board for about an hour or so; they will go brown in

Apple cider vinegar is a life-enhancing elixir, full of nutrients and enzymes, and acts both as a cleanser of toxins and a restorer of well-being.

contact with the air, and this oxidisation is what you want as it will speed up the fermentation.

Throw the pieces into a clean 5-litre jar – they should fill the jar by about one-third to a half. If they do not, add more chopped apple. Add enough filtered water to cover the chopped apples completely – the container should be more or less full, say to about 5cm from the top. Stir in the raw honey or rapadura until fully dissolved.

Ideally, you want to keep all the apples immersed as they ferment. Use a suitable object, such as an upturned beaker or a smaller jar, to press down and submerge the apples.

Cover the top of the jar with your cloth and secure with a large rubber band. Place the jar in a warm, quiet and dark place, such as an airing cupboard, or a warm kitchen cupboard. Let the mix ferment for about 1 week, stirring gently once or twice a day. It will start to fizz and bubble, and smell like a microbrewery, as the sugar ferments into alcohol. It will also start to cloud and thicken, making a viscous liquid. You've now made a very coarse if somewhat weak cider, known as scrumpy in the West Country of England. Agricultural workers there, and where there used to be an abundance of apple orchards, were once paid – in part – with flagons of scrumpy. It's very nutritious and lightly alcoholic.

After about a further 7–9 days, often when the apple pieces no longer float but sink to the bottom of the jar, the apple cider is ready to be converted to vinegar. It's perfectly acceptable to leave the jar to ferment for much longer, say 6 weeks, and as every batch is different, it's good to experiment. You will end up with different flavours and strengths of apple cider vinegar.

Stage 2: From apple cider to apple cider vinegar – the secondary fermentation

The apples have done their work, so strain off the pieces by pouring the cider through a sieve into the 4 x 1-litre glass jars. If you like, you can mash up the apple pieces and press their juices out, and add this to the jars. Cover each jar with a fresh piece of cloth and secure with a rubber band.

Leave alone in a warm, dark environment for a further 3–4 weeks to allow the acetic acid bacteria to transform the alcohol into acetic acid. During this secondary fermentation the odour will shift from a sharp alcohol to tart vinegar, and some sediment will form at the base as well as, thrillingly, a culture known as the mother. You see the mother as threads in the liquid and perhaps as a disc on the surface of each jar. The mother of vinegar is a living thing, perfectly harmless to consume and formed of apple residues, enzymes and acetic acid bacteria.

From 3 weeks onwards, gently push aside the mother to taste your apple cider vinegar to see if it is ready. Once it has the right level of sourness for you, remove the mother, if one has fully formed, keeping her immersed in a jar of apple cider ready for the next batch. Most commercially produced apple cider vinegars have a declared

Stage 1: The primary fermentation

Stage 2: The secondary fermentation

acidity (pH) of 4.5–5, where in pH terms, 7 is neutral and is most acidic.

Pour off the vinegar, leaving behind the residue, which you can compost. Store in clean glass jars with secure lids or snap-top bottles.

Because the vinegar is raw and alive, another mini mother often develops in each bottle as fermentation continues. In the airtight environment this will soon cease and the vinegar will become stable and very long lasting. However, if you leave the fermenting vinegar exposed to the air for a very long time, the acetic acid bacteria will transform the acetic acid to water and carbon dioxide, making the vinegar increasingly weaker. The answer? Taste your fermenting vinegar once or twice a week, and bottle and seal it as soon as you like its level of acidity.

Assisting the secondary fermentation

To speed up the transformation from cider to vinegar, add some of your mother from a previously made batch or from commercially made raw apple cider vinegar, with the mother, to your secondary fermentation.

Scraps method – eating your apples while making quick apple cider vinegar

Follow the overall method above, but rather than chopping up your apples, peel them very coarsely with a knife. Keep the flesh for making a pie or some compote, and let the skins, cores, pips and stalks sit out to brown.

Use these scraps to make your cider and your vinegar.

Use about half the recommended honey or rapadura sugar.

Shio-koji
Fermented rice condiment

100g dried koji rice (find it in specialist Japanese food stores or online)

Warm (more like tepid) filtered water

Sea salt (about 25g or to taste, can be 10–30% of koji rice by weight)

KOJI IS AN EXTRAORDINARY FOOD. Extraordinary in that it is created by the deliberate inoculation of cooked rice or soya beans with a fungus – a mould – and extraordinary in that this culture is a key flavour ingredient (known as umami) in soy sauces, miso, mirin, amazake, sake, rice vinegar and fermented vegetables. It is made by adding the fungus *Aspergillus oryzae* to cooked rice or soya and allowing its enzymes to digest their complex carbohydrates and also proteins. This creates the most wonderfully sweet fragrance. The mould-encrusted rice or soya is then slow-dried in a dehydrator. Once dried, the koji has a long shelf life, and that can be further extended by freezing it. Once reactivated by immersing it in water with some salt, the slow secondary fermentation of the shio-koji (salt koji) is a brilliant source of umami for so many everyday foods and drinks. The mould activity and fermentation creates a sweet–savoury balance of natural glutamate and simple sugars. Use it to add a complex salty–savoury depth to vinaigrette, dipping olive oil, porridge, omelettes, Bolognese sauce, soups and cooked rice. Shio-koji will also assist in fermenting vegetables, bread-making and will tenderise meats, as well as make a marinade for roast chicken.

Prepare the koji rice
Break up the koji rice clumps by hand, but don't break the rice grains. Place in a storage container with a lid and pour over enough warm water to immerse the koji rice completely.

Stir in the sea salt. The more salt you add, the slower the fermentation and the longer lasting the shio-koji. Adding 25g salt (25 per cent of the dried weight of koji rice) seems a lot, and does make quite salty shio-koji. However, as the shio-koji ferments, the saltiness is reduced.

Now rub the mixture together with your fingers to break up any of the remaining clumps of mould-covered rice, and encourage the formation of a rough sloppy paste.

Ferment, stir and taste
Leave at room temperature and stir once a day. Keep it covered with a cloth. Depending on the ambient temperature, the fermenting shio-koji will develop a delicious sweet–salty taste within 6–14 days, so taste it every day after stirring it. Add some water if it becomes too solid – the shio-koji thickens and becomes sweeter as it ferments.

Once it has reached the flavour you like, seal the container with an airtight lid and refrigerate it. It will keep for 4–6 months and for much longer when very salty. If you want it smooth, crush it using a pestle and mortar to whatever texture of paste you prefer. For even richer flavours, add a piece (about 3 x 3cm) of dried kelp (kombu) to the shio-koji.

Fermented lemons

7–10 thin-skinned unwaxed lemons, about 1 kg

Approx. 4 tablespoons sea salt

2 tablespoons whey (optional, see pages 41–43) or some water if necessary

PRESERVING FRUITS THROUGH FERMENTATION is a long-established tradition. Marmalade was originally lacto-fermented and as sugar was once very costly, this condiment was originally quite salty and far more tart and sour than today's version. Several cultures have a long tradition for pickling fruit as a way of extending its season. In Japan, for example, unripe ume plums (or Japanese apricots) are pickled in brine and sun-dried to make umeboshi, an invigoratingly tart and salty treat that is both palate-refreshing and rejuvenating. In North Africa whole lemons are pickled in salt and their own juices.

Brining and fermenting lemons with or without whey reduces their tart nature, creating a pleasant sour saltiness. In the process, the rind softens and becomes edible, eventually without any bitterness. You get the same result with limes, and you can, of course, lacto-ferment all citrus fruits, from oranges to grapefruits to satsumas.

When selecting lemons, choose a thin-skinned variety and, if possible, the wonderful Meyer lemons, which are available from November to March. These are not only thin skinned, but more complex in their citrus flavours, being a cross between a lemon and an orange, or perhaps a mandarin. It's also really important to select citrus fruits that have not been sprayed or waxed to increase their shelf life. As always, choose organic, and even so, wash the fruits thoroughly before you begin.

Saltiness. There's no fixed amount for the quantity of salt you use. Allow about 4 tablespoons of sea salt per kilo of lemons.

Marmalade was originally lacto-fermented.

Wash the lemons, squeeze the juice from 2 of them, and reserve, then slice them all, more thickly than thinly. Quarter the lemon slices.

Throw the lemon pieces into a 1-litre preserving jar, add the salt and mix them all together thoroughly. Use a rolling pin with a flat end or a kraut pestle or masher to press the lemons down into the jar. Leave a space of about 2.5cm at the top of the jar.

Mix the lemon juice with the whey (if using) and add this to the pressed lemons in the jar. It is important that the lemons are covered by the liquid. Use a weight, such as a small clean stone, to keep them submerged. Seal or close the jar tightly.

Leave out at room temperature, upending the jar once a day, and burping it from time to time. Whenever you open the jar ensure that the lemons remain covered by the brine.

After about 2 weeks taste your lemons. If they are too bitter, leave out to ferment for another week, before tasting again, and repeat again if necessary. Refrigerate once they are just right. They will keep for a very, very long time.

Mayonnaise – three ways

Makes about 500ml

3 egg yolks from pastured hens

Large pinch or ¼ teaspoon finely ground sea salt or shio-koji (page 67)

1 tablespoon apple cider vinegar (see pages 62–66) or freshly squeezed lemon juice

1 tablespoon water

About 350ml olive oil

Optional; all or any combinations of:

1 garlic clove, crushed

Minced fresh French tarragon or finely chopped chives

Dijon mustard

ONCE YOU'VE MADE YOUR OWN MAYONNAISE, you will be unlikely to go back to the shop-bought varieties. And there's a lot of choice out there. In principle, any shop-bought mayonnaise that lists ingredients you can pronounce and that you would be happy to use at home, is a perfectly sound and nourishing condiment; it will, of course, be pasteurised. Homemade mayonnaise is, however, in a different league. First, you're in control of all the ingredients, so you can select those that are of the very best quality, source, freshness and, therefore, nutrient density. This is particularly important for the selection of the eggs, which must be from pastured flocks. Secondly, you will be making it fresh, and so of course it will be raw and not pasteurised. Thirdly, you can vary the style of the mayonnaise to suit its use and the flavour profile of the accompanying foods, whether thick or thin, tart or neutral. Finally, the flavours. This is a classic example of the relationship between the unspoilt, nutrient density of a food and just how much more complex, flavoursome and deeply satisfying it tastes.

Some useful information when making mayonnaise

Thickness: this is determined by the thickness of the starting yolk-based mixture, before you add the oil or oils. You can make yolks thicker by freezing, by heating or by adding salt. Commercial mayonnaise manufacturers typically freeze the yolks, as they remain thicker even when thawed; this way the manufacturers can use fewer yolks, to a ratio of about one third of a yolk per 225ml of oil.

Increasing stability after you begin to add the oil: add some lemon juice or apple cider vinegar, or a mixture of lemon juice or apple cider vinegar and water – they are essential for the creation of a stable emulsion. These watery liquids are emulsifiers, keeping the oil droplets apart.

Room temperature please: if your ingredients are too hot or too cold, they will jeopardise the formation of a stable emulsion.

Add the oil slowly at first: this way you will be able to break up the oil into tiny droplets more effectively.

Splitting: whisk up another egg yolk, and then, while whisking, add drop by drop your split or separated mixture until it is combined, then continue to add the oil as before.

This is a classic example of the relationship between the unspoilt, nutrient density of a food and just how much more complex, flavoursome and deeply satisfying it tastes.

Everyday mayonnaise

1. By hand
Put the egg yolks into a bowl that will take your completed volume of mayonnaise and whisk the salt into the yolks followed by the vinegar and then the water. This is also the time to whisk in any of your extra ingredients.

The secret to emulsifying the oil is to add it, at first, very, very slowly as you whisk. Start one drop at a time. Yes, one drop at a time, until you have been whisking for about a minute, by which time the mayonnaise will have thickened and increased in volume.

Continue to whisk as you add the oil, not drop by drop, but slowly... in a fine drizzle, until all the oil is incorporated.

2. With a food processor
Combine the yolks, salt, vinegar and water, then pour in a few drops of the oil, make sure it is incorporated, and then add more oil, drop by drop at first, and then a drizzle.

Storage
Store in a sealed jar in the fridge; it keeps for 7–10 days.

Slightly fermented mayonnaise

Add 1 tablespoon of whey (see pages 41–43) to the egg yolks. Once made, seal in a jar and leave out at room temperature for 6–8 hours before refrigerating. This mayonnaise will keep longer, up to 2–3 months in the fridge, and will firm up over time.

Mayonnaise with coconut oil

Replace half the olive oil with coconut oil. You may have to gently warm the coconut oil to ensure that it remains a liquid as you whisk it into the eggs. This mayonnaise will be thicker, more like a spread, when chilled.

Gomashio
Japanese sesame salt

Makes about 300g gomashio with a sesame to salt ratio of about 15:1

3 tablespoons sea salt

300g whole (not hulled) brown or black sesame seeds

THIS IS A PERFECT CONDIMENT FOR PLEASURE and for health, as it combines toasted whole black or brown sesame seeds (goma) with sea salt (shio). Gomashio is a Japanese speciality, and it's used to bring life and flavour to rice dishes. Once you've tried gomashio you will be sprinkling it on salads, rice and even porridge, it's so good. Gomashio is extremely simple to make and you can vary the salt content as you wish, from about 5 parts sesame to salt, to a macrobiotic diet ratio of 18 parts sesame to 1 part salt.

Heat a dry frying pan over a medium heat. Add the sea salt and toast until it turns grey, then toast the sesame seeds until they start popping and, if using brown, colouring nicely, but not burning.

Remove from the heat and set aside to cool. Once the salt and sesame seeds have cooled, whizz in a blender or a coffee grinder with a blade for a moment or two, no more. The seeds need only to be cracked open to release their oils, not ground.

Gomashio should be a light brown, sandy-textured condiment. It will keep a long time stored in a sealed jar, but you will use it all before it has a chance to go rancid.

Once you've tried gomashio you will be sprinkling it on salads, rice and even porridge, it's so good.

Some very useful tomato sauces

Makes about 400g

1kg medley of super-ripe but firm, very fresh heirloom tomatoes

A bunch of fresh basil leaves, torn

80ml extra virgin olive oil

Big pinch of sea salt

THE AROMA OF FRESHLY PICKED TOMATOES, sun-ripened on the vine, is one of the most evocative sensory pleasures of summer. Their sweet juiciness, heightened by a pinch of sea salt flakes, is equally divine. Not so the year-round bulletproof so-called fresh tomatoes, often grown hydroponically, picked green and then ripened with ethylene. Fresh tomatoes, especially heirloom varieties, are the gift of the summer's sun, and their season should be anticipated and relished with gusto. For the rest of the year? Find a maker of tinned tomatoes you trust and like. Good tinned tomatoes are picked off the vine when fully ripe so their nutrient value, flavour and colour are naturally sun given.

Tomatoes are an excellent source of good nourishment, including vitamins B and C, carotenoids, including high levels of lycopene, calcium, phosphorus, potassium and magnesium. As ever, their nutrient value will vary wildly according to how fresh they are and how they have been grown.

Raw tomato sauce with fresh basil

Rough: Core the tomatoes and chop them medium–coarse, and put in a bowl. Add the torn basil leaves, oil and salt, toss, then cover the bowl with a plate or lid, and leave for about 30 minutes to 1 hour.

Smooth: Peel and deseed the tomatoes (see above) before chopping.

Enjoy with freshly made bread or some freshly cooked fresh pasta.

How to peel fresh tomatoes easily

Either don't bother, just cook your fresh tomatoes and then make a smooth sauce with a food mill. Or scald and prepare as follows:

Cut a divot from the top of the tomato, where the stalk was attached. Plunge the tomatoes, if necessary a few at a time, into a bowl of freshly boiled water, for about 30 seconds and up to 1 minute, and then, to prevent further cooking, into a bowl of cold water with some ice cubes. They should peel easily. Discard the skins. Cut the tomatoes in half across their middle, and then use your thumb to push out the pips and any surrounding flesh into a sieve sitting over a bowl. Press any remaining juice out of the flesh and pips into the bowl, and add to your chopped or halved tomatoes. Discard the pips.

Makes about 400g

4–6 good-sized garlic cloves, smashed and coarsely chopped

60ml extra virgin olive oil

1kg fresh, ripe tomatoes, prepared as on page 74, or 400g tin chopped tomatoes

Sea salt

Everyday fresh or tinned tomato sauce

Perfect with pasta, pizzas and frittata. In late summer or early autumn, when there are lots of tomatoes going for a song, make plenty and freeze it.

–

Prepare the garlic 5 minutes before you cook it, and its nutrients will be more bio-available.

Heat the oil in a small- to medium-sized heavy saucepan over a medium heat. Throw in the garlic and let it sizzle for just a few seconds before adding the tomatoes with all their juice. Add a large pinch of sea salt. Stir, bring to a simmer, then reduce the heat to keep it simmering. It will be ready in about 15–20 minutes, but for a really rich sauce, let it simmer gently for at least 30 minutes, stirring from time to time.

For a less lumpy sauce, use a potato masher and mash the sauce in the pan. For a really smooth sauce, pass it through a food mill.

Easy variations on the above

At the beginning: sauté a small diced onion or shallot in the hot oil until lightly coloured and soft before adding the garlic.

At the end: chop or tear up some fresh herbs and add to the sauce just before serving. Basil is the perfect companion, or flat-leaf parsley.

Vinaigrette, many different ways

1 tablespoon apple cider vinegar (see pages 62–66)

Sea salt

Freshly ground black pepper

3–4 tablespoons olive oil

THERE ARE TWO WAYS TO MAKE A VINAIGRETTE WONDERFUL. First, by using the very best-quality ingredients, especially the oils, which must be fresh, cold-pressed and extra virgin, without any filtering or refining. Secondly, by introducing an imaginative array of flavours, complete with their nutrient-dense goodness, be they fresh herbs, sweet miso paste or bacon dripping. Whatever the ingredients, the principles remain the same: vinaigrette is made with 1 part vinegar to 3 or 4 parts oil. Make more than you need because stored in a sealed glass jar, vinaigrette keeps pretty well in the fridge. Finally, always taste as you go; dip a finger in the mixture as it is being assembled to assess the balance of flavours.

Simple olive oil vinaigrette

Pour some vinegar into a small bowl that you can use a small whisk in, and then sprinkle on some salt. Stir to dissolve the salt, and taste. Adjust or not, and then add some black pepper. Taste again. Whisk in a little of the oil, then some more. Keep tasting as you add some more oil, and stop when you are happy with the flavour profile and thickness. It should be neither oily nor too acidic.

Ideas for ingredients and flavourings:

Fresh herbs. Add 1 teaspoon of finely chopped herbs to the finished mixture, such as French tarragon, oregano, basil or flat-leaf parsley. Use immediately.

Garlic. Crush, mince or finely chop garlic. Add to the vinegar and salt, to make it as pungent as you like.

Mustard. A teaspoon or more of smooth or coarse grain Dijon mustard thoroughly mixed in with the vinegar and salt will thicken the vinaigrette, adding a real punch, especially with garlic.

Cream, soured cream or crème fraîche. Add after making the vinaigrette, or replace some or all of the oil you use with these creams for a dairy rich dressing.

Vinegar. Use red wine, white wine, balsamic, sherry, rice wine or coconut vinegars, or freshly squeezed lemon juice.

Nut oils. Swap the olive oil for some other oils, such as freshly made walnut or hazelnut oils.

Fruit oils. Instead of the olive oil, or some of it, use gently warmed coconut oil or avocado oil.

Seed oil. Sesame oil, not toasted (as it's too strong) makes a very light vinaigrette.

Bacon dripping. Add warmed dripping/fat from frying bacon; this lends wonderfully pungent saltiness to the vinaigrette.

Salt. Use shio-koji (see page 67) instead of salt.

Sweetness. Add some raw honey.

Sweet miso. Mix well some sweet miso with some rice wine vinegar and some freshly grated ginger. For oil, use either warmed coconut oil or plain sesame oil. For salt, if needed, use some shio-koji.

Chicken stock

Makes approx. 3.5–4 litres

8–10 raw chicken feet

1 whole chicken, or 1.5–2kg
raw chicken parts, such as the
carcasses, wings, etc, with skin on

1 or 2 raw chicken heads

3 tablespoons apple cider vinegar
(see pages 62–66)

Water – about 4 litres

1 large onion, unpeeled and
quartered (the skin contains fibre,
and the plant pigment quercetin,
which can help reduce blood
pressure, so leave it on)

1 large carrot, topped and tailed
as necessary, peeled and very
coarsely chopped

1 celery stick, coarsely chopped;
include any celery tops/leaves –
they are rich in magnesium

1 or 2 leeks, rinsed of their earth
and coarsely chopped; add any
leftover green leek tops

1 unpeeled large garlic bulb, cut in
half across its width

Some sprigs of thyme and a
bay leaf

1 tablespoon whole black
peppercorns

A bunch of flat-leaf parsley

INEXPENSIVE, CONVENIENT, HEALTHY, DELICIOUS, VERSATILE – what's not to love about homemade soup? It's the original fast food. The basis of a good soup is a well-made, nutrient-dense stock. Our ancestors the world over were wholly acquainted with making meat and fish stocks as a perfectly natural and responsible way to get the most out of the precious animals and fish that were reared or caught with thanks and respect. A bubbling cauldron or stockpot was a central part of the kitchen landscape until very recently, and the stock-making would be a continuous process, adding scraps, seasonal ingredients and windfalls to create a unique and ever-evolving unwritten recipe. We must return the stockpot to its rightful place, as the most important provider of everyday nourishment and efficient digestion and, as a consequence, strength and wellness.

Stock, and especially chicken stock, has a long association with health as well as the sensory pleasures. Chicken soup may well be known as Jewish penicillin, but its value is universally appreciated: across Asia, chicken stock is the basis for an endless selection of recipes, largely divided into those that will cure illnesses and those that will fight off illness. Chicken broth is the perfect example of an ancestral food whose benefits have truly stood the test of time, so much so that freshly made chicken broth made from the best ingredients should be doled out as a delicious medicine in hospitals the world over for convalescence and healing. This was wholly understood until relatively recently; chicken and other meat broths and stocks were featured and recommended in many pre-World War II cookbooks as the best foods to strengthen, protect and cure.

When made from the most nutrient-dense meat and vegetables, stocks are richly endowed with easily assimilated minerals derived from the marrow, cartilage and bone, as well as the vegetables. Adding vinegar before cooking the stock helps to draw out these minerals. Meat stocks are especially rich in gelatine, as well as cartilage components and collagen; interestingly, gelatine was heralded as a superfood and a miracle food in the late nineteenth and early twentieth centuries. Although gelatine's hydrophilic or water-loving nature has been proven to increase the digestibility of meat and beans, and to assist in releasing proteins from wheat, barley and oats, it is not a complete protein solution in itself. This historical precedent for an obsession with a supposedly miracle protein has as its modern counterpart the equally misguided trust in soya as a suitable form of nourishment for humans. As the Japanese, Chinese and Indonesians have discovered, soya is indeed nourishing for humans, but not until it has been properly prepared (pre-digested) by fermentation, with or without the assistance of fungi.

We must return the stockpot to its rightful place, as the most important provider of everyday nourishment and efficient digestion.

Ask your butcher for the fresh chicken feet and heads. They should be delighted to oblige. If not, find another butcher.

Remove the membrane from the feet

Wash the feet carefully and cut off the talons. Pour boiling water over 2 or 3 feet at a time, leave for 30 seconds, and then plunge the feet into iced water. This scalding will make it really easy to remove the yellow membrane. Always use freshly boiled water for each small batch of feet.

Push a sharp knife across the yellow membrane and it will tear away from the foot. Continue to scrape, cut or tease the membrane off the scaly foot. You will often be able to peel the membrane off like a sock; it's fiddly but very satisfying work. If there's a hard, soil-packed pad in the sole of the foot, slice it off with a sharp knife. Wash the feet after removing the membrane.

Prepare the chicken, then rest the lot

Remove fat glands and any innards from the whole chicken – they'll be a treat for a pet – or keep the fat and render it for use as highly nourishing chicken fat (see pages 87–89).

Put all the chicken pieces in a large stockpot, add the cider vinegar and fill with water so that the bones are covered. Leave to stand for about 1 hour.

Cook very gently

Place the uncovered pot over a medium heat, bring to a very gentle boil, then turn down to a bare simmer. Remove any scum with a small sieve or skimmer.

Add all the vegetables, the thyme, bay leaf and peppercorns. Cook, partially covered and at no more than a gentle simmer, for about 4–6 hours. If necessary, remove any scum and replenish the water so that the bones are always covered.

Or

Cover the simmering pan and transfer to the oven. Cook at about 60°C/gas ¼, but check and adjust the temperature as necessary so that it is simmering gently, for about 18–24 hours.

In the last 30 minutes of cooking add the flat-leaf parsley.

Remove the bones and strain

Whole chicken: remove and let cool before pulling away the meat from the carcass, which will be ideal for sandwiches and salads.

Carcasses and other pieces of chicken: Press the bones down into the pan with a potato masher to extract all the juices and goodness from the bones and membranes, and then remove.

Pour the liquid and vegetables into a large glass or ceramic bowl through a fine mesh sieve or strainer, lined with muslin if you like. The stock is now ready for use.

Store the stock

The stock will keep well in the fridge for 3–5 days or, frozen, for months.

Before you chill in the fridge or freeze, cool the stock down. Set the bowl in a sink of cold water, refreshing the cold water often. When tepid, ladle or pour the stock into storage jars or pots. Place in the fridge with the lids ajar for 2–3 hours, until the fat congeals on the surface. Remove this fat and reserve (it's chicken dripping – delicious spread on toast or bread and butter), then cover the pots securely and continue to chill or freeze.

Thicker or a more jelly-like stock?

Once strained, boil the stock to thicken it, and for more of a jelly consistency, add more chicken feet or indeed a split pig's foot or two to your stockpot. You can also cheat a little by adding some powdered gelatine, though it's hard to find gelatine from a trusted source of beef.

Dark or light stock?

The longer you cook the stock, the richer and darker it will be, and, generally, the higher its levels of amino acids.

A trendy new beverage

You'll be amazed. Have a cup of warm chicken stock and your coffee cravings will disappear...

Clear or cloudy?

Most of the time the stock will be slightly cloudy. Reduce cloudiness by slow heating at the start, removing all scum, and by not allowing the stock to boil. It should simmer. Once you have chilled your stock, the heavier particles will settle to the bottom of the jar. Pour off the clear stock and discard the cloudy residue.

To make your stock even more appealing, gently heat it with a tablespoon of sweet (white) miso paste, and throw in some finely chopped parsley or coriander. Once the miso is added don't boil the stock or you will damage the miso nutrients.

Lard

Makes approx. 600g lard from 1kg fat

1–2kg chilled leaf or back fat from a pastured, fat-rich pig

LARD: THE RENDERED FAT FROM A PIG. Lard, fat and pig. These very words are simplistically associated with our recent, grotesque fear and misunderstanding about the nature of fats, and most importantly, good fats. Good animal fats include butter and its rendered derivatives clarified butter and ghee, as well as suet (the raw fat from the abdominal cavity and especially from around the kidneys of cattle and sheep) and rendered beef and sheep fat, known as tallow (see pages 86–89). Raw pork fat from the back of the pig when salted and aged (cured) is called lardo, while rendered pork fat from any part of the pig is known as lard. Not forgetting caul, the lacy membrane of fat that surrounds the intestines of a pig. Rendering? This is the process of heating fat to stabilise it by separating the fat from any water and meat.

People have relied and thrived on animal fats, primarily from pigs and beef cattle, for millennia; indeed, it is only in the last few hundred years that butter has joined tallow and lard as one of the principal animal fats in northern European cuisines, especially in French cuisine. Olive oil is of course the butter of the Mediterranean basin.

Making lard is extremely easy. But before you rush off to the butcher for some pork fat, take a moment to know more about it, as not all pork fat is the same. First, ask for the fat from a fat-rich pig that is of a good age, and one that has been pastured for as much of its life as conditions and the seasons allow. Secondly, consider what you intend to do with the lard, because fat from the different parts of a pig has different qualities, which you can match to your cooking and eating requirements. These are the different types of pig fat:

Leaf or flare fat
This is the very best fat for lard, found within the abdominal cavity and around the kidneys. There's not much of it in comparison with back and belly fat. It is very neutral tasting and wonderful for pastry making, in combination with butter.

Back fat or fatback
This is very firm fat found just under the skin on the pig's back. Next time you're close to a pig, feel the back, it's solid to the touch. Used for making lardo and, once rendered, lard. Being more or less solid fat, back fat is easy to render and makes a good general-purpose frying fat.

Belly of pork
Here the fat is layered with muscle, and may be sold with the skin (crackling) and bones attached (spare ribs). Streaky bacon comes from pork belly, and it also makes a perfect joint – by slow cooking it you get lots of lard in the dripping as well as a succulent feast of roast pork.

Caul fat or lace fat

This is a string vest-like membrane of fat surrounding the intestines of a pig. You won't want to render this fat, but it makes a brilliant self-basting wrap for lean meats. The white lacy wrap around a traditional faggot is caul fat. Try wrapping a whole chicken in caul before roasting; this will make up for the lack of fat hens and prevent the meat from drying out. Quick-reared chickens are almost entirely devoid of fat – either under their skins or within their body cavities.

Rendering lard

To render a relatively small amount of fat, say less than a kilo, heat the fat gently and slowly in a cast-iron or enamelled saucepan on the hob until it melts. For larger quantities, use a larger pan or a Dutch oven, and heat it in the oven following this recipe.

Prepare the fat

Chill the fat before cutting it up – it'll be much easier to handle.

Remove the papery membrane from leaf lard and the skin from back fat. Cut the fat into the smallest pieces you can manage or, better still, ask the butcher to mince it. The smaller the pieces, the more lard you will make.

Preheat the oven to 120°C/gas ½.

Heat, stir and be patient

Put the fat in a heavy cast-iron or ceramic saucepan or Dutch oven and add about 80ml of fresh filtered water per 500g of fat. Rendering with water, known as wet rendering, will help to ensure that the fat does not burn and taint the lard. Put the pan in the oven, uncovered, and set a timer for 30 minutes.

After 30 minutes, stir the fat, and then again every 15–20 minutes for 4 hours or more, depending on the fat you are rendering – leaf fat renders faster than back fat. You will see the fat melting and the water will evaporate. The larger pieces of fat, being slower to melt, will be floating about. Press these against the side of the pan to help them melt.

Remove from the oven when any of the pieces of fat start to colour and let the pan cool a little.

Strain and store

Line a sieve with muslin and pour the fat through this into glass storage jars. Discard any pieces of fat that won't render or put them out for your garden birds.

Once the jars are cool, label and seal them. Lard will keep for a long time in the fridge and pretty well indefinitely when frozen.

Using lard

If you like deep-frying, using lard will be a revelation. Lard is a clean, sweet-smelling fat compared with vegetable oils, and leaves no lingering unpleasant and rank oily odours. For sautéing and for roasting potatoes and vegetables, it's also brilliant. Your vegetables will be crisp and dry, and retain their flavours.

You can reuse lard for frying again, perhaps two or three times, but make sure you strain it through a muslin-lined sieve and do not use lard that is no longer white, or slightly off-white.

The best lard, such as leaf lard, has so little piggy flavour that you can use it for frying or sautéing delicately flavoured food, such as fish.

Lard pot

Keep a small ceramic pot with a lid by the hob and pour any bacon fat or lard left over from shallow frying into it. Use this for more frying, or when you're starving, cut a slice of sprouted spelt sourdough, lash on the lardish dripping from your pot, and enjoy with a side of sauerkraut and a cold glass of weiss beer or a natural red wine.

A note on mass-produced lard:

Not all lard is the same – most mass-produced lard has been hydrogenated (to improve stability at room temperature) and is also often treated with bleaching and deodorizing agents, emulsifiers and antioxidants. Do not use mass-produced lard.

Pork belly

Caul

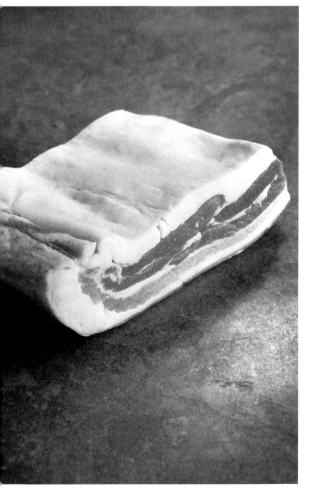

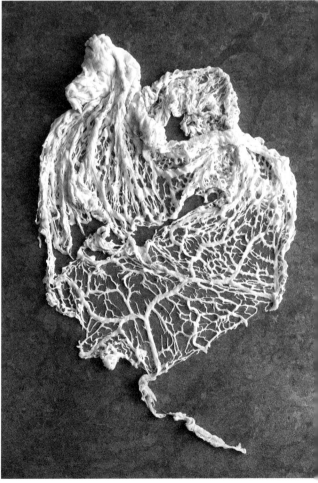

Fats from beef, lamb, mutton and poultry

Tips for rendering tallow

Prepare the suet (see right); grating it will ensure it melts quickly.

Chop up any other beef or sheep fats you intend to render, as small as possible.

Render the fat in a heavy cast-iron or ceramic saucepan or Dutch oven, by adding about 80ml of freshly filtered water to every 500g of fat. Rendering with water is known as wet rendering, and will help to ensure that the fat does not burn and taint the tallow.

Cook on the stove, uncovered, over a very low heat, and stir often. Or cook uncovered in the oven at 120°C/gas ½ and stir about once every 30 minutes. It takes 3–7 hours to render the fat.

Keep an eye on the colour of the lumps of fat or fat and tissue that won't melt. Once they start to colour, it's time to stop rendering.

Let the fat cool a little and then strain it through a muslin-lined sieve into your storage jars. Label the jars.

Once cooled, seal and refrigerate. Tallow freezes well, and will keep for at least a year.

THE PIG IS THE REIGNING CHAMPION OF FAT PRODUCTION, certainly in terms of the yield of fat per animal, but there are equally high-quality and nourishing fats available from other animals.

Beef, lamb and mutton

The generic name for all rendered fats from cattle and sheep is tallow. Tallow, historically, was not only a valuable fat for cooking, but was also used to make candles and soap. More recently, tallow has been used as a biofuel.

Sheep and cattle store their fat in three places: under the skin, within the meat and in the body cavity, especially around the kidneys. Sadly, as with pigs, the twentieth century fear of fat resulted in breeding reduced-fat animals, so the only way to acquire lots of good fat from beef, lamb and mutton is to seek out a butcher who buys in carcasses from farmers who raise traditional or native breeds in a high-welfare environment, and keep them pastured for as much of the year as possible. It's also important to seek out older animals; those will always have more fat within the meat, known as marbling, consequently the meat will have a far better flavour, and the fat itself will be more appetising, and there will be more of it. Fat from lamb, in particular, is nowhere near as unctuous and tasty as that from mutton, which is the meat from a full-grown adult. If you want to test the theory, find some lamb chops and compare them to chops from an older lamb or young mutton sheep. You won't choose young lamb again.

Suet is the hard, brittle fat found within the body cavity and especially around the kidneys of sheep and cows. It is only called suet in its raw form. Simply grated it is ready for use. Most suet is beef suet, which is traditionally highly prized for making pastry, steamed puddings, mincemeat and dumplings. In its rendered form, when it is known as tallow, it is ideal for deep-frying. Next time you buy chips, ask what oil they use, and if the answer is not tallow, suggest that they do; they'd be both traditional and trendy. Look how much gourmet excitement chips triple-fried in tallow creates. Chips fried in tallow are crisper, drier and far less greasy than chips cooked in vegetable oil; in fact, potatoes absorb half as much tallow as vegetable oils.

Beef and sheep fat, depending on the breed and the way the animals are reared, has an excellent balance of saturated and monounsaturated fats, and is low in polyunsaturated fats. This makes it stable at room temperature, and because it possesses a high smoke point, around 200°C, it is less likely to burn and taste unpleasant. Most sheep are less intensively reared than beef cattle, so it's important to be very careful when you buy your beef; select only beef that's been able to graze freely, and when indoors, fed predominantly on dried grass (hay) or fermented

Tips for preparing suet

Buy suet from a supplier who sources pastured animals only.

Trim or cut away any traces of blood or organ meat from the suet and peel away the papery membrane.

Grate or finely chop the suet as required.

Store, almost indefinitely, in the freezer. Use from frozen.

Vegetarian suet is made of hydrogenated vegetable oils; better used for soap or candle making.

grass (silage). The fat from grass-fed beef and sheep, especially those that graze outdoors, is rich in omega-3 fatty acids, as well as conjugated linoleic acid and vitamin D, all essential for our health and well-being.

Dripping usually refers to beef dripping, but of course when you slow-cook fatty joints of pork, you get a lot of dripping which, as it sounds, is the fat and meat juices that seep from meat as it cooks. Whenever you cook a joint of meat, collect the dripping and let it cool. The fat will rise to the top, leaving a meat juice jelly underneath. Enjoy this as a thoroughly moreish and nourishing spread on toast, or if there's a lot of fat, scrape it off, heat it gently, and once liquidised, pour it through a sieve lined with muslin and use as tallow next time you're making chips.

Poultry: goose, duck and chicken

Poultry fat is the stuff of health legends. Think of chicken broth, known as Jewish penicillin – and for good reason. All poultry fats are rich in monounsaturated fats, of which palmitoleic acid is the most renowned, as it is evidently one of the immune-boosting elements we benefit from by eating properly made chicken broth or stock (see pages 78-81).

Not all poultry is equal. Geese and ducks are water birds and possess a lot of fat as insulation; they are also programmed to lay down more fat in autumn in preparation for migration or the rigours of winter.

Being less easy to rear and fatten quickly, unlike chickens, these fowl have largely escaped industrial production, which is not (factory) farming, but rather a white meat processing concentration camp.

Getting any fat from mass-produced chickens is almost impossible as so much of the fat has been bred out of them. They are also slaughtered too young, and their feed encourages muscle growth at the expense of skeleton bone and fat. Cheap chicken is not a civic right, it's an environmental, welfare and ethical disaster. Whatever happened to a fat hen? Lean chicken is tasteless, which is, one supposes, the intention of the process.

Forget cheap, lean and tasteless chicken: find a butcher that sources his chickens from a farmer with small flocks that really are pasture reared. It's best to visit the farm to see that they do, as the label 'free-range' can often be meaningless if the birds are not encouraged or made to venture out of their sheds to peck for tasty worms, beetles and other insects. Chickens are omnivores, and they desperately need their animal protein. You want as old a chicken as possible; in essence you want a plump chicken. Chicken fat is found beneath the skin and most of it in the body cavity, so make sure that the butcher does not discard any when he is gutting the bird. Overall there's not much fat, so you end up rendering the skin, the cavity fat and any fatty pieces of meat to collect the precious substance.

By contrast, the fat on a goose or duck is self-evident. When roasting a bird, collect the copious dripping, separate the fat from the meat juices by straining through a muslin-lined sieve, and use the fat for roasting potatoes or sautéing and frying in general. The smoke point of poultry fat is about 190–200°C, comparable to tallow (see page 86).

You want as old a chicken as possible; in essence you want a plump chicken.

Rendering poultry fat

Collect together and chop up as small as possible, all the skin, fat and fatty parts of the bird, and place in a heavy saucepan or big iron frying pan. Add about 80ml of fresh filtered water to every 500g of poultry bits.

Set the pan over a low heat and stir often. The water will evaporate, the fat will liquefy and after anywhere between 2 and 4 hours, the pieces of poultry will begin to colour. Turn off the heat and let the pan cool a little.

Pour the fat through a sieve lined with muslin into storage jars.

You can return the coloured pieces of poultry to the pan again and continue to heat slowly and gently; you will obtain a little more fat from further cooking. And you'll be left with a real treat: poultry cracklings.

Drain the cracklings, and while still warm, sprinkle with some flaked sea salt, freshly ground black pepper, and enjoy as a snack, or scatter on salad or over soup.

Seal and label your jars of precious poultry fat. It will keep well in the fridge and when frozen, for at least a year.

Apple, pear and apricot butters

Makes 2–3 jars

750g dried apricots, or 500g dried apple or pears, with skin on

Approx. 100g raw honey

60ml whey (see pages 41–43)

1 tablespoon sea salt

WE'RE EXTREMELY FAMILIAR with the link between apples and health. Apples are a truly ancestral fruit, steeped in lore, mythology and meaning. Grown well and used fresh, or stored sympathetically, they are particularly refreshing and a great source of vitamin C and fibre. The skin is particularly high in antioxidants, which may help reduce the risk of developing cancer, diabetes and cardiovascular disease. Cut an apple in half around its equator, rather than down past the stalk. The cross-section you'll find is particularly wonderful, as the central star-like form evocatively mirrors the shape of an apple flower.

Pears and apricots too have long-held and proven health benefits. Pears, a relative of apples, share similar qualities. Apricots, a relative of plums, peaches, cherries and almonds, have been long cherished for both their sweet flesh and their seed, or kernel. Apricots are rich in fibre too, as well as antioxidants, including lycopene, and also copper and potassium.

Making apple or pear butter is a traditional harvest pastime in the tree fruit-growing world. In fact, there's no butter involved, it's merely a highly concentrated form of apple sauce – a thick spreadable syrup. Since the Middle Ages, making such preserves has been the simplest way to conserve the fruit after the harvest in order to make it last almost indefinitely. Making fruit butter was historically a community endeavour, everyone taking turns to stir large bubbling vats of slow crystallising fruits, water and sometimes cider.

This recipe requires no heating, reducing or caramelising, but rather the slow drying of the fruits with their skins on, followed by processing to a sauce and subsequent mild fermentation. It's possible to use bought-dried fruits for this recipe, as long as you select fruits without the preservative sulphur dioxide or added sugars, but you could prepare and dry fruits yourself. Invest in a simple domestic electric dehydrator, one with trays to lay out the sliced fruits, which is capable of drying food for as long as it takes at a steady low temperature ranging, as necessary, from 35–75°C. Once you have a dehydrator, you can dry, crisp and preserve all manner of fruits, vegetables, herbs, meats and fish.

–

Soften the fruit by gently heating it in some water, as much as it takes to allow the fruit to rehydrate.

While soft and warm, put the fruit in a food processor and blend with the honey, whey and salt. Taste for sweetness and saltiness and adjust as you like.

Fill preserving jars to about 2.5cm from the top, let cool and then seal, and leave out at room temperature for a few days. Burp the jars morning and evening. Refrigerate after 2–3 days. Enjoy within 2–3 months on pancakes, waffles, porridge, ice cream and with yogurt or crème fraîche.

Nut and seed butters

Makes 2–3 jars

500g activated almonds, with or without the skins – your choice (the butter will be darker if you leave the skins on. However, the tannins in the skin are not so easy to digest)

1 teaspoon sea salt (for a mildly salted almond butter)

Coconut oil (optional)

Making nut butter at home is completely straightforward, quick and easy. After all, many health food stores have a nut butter maker on site that delivers freshly ground nuts while you wait. Making your own nut butters means you have complete control over the quality of the ingredients. You can activate or sprout the nuts and seeds (see pages 98–105), you can also roast them, and of course, you can make your own bespoke mixtures of different nuts or seeds, or a combination of the two. Finally, if you want extra ingredients for flavour or for extra goodness, you can add sea salt, honey or coconut oil as you wish. All you need is a food processor.

–

Almond butter – roasted or raw?

If you want to keep your activated almonds raw, omit the roasting step. If you do want the roasted almond flavour, leave the skins on after activating and drying for the richest roasted flavour.

Roast (optional)

Set the oven to 190°C/gas 5. Spread the almonds out on a baking sheet in a single layer. Roast for 8–9 minutes and watch them carefully. You want a slightly coloured nut with a sweet aroma. Any sign of burning is a disaster and you'll have to feed the nuts to the birds. Always roast less rather than more. Allow the almonds to cool until warm to the touch before processing.

Throw the almonds into the processor and start the machine. Within a minute or two you will have finely broken almonds. Continue to process; after another 4 minutes or so the oil from the almonds will be fully released and you will create a creamy paste. It may take longer – up to 15 minutes – depending on the freshness and nature of the nuts. Once the paste is as creamy as you like, add the salt and pulse to integrate. Taste. If you're using activated nuts or seeds and they refuse to cream as you would like, add some coconut oil.

Store in a jar or container with a tight-fitting lid. The butter will keep for months in the fridge.

Cashews or peanuts?

Follow the same instructions using cashews or peanuts. Peanuts are, of course, a legume, and not a nut.

Crunchy or smooth?

If you like your nut butter crunchy, reserve some nuts before processing them, chop these nuts to any size you like, then mix into your butter before you transfer it to your storage jar.

Mixed butters

Try mixtures of your own, with or without salt, crunchy or smooth, roasted or not. How about:

Almonds, cashews and sunflower seeds

Cashews, almonds, brazil nuts, chia and pumpkin seeds

Peanuts, cashews, almonds, sunflower and flax seeds

For a decadent version, break up some dark chocolate (at least 70 per cent cocoa solids) into slivers or crumbs, and add this to your mixture at the end

Making nut butter at home is completely straightforward, quick and easy.

Maple butter

Some Grade A maple syrup

Sea salt (optional)

Equipment

Sugar thermometer

500ml glass storage jar

WHEN YOU CRAVE SOMETHING SWEET, choose the best, preferably wild, and pure. Raw honey and tree saps are nature's gift of wild sweetness. Until people learned how to preserve cane juice by evaporation and the subsequent further refinement over recent centuries into table sugar, all sources of sweetness were not only wild but seasonal, and largely serendipitous.

The most well-known tree sap comes from the sugar maple, yet that is but one of scores of trees the world over that can be tapped for their sweet sap, which usually rises as the tree wakes from its dormant period in the late winter and spring. The quality and quantity of the sap is often dependent on the severity of the winter. Tree sap can be harvested from the many species of maple, as well as species of walnut, birch and sycamore. Some, like birch, are consumed as a drink or fermented to make beer. Fresh birch sap is a most extraordinary drink; it is neither sweet nor sour, but clear, refreshing and invigorating. Don't miss the opportunity to try it in spring. It does not keep.

Maple butter is the simple transformation of maple syrup (which is the sap boiled down into syrup – it takes about 40 litres of sap to make 1 litre of syrup) into a more solid substance; now you can have the pleasure of maple syrup on your toast or waffle without it becoming soggy. It's easy to make, if rather tiring – you don't get something wonderful for nothing, you know.

Maple syrup is graded (America uses A, B, C; Canada uses 1, 2, 3) according to its translucency; choose your colour – the darker syrup has more flavour. You will lose about 35–40 per cent of the syrup through evaporation, so 750ml of syrup makes about 500ml of butter. Don't fret about the cost; it's a truly delicious special sweet treat and keeps well, if you can manage not to eat it too often.

–

Prepare
You will be heating the maple syrup to 113°C, cooling it rapidly to 38°C, then beating it until it is transformed (it crystallises) into maple butter. Prepare by setting a saucepan or bowl into a large bowl of ice cubes, as this will be your cooler.

Boil
Heat all the syrup in a separate saucepan until it boils and add a pinch of salt if you want to temper the sweetness. Do not stir the syrup. Monitor the temperature with a sugar thermometer or equivalent. Once you are sure all the syrup has reached 113°C remove it from the heat and pour the syrup into the pan/bowl on ice and let it chill without stirring.

Raw honey and tree saps are nature's gift of wild sweetness.

Chill and stir

Wait until the syrup has reached 38°C, then remove it from the ice bath and start stirring with a wooden spoon. Not fast, but steady as you go. You'll be stirring for about 30 minutes, so it's worth making this a community effort and sharing the task with another, or others. After about 10 minutes the syrup will lighten and start to solidify through crystallisation. Don't give up; keep stirring. You want a consistency of pourable batter.

Quickly now

Have a storage jar ready. Once it's on the slightly runny side of pourable, pour and scrape it out of the bowl quickly into the jar, as it will thicken very quickly and be difficult to handle.

It keeps for months in the fridge, but goes quite hard, so treat it like ice cream and remove well before you need it so that it warms to the consistency of a nut butter.

Sprouting

Seeds, nuts, pulses or grains specifically for sprouting

Equipment

Sprouting jars with stainless steel mesh lids, with a draining rest

> The seed, on germination, becomes a vital, energised life form.

THE SPROUTING OF SEEDS, nuts, pulses and grains has a common theme and goal: to wake up what is, in reality, a dormant or sleeping life form in order to make the bound-up energy and goodness more available for our benefit.

A dormant seed – here we'll call all the dormant forms a seed – is waiting for the right time to germinate. Its nutrients are locked up and well protected, which for us, with our relatively simple digestion system, makes a dormant seed hard to digest. It simply does not want to be destroyed by any of a host of nature's challenges, such as drought, sub-zero temperatures, or digestion by birds and beasts; that seed is built to wait for the right moment to germinate, then to grow and finally to reproduce.

When soaked in water at a suitable temperature, the seed considers that it's time to wake up and so starts to sprout, or germinate. Enzyme activity breaks down growth inhibitors, transforming and multiplying nutrients into their more easily digestible forms. The seed, on germination, becomes a vital, energised life form, and we are fortunate indeed to be able to recognise this and to harness this process in order to take advantage of this wonderfully generous gift of nature.

In times past, sprouting seeds was either a deliberate act or part of the natural rhythm of the harvesting and storage of grains. Chinese seafarers carried sacks of mung beans on board which they sprouted to boost their vitamin intake. Haphazard sprouting of grains was inevitable before the arrival of the combine harvester; dependent on the warmth and the humidity, some grains would sprout in the stooked-up sheaves standing in the fields after harvest. In principle this would not spoil the storage of the grain as farming was mostly small scale and very local, with at least one mill and a baker in every village.

More recently, sprouting has been popularised in two different ways. One, stemming from the 1970s as part of the nature aware movement, is a passion for sprouting for salads and microgreens, and the second, more recent development, is the sprouting of grains, their subsequent milling and use in baking. This trend was driven initially by the pursuit of the rich fresh flavours that sprouting brings, and now by the realisation that sprouted gluten grains possess less gluten and are more digestible than their unsprouted forms.

Both microgreens and sprouted grain flours are bursting with flavour because their complex sugars have been broken down to simple sugars and, since these are baby plants in their prime, they have a greater concentration of proteins, vitamins, minerals and enzymes than at any other time in the life of the plant. All this rich nutrient density provides supremely satisfying flavours.

Once a seed has sprouted there are many ways to realise its nutrient-rich benefits, depending on the nature of that seed. It's also important to know that, aside from the delicious taste, sprouting in all its forms brings terrific advantages for health, the environment and cost too.
By sprouting you get:

· Deep nourishment from natural food that is more digestible
  – the food is alive, fresh and raw.

· Ravishing flavours and a big choice of seeds to sprout.

· Known source – as long as you buy organic seeds from a trusted supplier, you know that what you are eating is what you have grown.

· Year-round freshness – you can sprout seeds at any time of year.

· Economical and environmentally friendly food – all you need are some seeds, water and sprouting jars – it's a convenient, simple and quick process.

Sprouting for increased nutrient availability in the seed
First, let's consider sprouting as a means of increasing the bio-availability and nutrient density of the seed itself.

Grains
Grains can be sprouted, crushed and used as a wet mash for immediate baking, cooking or for gruel; or they can be sprouted and then slow-dried at a low temperature to preserve as much of the valuable nutrients as possible. When stone-ground at a low temperature, you end up with a raw, wholegrain sprouted flour, ready to use. Alternatively, you can flake the sprouted grain, ready for making into porridge, or for baking.

Pulses
Sprouting dried pulses, such as garden peas, lentils and beans is easy and requires the minimum of equipment, space and preparation. Simply soak some dried pulses (bought from a specialist sprouting seed grower) in water in a sprouting jar, drain, rinse twice a day and let sprout. Within 4 days you will see the pulses springing to life with their little tails, full of released, enhanced and bio-available nutrients and flavours. Use this method to make the sprouted garden pea soup on page 133.

Nuts
Once removed from their hull, some nuts won't sprout at all: brazils, hazelnuts, pecans or walnuts, for example. Instead, you can activate them, which involves soaking in a mild saline solution, washing and slow drying (see pages 102–105). Other nuts, such as truly raw almonds and cashews, will sprout. Ideally, you want to allow these to sprout but only a little, and then use them immediately, for baking or in a smoothie for instance, or to preserve them by dehydration. If you let them sprout for too long they don't taste good, and most of their energy has been lost into the sprout.

Seeds
Many seeds, sunflower seeds for instance, will sprout readily whereas some, such as chia, are reluctant to germinate and, like flax, they become gelatinous when soaked, and so require more specialist skills

and equipment. Other seeds are better activated (see pages 102–105) rather than sprouted, and then slow-dried for enjoyment as a snack or as an ingredient.

–

Sprout and dehydrate
Soak the nuts, seeds, pulses or grains for up to 12 hours (see also the chart on page 105 and read the seed supplier's instructions). Drain, then rinse with plenty of cold water.

Let the jars sit and sprout, draining on the rest. Do not leave in full sun.

Rinse 3–4 times a day, returning the jar to the draining rest each time. After about 24 hours you should see the sprouts emerging.

Rinse for a final time, gently pat dry on kitchen paper, then dry in a suitable oven or dehydrator at about 70°C for 16–20 hours until they are completely dry and crispy when you bite into them.

Store in an airtight jar. They'll be good for weeks, if not months.

Sprouting for fresh microgreens
The other way to gain the benefit from this energy-rich life stage is to harvest the microgreens or sprouts.

Activating nuts and seeds

Raw, untreated nuts and seeds

Flaked sea salt, quantities as specified

TO ACTIVATE NUTS AND SEEDS the simple principles are: soak in salted water, rinse well and dry slowly at a low temperature (see page 105 for soaking and sprouting times).

Salted water not only activates enzymes that neutralise the enzyme inhibitors but also washes them away too. But be aware that not all seeds and nuts can be activated – many have already been killed and some, by their very nature cannot be activated or sprout. Most plain seeds and nuts have either been roasted or boiled (or both) or otherwise treated to prevent them from spoiling or, indeed, from sprouting out of control. Fundamentally, these destructive treatments increase the overall shelf life of the food, but at the expense of nutrient availability. Look out for raw, untreated nuts and seeds from a trusted source.

Drying nuts and seeds in an oven set to a very low temperature works fine but is rather wasteful of energy and somewhat limited, especially once you realise how often you will want to dry your activated seeds and nuts. A small dehydrator is the best solution.

Whatever your drying method, always ensure that your nuts and seeds are fully dry and completely cooled down before storing. If you don't, they will go mouldy. In ideal conditions, they will store for months.

-

Look out for raw, untreated nuts and seeds from a trusted source.

Wash the nuts or seeds in filtered cold water and leave to soak completely immersed in the salted water. Soak for the specified hours, usually 4–12, covering your bowl with a plate. If you can, use a plate to press the nuts or seeds under the water.

Drain and rinse well – you will be surprised at the colour and cloudiness of the water, especially from nuts. Continue to rinse until the water runs clear. Pat dry with kitchen paper and then spread out evenly in a single layer on a baking tray and slow-dry until crisp at the lowest possible temperature your oven allows, ideally about 50°C, turning or shaking the tray occasionally and testing for crispiness from time to time. This should take 4–5 hours. If you have a dehydrator it will take about 18–24 hours at 38°C.

Crispy pecans

A mature pecan tree is a magnificent sight – a massive wide-spreading tree with a generous girth. The roots extend deep into the earth, providing a rich source of trace minerals to the nuts, particularly manganese, and also selenium, phosphorus, iron and calcium. Pecans contain about 70 per cent fat, mostly monounsaturated oleic acid, which is a very stable oil, giving the nuts excellent keeping qualities.

100g of pecans is 1 cup. Use ½ teaspoon of salt per cup. Soak for 6 hours. Soaking then slow drying pecans is a revelation, releasing a buttery

intensity in flavours that is completely compelling. Pecans will not sprout. Store in an airtight container.

Crispy walnuts

Walnuts, when raw and fresh and freshly shelled, contain the highest level and potency of antioxidants of all the varieties of tree and ground nuts. They are less moreish than pecans or almonds, but pair brilliantly with well-made artisan raw milk cheeses.

100g walnuts is 1 cup. Use ½ teaspoon of salt per cup. Soak for no longer than 4 hours. Slow dry for 4–5 hours. Once dry, store in the fridge. Like pecans, walnuts will not sprout.

Crispy almonds

Look for raw almonds complete with skin. This is less easy than it sounds as it is permitted for almonds to be sold as raw when they have in fact been steamed, roasted or irradiated. Buy from a trusted source, from a known origin or grower who you can trace or challenge, and from a region that grows almonds sustainably.

Blanched or skinless almonds have already been soaked in hot water to remove their skins and therefore arc unsuitable.

170g almonds is 1 cup. Use ½ tablespoon of salt per cup. Soak for 12 hours, and either leave the skins on or push the skin off between thumb and fingers. (This is a soothing pastime, especially with company.) Skinless almonds are easier to digest. Slow-dry for 4–5 hours. Dry and store in an airtight container.

Fresh and raw almonds are particularly rich in vitamin E, good oils (almond oil is a popular massage oil) and contain a wide variety of essential minerals such as zinc, manganese and phosphorus. Some almonds will sprout after about 3–4 days (see opposite).

Crispy cashews

A cashew is an extraordinary tropical nut or, more correctly, a seed, as it grows from beneath the cashew apple. Juice from the cashew apple is delicious and refreshing, with a highly attractive sweet–savoury flavour combination. It also has five times more vitamin C than an orange.

The nut is protected by a double shell that contains a poisonous oil related to the toxins found in poison ivy. The great majority of cashews are mechanically processed by a combination of cracking, boiling and roasting to rid the nut of its toxic oils. Despite this treatment it is permitted to sell these cashews as raw.

The only truly raw cashews are extracted by hand, and as this is a process that is very time-consuming to do safely, the nuts are extremely expensive and difficult to find. They are, though, especially delicious and worth every extra penny.

170g cashews is 1 cup. Use ½ tablespoon of salt per cup. Soak for no longer than 2–3 hours and dry at a slightly higher temperature or, if they are not truly raw, you can even roast them at about 95°C for 2–3 hours. Store in a sealed container. They do not always sprout – see the chart opposite.

Cashews are a comparatively starchy nut, popularly used in Asia as a thickener for soups and sweet foods. They are also rich in antioxidants and good oils, and possess, along with most nuts, a powerful selection of beneficial and essential minerals.

Caramelised nuts

Caramelised nuts

100g crispy activated nuts

For the caramel

50g rapadura sugar, coconut palm sugar or date syrup

¼ teaspoon ground cinnamon

Large pinch of nutmeg

Large pinch of sea salt

1 teaspoon vanilla paste or essence

15g butter, preferably raw

For an indulgent treat, coat your crispy activated nuts in a salty caramel and spice mixture. Use whole or half nuts; chopped nuts tend to burn.

Mix together the sugar, spices and salt

Warm a frying pan over a medium heat and add the butter and the crispy activated nuts. Stir to coat the nuts in butter, then stir continuously as you add your sugar and spice mixture. Keep turning the nuts over to coat them evenly with the caramel, for 3–5 minutes.

Tip the nuts onto a baking tray and after 5–7 minutes the caramel will have set. Break the clusters apart or enjoy in random clumps.

Toasting seeds with tamari

Toasting seeds with tamari

1 tablespoon coconut oil

60–70g seeds, ground or cracked (see page 241)

1 tablespoon tamari (wheat-free soy sauce)

Seeds toasted with tamari and coconut oil make for a truly moreish snack; scatter over salads and cooked greens too.

Warm the oil in a pan over a medium heat and add the seeds. Stir to prevent the seeds from burning, and, once they start to colour, remove from the heat and add the tamari. Continue stirring to coat the seeds evenly. Leave the seeds to cool for 3–5 minutes before serving.

Crispy pumpkin seeds

Central American peoples have been soaking, flavouring and drying pumpkin and squash seeds – known as pepitas – for millennia, typically

enjoying them spiced with chilli. Munching on pumpkin seeds is also popular in Russia and Ukraine, and a lot of pumpkins are grown for their seeds in Hungary and Austria.

Slow-dried for 3–4 hours, pumpkin seeds keep well, and provide a lot of energy and nutrients in a small package. They are especially rich in iron and magnesium. Soak for 8 hours, with ½ tablespoon of salt per 130g/1 cup. Slow-dry. Store in a sealed container. Pumpkin seeds will sprout after about 3 days (see chart below).

Crispy sunflower seeds

Sunflower seeds are packed with vitamin E, as well as B vitamins, and are a very good source of folic acid, calcium, iron, manganese, zinc, magnesium and selenium. Cracking open and spitting out the hulls of sunflower seeds while eating the kernels is a useful skill, one much practised in Mediterranean and Asian countries.

Activate hulled sunflower seeds by soaking for 6–8 hours with ½ tablespoon of salt per 140g/1cup. Slow-dry. Store in a sealed container. Sunflower seeds will sprout after about 12–24 hours (see chart below).

Food	Soaking time (hours)	Sprouting time (days/hours)
Almonds	8–12	No sprouting or 3 days
Brazil nuts	None or 2–3	No sprouting
Cashews	2–4	No sprouting or 12–24 hours
Chickpeas	8	2–3 days
Flaxseeds	½	Will form a gel; sprouting in a jar not recommended
Hazelnuts	8–12	No sprouting
Macadamias	2	No sprouting
Peanuts	6	2–4 days
Pecans	4-6	No sprouting
Pistachios	None or 8	No sprouting
Pumpkin seeds	8	3 days
Sesame seeds	8	2–3 days
Sunflower seeds	8	12–24 hours
Walnuts	4	No sprouting

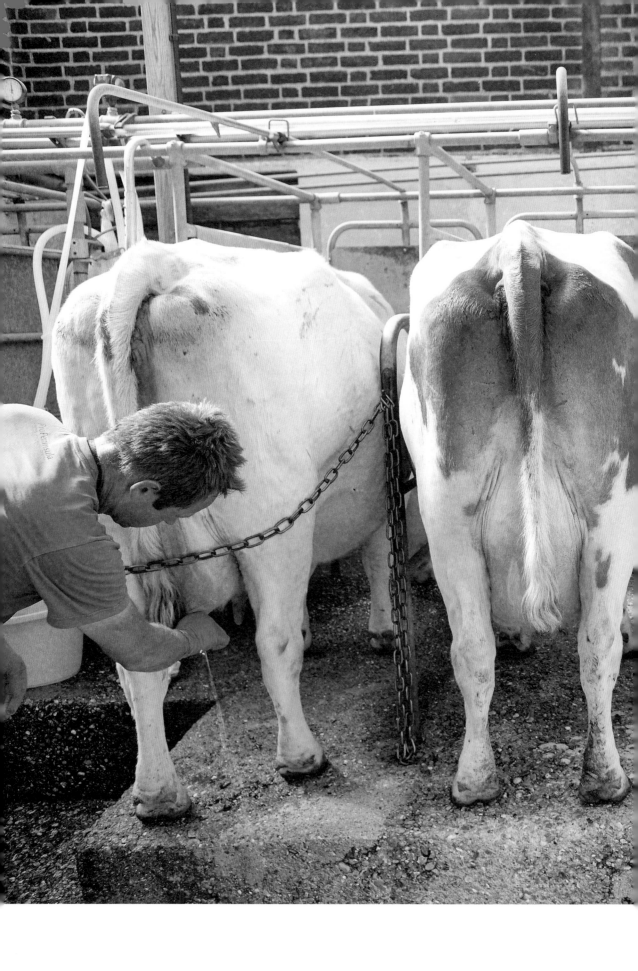

BREAKFAST

Eggs: boiled, fried, poached and scrambled

It should come as no surprise to know that our ancestors consumed eggs with gusto.

NOW THAT EGGS HAVE BEEN QUIETLY REHABILITATED from their lost decades in the nutritional badlands, it should come as no surprise to know that our ancestors consumed eggs with gusto. They were lucky, as all their eggs would have come from pastured omnivorous birds, free to roam and hunt for insects, bugs and worms as well as their treat of occasional grain. Sadly, the majority of eggs in our so-called civilised society are from hens cruelly confined in massive industrial-style sheds, fed a relentless, unnaturally vegetarian, grain-based diet. Their eggs are not as delicious or as nutrient-dense as those from pastured hens. Eggs from pastured chickens have dark yellow, orangey yolks and are of such quality they are worth seeking out and enjoying on a daily basis, especially because they can be cooked in so many ways, to suit all ages and sensitivities.

Boiled egg

This is a guaranteed no-crack soft centre cooking technique.

Fill your egg pan with enough water to cover an egg. Place your egg, or eggs, in the pan; it doesn't matter if they are straight from the fridge. If they float, they are too old and probably inedible. If they half float, they are acceptable. If they sink and stay submerged, they are fresh. Cook uncovered on the highest heat until the water boils. Remove the pan from the heat and let sit for 3 minutes. That's it. Ready to eat.

Fried egg

Most children will eat fried eggs, especially when cooked gently in quality butter or, even better, in ghee. Frying eggs in lard or other animal fats, and also coconut oil, is highly recommended too.

Warm a heavy, well-used and seasoned cast-iron frying pan over a medium heat and add a big knob of butter. Immediately turn the heat to low. Let the butter melt and begin to froth but not burn, swirl it around, and then slide the egg into the pan. Cover with a lid, turn down the heat a little and let the egg cook until the white has set and the yolk is looking less glossy.

Or, if you want to flip your egg over, leave the lid off and cook the egg until the white is almost set. Gently ease a spatula under the egg and then in one motion, turn it over. Cook for about 30 seconds more if you want a soft yolk, and for a minute if you like a firm yolk.

Serve immediately, pouring the melted, slightly caramelised, butter over the egg.

Serves 4

6–8 eggs from pastured hens, plus 2 yolks (extra yolks optional)

Cream (optional), preferably raw, otherwise Guernsey or Jersey

Chopped fresh herbs – chives, parsley or dill, or combinations of (optional)

Butter, preferably raw

Sea salt and freshly ground black pepper

Scrambled egg

Crack the eggs into a bowl, stir to break the yolks and blend all together. Do not whisk or beat. Stir in the extra yolks and 3–4 tablespoons of cream, if you like your scrambled eggs rich. Season with 2 and a bit large pinches of salt, black pepper and some herbs, if you wish.

Warm a heavy saucepan over a medium heat. A pre-warmed pan will reduce the degree to which the eggs will stick to its surface. Throw in a large knob of butter and let it sizzle; once it foams, add the eggs, and do not stir. Reduce the heat to a low–medium and watch the eggs begin to set. When they do, stir gently so that they cook evenly as wet or as dry as you prefer.

Remember to take the pan off the heat and serve the eggs when they are a little wetter than you like as they will continue to cook rapidly in the pan when off the heat. Serve straight away.

Poached egg

There are four secrets to making the perfect poached egg: a cup to crack the egg into, vinegar, a gentle pre-simmer and proper draining.

Carefully crack an egg into a small cup or mug with a handle.

Bring a saucepan of water to a gentle pre-simmer, no more, and add a big glug of apple cider vinegar.

Ease the cup with egg into the water and hold it under so that the egg is immersed, then let it slide gently into the pan. Leave the egg alone, for about 3 minutes, perhaps 4.

Use a slotted spoon to lift the egg out of the water. If it looks set, it is ready. If not, allow it another 30 seconds. Let the water drain through the slotted spoon and dab the egg with kitchen paper before serving.

Breakfast fry-up

Lamb's kidneys, prepared

Sourdough bread
(see pages 278-280)

Garlic

Flat-leaf parsley

Lard (see pages 82-85)

Pancetta

Ghee (see pages 36-39)
or butter

Mushrooms

Eggs, from pastured hens

BRITAIN MAY NOT BE RENOWNED FOR ITS SOPHISTICATED INDIGENOUS CUISINE, but it's certainly respected for its hearty cooked breakfast. The Full English Breakfast. Where else in the world can one be offered a fry-up breakfast that is suitable for every meal of the day?

The secret of a truly satisfying fry-up is not only the quality, provenance and freshness of the food, but also the choice of fat you use for frying. Use butter, ghee or lard. Talllow is also good, but has perhaps rather too strong a flavour for breakfast time.

Egg and bacon might seem a given, but kidneys are a nutrient-filled treat, especially when they come complete with the fat or suet, clinging to them. All organ meats are rich in fat-soluble vitamins A and D, as well as long-chain fatty acids and trace minerals. Our ancestors knew this and prized the organ meats accordingly, often eating them fresh and raw, and giving them to their babies, pre-chewed of course, as weaning food. Remember that in the wild, predators, especially the big cats, eat the organ meats of their prey first, and leave the muscle meat and bones to the scavengers. This is in complete contrast to our muscle-obsessed meat culture.

Preparing lamb's kidneys
Pare off the suet and keep it for pastry or if you have been lucky and found some extremely fresh young and milk-fed lamb's kidneys with their fat, then slice in half and barbecue or griddle, complete with the fat. Exquisite.

Leave whole or cut the kidneys in half lengthways, snip out the core of white gristle, wash well, then soak either in a bowl of salted water for about 30 minutes, or in some lemon juice or apple cider vinegar for 1–2 hours, or overnight in milk. Soaking will make them taste less strong and wash out any residual impurities. Rinse again after soaking and blot dry.

Prepare the kidneys, if necessary the night before (see above). Wipe off any grime and dirt from the mushrooms with a damp cloth and dice roughly, or if very small, leave whole. Slice the bread thickish and cut into rough triangles or squares. Smash 2 or 3 garlic cloves, remove the skins and chop roughly. Pull off a handful of parsley leaves and leave to one side ready to chop at the last minute.

Heat a cast-iron frying pan over a medium heat with a very generous wedge of lard and start to fry the pancetta. Keep an eye on it; if it starts to cook too quickly, move it up against the sides of the pan.

Heat a second cast-iron saucepan over a low–medium heat and add 2 tablespoons or a large knob of ghee. This is for your mushrooms.

Where else in the world can one be offered a fry-up breakfast that is suitable for every meal of the day?

Start to cook the mushrooms, turning them over in the ghee.

Ease the pancetta to the sides and place the kidneys in the pan, cut-face down. Turn up the heat and cook for about 2 minutes. Add some of the bread alongside the kidneys, adding more lard if it soaks up too much of the fat.

Start to fry your eggs in some ghee or butter.

Flip the kidneys over and press down onto the pan with a spatula. Cook for no more than 2 minutes. Turn the bread over too. The bread is best and ready when full of fat and browning lightly.

Turn up the heat under the mushrooms, they should glisten with the ghee and then start to brown a little. Throw in the garlic, add a pinch of salt and a grinding of black pepper, and stir.

Chop the parsley coarsely and add at the last minute to the mushrooms.

Serve this magnificent fry-up immediately, pouring any remaining fat onto the fried bread.

Pineapple and bacon

Serves 4

1 ripe pineapple

A little lard (see pages 82–85) or coconut oil

Streaky bacon – smoked or unsmoked

PINEAPPLE IS APPRECIATED PRIMARILY FOR ITS UNIQUELY APPEALING and delicious sweetness. It is an extraordinary fruit as it is formed when a hundred or more fruits from the pineapple flowers coalesce, which explains its unusual structure.

A native of South America, pineapple is often paired with meats, and particularly pork. The fresh, bright and sweet flavour of pineapple brings not only character but also helps digest meat, as it contains bromelain, an enzyme that breaks down protein. Its presence also explains why other fruits in a fruit salad made with fresh pineapple go soggy. Pineapple is high in fibre, manganese, carotenoids, B-complex vitamins and vitamin C.

This simple recipe is quick and easy to make, and is an ideal sweet–savoury breakfast surprise for children.

You will know that your pineapple is ripe when the leaves can be pulled off quite easily and it smells sweet. Cut off the base and the leafy top of the pineapple, then cut away the rough outer layer. Slice into thick rings, remove the hard core and then dice the flesh into chunks.

Melt the lard or oil in an iron frying pan and fry the bacon until lightly crispy, chop into short lengths and set aside in a warm oven.

Fry the pineapple in the same pan over a high heat, turning the chunks from time to time to ensure that they colour and caramelise as much as possible.

Serve the hot chunks in a pile with a generous topping of bacon pieces. If there is any oil left in the pan or warming dish, drizzle this on top.

Soaked oatmeal porridge

Serves 4

140g pinhead (steel-cut) or medium-grade oatmeal, or a mix of both

300–400ml freshly filtered water

Sea salt flakes

PORRIDGE IS NOTHING MORE THAN GRUEL MADE WITH OATS. Most cultures have a recipe for cooking or soaking a soup or mush of grains or pseudograins to pre-digest and release nutrients, such as polenta, mealie meal or grits (corn), muesli or porridge (oats) and kasha (oats, barley, buckwheat, millet or rye).

Until the early twentieth century, porridge was always made with cut or ground dehulled oat seeds (groats), what we know as oatmeal. Oat flakes were milled thick and coarse and usually fed to animals, particularly horses. Industrial steaming of oat groats and high-pressure roller milling created 'quick' oats, one of the first convenience foods, as the thinner, part-cooked flakes cook in minutes without pre-soaking.

Porridge made with oatmeal is tastier and more nourishing than everyday oat flakes, and when you soak the oatmeal overnight you will be reviving a simple and grounding time-honoured rhythm, as well as an understanding of how to persuade a reluctant/selfish seed to give up its goodness and energy. Soaking oatmeal the night before in warm water neutralises the phytic acid present in most grains and legumes that binds minerals and other nutrients. Pre-soaking the oatmeal means those nutrients are made available to us, and allows for gentle and effective digestion, as well as speeding the cooking time in the morning.

–

The night before, tip some oatmeal into a bowl and add sufficient warm to tepid water so that the oats are just covered and fully soaked. The water must be skin temperature and not scalding or the oatmeal will be lumpy. Stir as you add sufficient water to make a very thick soup. Smell the warm oatmeal – it's wonderfully comforting before bed – a rich aroma that comes from the good fats. Cover and leave to one side; it will soon thicken and set.

In the morning bring about 200ml of cold filtered water to a simmer in a small pan and add a generous pinch of salt. Slide the soaked oatmeal into the pan, stir and bring to a simmer.

Keep a jug of water by the stove: far better to add water to a mix that's too thick than boil down a watery gruel. Stir vigorously and cook so that the oatmeal is lump free and very hot. Taste for salt. The oatmeal should taste neither salty nor dull and should have a pourable but not runny consistency. Within 3–5 minutes your oatmeal should be ready. Taste to be sure, then turn off the heat, put a lid on the pan and let it rest for a minute or so.

Porridge made
with oatmeal
is tastier and
more nourishing
than everyday
oat flakes.

Sweet – serve with honey, maple syrup, rapadura or coconut palm sugar, or add chopped fresh or dried fruits.

Imaginative – add as much coconut oil as you like, and sprinkle over some bee pollen.

Savoury – chopped streaky bacon fried in lard and a scattering of grated strong Cheddar cheese.

Serve with a bowl of cream – dip your spoon into the cold cream and then take a scoop of porridge. It's not only a taste sensation but a traditional Scottish crofter's breakfast.

Lightly ferment your overnight soaking oatmeal with a spoon of live yogurt – it will make it slightly sour, which may be an acquired taste, but it's extremely good for you.

Try a wedge of good butter on your oatmeal porridge – another time-honoured tradition that is also rudely nourishing as the fats in butter and cream further increase the satiety of the dish, and enhance its oaty flavour.

Leftover porridge fries up beautifully to make tasty fritters (see page 262).

Not all oats are the same

Oats are now firmly established as the nourishing grain of choice. This would come as no surprise to our oat-growing ancestors who knew that a serving of oats cooked in water and salt and garnished with a slab of butter or cream was packed with sustaining energy. The Scots liked to eat their porridge standing up, so as to cram in more before a day at work. Oats contain a better balance of good fats, carbohydrates and protein than the majority of grains, and they are rich in B and E vitamins, calcium, iron, magnesium, potassium and phosphorus.

Oats are, however, quite reluctant to give up their goodness as they are rich in phytates – antioxidant compounds that block mineral absorption. Our grandparents would be familiar with the need to soak oats overnight before making porridge – this simple process neutralises most of the phytates and also speeds the cooking process the next day. You can achieve similar, if not better, results by sprouting oats – the vitamins B2 and B5 content rises by as much as 200 per cent and B6 by up to 500 per cent. You do need to find a source of living whole oat seeds (groats) though, because all oat seeds for milling are stabilised before processing to ensure that they will not sprout.

Oats in their natural uncontaminated state do not contain gluten, but they do contain a protein called avenin, which can be tolerated by some coeliacs. Oats described as gluten-free are grown, harvested and handled in isolation from all other gluten crops, and as this process is both time consuming and difficult it's not surprising that these so-called 'pure' oats are more expensive.

If you're after a diet based on raw food, then it's also important to be aware that pretty much all cut, ground or flaked oats have been cooked – not once but up to three times. These oats are not raw. When, and why are oats cooked? First off, the whole oats are steamed to ensure they will not germinate (sprout) and to prevent rancidity. This is known as stabilising, and it increases the keeping qualities of the oats. If the whole oats are destined to become oatmeal, they are sold as groats or, when cut into three pieces, as steel-cut oats or, when milled, as ground oatmeal in varying grades. So far, they have been cooked once only.

Then, if they're to be flaked, the groats are steel cut or left whole, steamed and rolled into flakes, then cooked again to reduce the water content – again to increase shelf life. A jumbo oat flake is made from a groat that has been steamed and rolled to varying thicknesses; a porridge oat flake is a piece of the groat, steel cut or broken, that has been steamed and rolled, and these flakes are therefore smaller. All these oats have been cooked three times.

Why steam before flaking? Convenience. Steaming a groat softens it, which allows it to be flaked at a high pressure, and that forms a thinner flake. Thinner, part-cooked flakes take less time to prepare. This was an invention of the nineteenth century, marketed as a time-saving marvel called 'quick oats', which dispensed with the need for soaking or onerous cooking times. Not surprisingly, this pursuit of oaty convenience is not a healthy one: the processes reduce the nutrient density of the food, and do not remove or neutralise the anti-nutrients. Most oats sold today are quick oats.

So, in theory, the only raw oats are oat groats that have not been stabilised, which are then steel cut or ground into oatmeal, or roller milled into coarse, broken flakes. If you can find a source of dehulled raw groats, you could flake these yourself with a simple domestic roller mill. Some farmers sell coarse raw oat flakes, and sprouted porridge oats are usually not steamed or baked, and are therefore sold as raw.

Oats contain a better balance of good fats, carbohydrates and protein than the majority of grains.

Fruity date:
a world-champion porridge

Serves 4

75g mix of medium-grade oatmeal and pinhead oatmeal

75g mix of porridge oat flakes and jumbo oat flakes

450ml Guernsey or non-homogenised milk, preferably raw, or a mixture of milk and water

Pinch of ground cinnamon (to taste)

1 tablespoon apple powder, or (as it's not easy to find) dehydrate some fresh apple and grind

A handful of freshly chopped dates

A handful of freshly chopped dried apple, either from rings or as cubes, with or without skin

A handful of freshly chopped dried apricots

To serve

Guernsey cream, or raw, or clotted

Coconut palm sugar (optional)

EVERY YEAR, in October, and for more than two decades, competitors from the world over arrive in the quiet Scottish Highlands village of Carrbridge in the Cairngorms to take part in the quest for porridge world championship glory. That's for cooking porridge, not for how many bowls you can eat in one sitting. There are two categories and winners: one for traditional Scottish oatmeal porridge, made only with oatmeal (not jumbo or porridge flakes), water and salt; the second for a speciality porridge dish, which can be savoury or sweet but must contain oats.

This event is called The Golden Spurtle, named after the trophy awarded for the best bowl of traditional porridge (a spurtle is, of course, a porridge stirring stick), and takes place in Carrbridge village hall. It is a unique and entertaining spectacle, watching contestants vying for the trophies with their imaginative recipes and ingredients. This recipe won the speciality trophy in 2014; the judges declared it is so simple that a child could make it. Praise indeed.

–

Combine the oatmeal and the oat flakes mixtures.

Heat the milk, or milk and water, in your favourite porridge pan. Add the oatmeal and flakes, and start to stir with your spurtle. Now add the cinnamon and apple powder, and most of the chopped fruits – save some to sprinkle on the top of each bowl.

Simmer for as long as necessary until just right – usually about 4–6 minutes. Add some extra milk, or water and milk, if the porridge becomes too thick. It should be thick and creamy but pourable.

Serve, sprinkling some of the reserved dried fruits on top, before pouring over, generously, as much cream as you like. Sweeten some more, if you wish, with a shaking of coconut palm sugar.

Or, if you want to appreciate the cream cold with the hot porridge, serve the cream on the side in its own bowl. Dip your spoon into the hot porridge and then into the cream, hot and cold, cream and oats... a heavenly combination.

This recipe won the speciality trophy in 2014; the judges declared it is so simple that a child could make it. Praise indeed.

Sprouted oat porridge

Serves 4

150g sprouted rolled oats

400ml freshly filtered water, plus extra for wetting the oats

Sea salt

ALL GRAINS ARE RELUCTANT TO GIVE UP THEIR NOURISHMENT WITHOUT A STRUGGLE. After all, they are seeds and want to germinate, thrive and reproduce, rather than be plucked, dried, ground or flaked and then eaten. Oats are no exception, which is why our ancestors would never prepare, cook and consume a bowl of porridge in moments. Instead, they would soak and often ferment their grains overnight before cooking them to release the nutrients in the raw oat groat or seed. They may not have understood the nutritional science, but they embraced the symbiotic powers of fermentation, and before industrialised harvesting they would also have been aware that some of their grains sprouted or germinated naturally. Once sprouted, then dried and stored correctly, such grains provided an easily digestible source of bio-available nutrients, including soluble fibre, and rich flavours without the need for soaking or fermentation.

Oat porridge is such a simple dish, no more than a gruel in reality, yet when made with raw sprouted oats it is transformed into the realms of deeply satisfying moreishness. You will enjoy your porridge more, eat less of it, and feel satisfied for longer, after preparing and cooking it within minutes. With sprouted grains you really can have the best of both worlds: time-honoured nourishment and modern convenience.

Which water, salt or how about shio-koji?

If you want to up your porridge game and prepare for The Golden Spurtle (see page 118), you will be wanting to pimp up your ingredients.

Water: unless you have your own spring, try your favourite bottled spring water.

Salt: the subtle oat flavours should be enhanced gently by salt, not destroyed by a harsh saltiness. Find a fine flake sea salt that's sweetly salty.

Shio-koji: it's salty and mysteriously sweet (see page 67). Perfect umami for porridge. Try it.

Pour your oats into a bowl and cover them with warm water (skin temperature not scalding), just enough to wet them. Stir to combine. This will ensure that your porridge is not lumpy. If you want to reduce the cooking time, leave the oats to soak for 15–25 minutes.

Pour about three-quarters of the filtered water into your favourite porridge pan, and bring it to a simmer. Throw in 2 big pinches of salt, followed by the wet oats. Reduce the heat to a gentle, plooping simmer, and cook for 2–3 minutes or so, stirring frequently, before tasting and adding more water or salt if necessary. Finer flaked sea salt makes this easier, and also add a splash of water.

Good porridge should not be salty or dull and it should be just pourable, not runny, nor solid. Simmer, stir, taste and adjust, and then cook for a further 7–9 minutes (3–4 minutes if soaked for longer).

Taste for a final time, then serve piping hot. This, like all porridge, must be eaten forthwith before it solidifies and cools.

Multigrain and super seedy sprouted porridge

The majority, say 75 per cent, of your recipe should be oat flakes, but mix it with sprouted barely, rye, quinoa and buckwheat flakes, and some sprouted or activated seeds, such as golden linseeds, linseeds, pumpkin, sunflower, poppy and chia. Cook as above.

Bircher muesli:
the original muesli

Serves 4

75g rolled oats – a mixture, as you like, of porridge and jumbo oats

Freshly filtered water

Some lemon zest or lemon juice

Clotted, Jersey or Guernsey cream

1 apple, unpeeled

Some hazelnuts, almonds and sunflower seeds

The nineteenth century was a time of dietary introspection for new wealthy urbanites in Europe and the USA. The obsessions were digestion and vegetarianism. Religious zealots such as the Rev S. Graham and the Kellogg brothers preached the abstinence of meat, alcohol and sex, inventing in the process Graham flour and cornflakes – temperance foods indeed. Meanwhile, out walking in the Swiss Alps, a Zurich doctor, Maximilian Bircher-Benner, rediscovered a peasant dish of oat gruel – now known as muesli – that he adapted for his sanatorium. Muesli is of course really nothing more than cold oat porridge. Muesli in Swiss-German means 'mush', which is a common expression in the USA for porridge.

–

The night before, soak the oats in just enough water to make the oats sodden, add a generous squeeze of lemon juice or a sprinkle of lemon zest, and stir. Cover and leave to one side.

Mix as much cream into the soaked oats as you like. Coarsely grate the apple over your mush, then stir in if you wish. Serve with a generous sprinkle of crushed or powdered nuts and sunflower seeds.

Fermentation. The folk of the Swiss Alps knew, from tradition, that an overnight fermentation of the oats was necessary to neutralise the anti-nutrient phytic acid so that the nutrients in the oats would be available for digestion. Rather than lemon juice, they would have used whey, yogurt or buttermilk to ferment their gruel. Stir 2 teaspoons of any of those dairy products into your overnight soaking oats rather than lemon juice or zest.

Raw Bircher? Not all oats are the same. You will find that sprouted oat flakes are much more inclined to ferment when soaked. This is because when germinated, the starches have been converted to simple sugars. So, unless you're looking for the sour ish fermented taste, refrigerate the soaking sprouted oat flakes overnight and make only enough for each morning bowl of bircher. For more information on sprouting and sprouted grains, see pages 98–101.

No cream at breakfast? Use plain yogurt (see pages 26–29) or kefir (see pages 22–25).

Nuts. Sprout or activate your nuts (see pages 98–105) and try pecans and brazils too.

Seeds. Sprinkle a variety of freshly ground or whole seeds, such as poppy, chia, hemp, pumpkin and linseed onto your muesli, sprouted if you like (see pages 98–101).

Granola

Grains – a combination of oat, spelt, rye, barley and buckwheat flakes: about a third of the mix

Seeds and puffs – as you like, such as sunflower, chia, pumpkin, puffed amaranth and puffed quinoa: about a sixth of the mix

Nuts – broken or whole almonds, pecans, hazelnuts, Brazils and coconut chips: about a sixth of the mix

Unsweetened fruits – soft dried figs, raisins, apple, apricots, mango, wild berries, Cape gooseberries and dates: about a third of the mix, or for a fruit-free recipe, substitute with grains and seeds

Oil – use 2 tablespoons cold-pressed coconut oil, gently warmed to a liquid

Sweetness for binding and flavour – one or simple combinations of maple syrup, rapadura sugar, coconut palm sugar, honey and date syrups, to taste and to make the granola more or less crunchy/clumped. If you use a sugar, melt it gently with the oil so that it blends more easily

Spices – vanilla, cardamom or cinnamon

GRANOLA IS NOTHING MORE THAN BAKED AND SWEETENED GRAINS. It has a surprisingly long pedigree, as it was originally conceived in America in the mid nineteenth century as a mess of smashed-up tray-baked Graham (wheat) flour and known as 'granula'. In the doldrums as a breakfast cereal until the 1960s, granola was rediscovered and reinvented, more often than not as crudely sweet and crunchy oat cereal, often with miserably hard, dried fruit and stale nuts.

Fresh homemade granola, by contrast, is a real treat – and you can easily create your favourite combinations of grains, seeds, nuts and fruits, and make your granola clumpy or broken, crunchy or soft, and as sweet or savoury as you wish. If you must add dried fruits, do so late in the baking time so that they do not cook rock hard.

Make enough to last you a week. Fresh granola is best eaten as soon as possible.

–

Preheat the oven to 150°C/gas 2.

Mix your selection of ingredients (without any fruit) in a bowl and make sure they're all coated in the sweetness and oil.

Tip onto a baking dish or tray with sides and spread out roughly but evenly. Bake for 15–20 minutes, mix in your fruits and bake again for 10 minutes.

When cool, store in an airtight jar, and not for long. Homemade granola really does taste best when very fresh.

It is delicious with plain yogurt or milk, or snacking straight from the jar.

Sprouted and activated – use sprouted grains, seeds and activated nuts for more nourishment (see pages 98–105).

Toast nuts and seeds before baking your granola – this will give you more crunch.

Gently sauté some nuts and seeds with one of your sugars or syrups, and add to the baked granola for a sweet crunch.

Sprouted spelt American pancakes (and waffles)

Makes about 8 American-style pancakes

130g sprouted spelt flour (or sprouted wholewheat flour)

¼ teaspoon finely ground sea salt

½ teaspoon bicarbonate of soda

1½ teaspoons rapadura sugar, jaggery or coconut palm sugar

30g unsalted butter, preferably raw, melted

275–300ml raw buttermilk, or use yogurt or soured raw milk from pastured cows (you will need less soured raw milk than buttermilk or yogurt)

1 egg, from pastured hens

Ghee (pages 36–39), for sautéing

To serve

Raw butter

Maple syrup

SIMPLE PANCAKE AND WAFFLE RECIPES made with sprouted flours are alive with flavour, tasting fresh and light, with a melting texture. Sprouted flours not only taste more exciting, they are so much easier to digest, and they are also easy and convenient to use, as they don't require soaking or any fermentation before cooking.

In simple terms, a seed, once it sprouts, has undergone a complete transformation; from a locked-up store of energy and goodness, to, in essence, a plant. A seed does not want to be digested, it wants to be dispersed to a new home in the soil, where it can sprout and grow into a new plant when conditions are right. As a seed it therefore protects itself and resists digestion by animals not only by virtue of its tough fibrous structure, but also by containing a sophisticated selection of natural chemicals such as anti-nutrients and enzyme inhibitors.

Our ancestors knew this very well, and so they would take the necessary steps to sprout or ferment their grains before cooking and eating them.

We have not only lost sight of the wisdom of sprouting and fermenting grains to increase the bio-availability of their nutrients, we have also lost our relationship with, and understanding of, the importance of eating a variety of grains. For about 100 years we have been consuming more and more foods either made from or containing grains, particularly wheat, that are not suitably prepared for digestion at all. Imagine a daily diet of wheat flakes for breakfast, along with toast, made from mass-produced bread. Lunch? How about a sandwich? And for supper, a bowl of pasta, made from highly refined and extruded wheat flour. Call that variety? This is a grain-based diet.

And how about the varieties of wheat? Farmers used to grow and nurture their own seeds that had evolved to suit their local ecosystem. Each country, region and community had its own unique selection of wheat, often suited to, and bred for, fields or areas on each individual farm. Now something like 90 per cent of all wheat grown today comes from just three varieties of dwarf wheat, bred for commercial efficiency and industrial-style agriculture. Combine this lack of variety with our delight in the shallow but moreish flavours of modern processed food with its obsession with convenience and it's no wonder that we're becoming increasingly intolerant of highly refined wheat. Thankfully, some of the traditional varieties of wheat, such as spelt, einkorn, emmer and khorasan (aka Kamut®), are being rediscovered and grown more widely.

Spelt was the staple variety of wheat in Europe and the Near East from ancient times to the Middle Ages. It's very suitable for less intensive and organic farming practices, being tall, disease resistant and requiring less fertilising than its modern dwarf relatives. Although spelt is not gluten-free, its primitive nature makes it more digestible than modern dwarf

hybrid wheat. As with all wheat, spelt contains lots of protein, is high in fibre and, when grown in nutrient-dense healthy soils, it is a good source of B vitamins, calcium and iron. What's more, it has a delicious nutty flavour, which comes through in this batter for making pancakes or waffles.

–

Sprouted spelt waffles

Use the same recipe for pancakes, but make the batter lighter by separating the yolk from the white. Mix in the yolk as before, and then whisk up the white until stiff and fold into the batter.

In a medium-sized bowl, mix the flour with the salt, bicarbonate of soda and sugar. In a separate bowl, mix the melted butter with the buttermilk (or soured milk, or yogurt) and egg.

Little by little add the wet mixture to the dry ingredients, stirring all the while to make a very smooth batter. Stop adding the wet mixture when you've made a just pourable thick and super-smooth batter.

Heat a heavy frying pan over a medium heat. Add a small wedge (if cold) or a glug of warmed ghee to coat the hot surface thinly, and reduce the heat a little.

Ladle in your batter and swirl around if need be to spread evenly. Let bubbles form on the surface of the pancake – and then flip – it should be golden brown underneath. Once you have cooked your first pancake, throw it away – it's never any good.

Cook the remaining pancakes, making sure that you have got a queue of hungry customers waiting to eat them straight from the pan.

Serve with lots of raw butter and maple syrup.

Sprouted buckwheat with spelt pancakes (blinis)

Serves 4, and makes lots, which is good (see leftovers on page 128)

400ml raw milk

200ml double cream, preferably raw, otherwise Guernsey or Jersey

2 teaspoons active dried yeast

130g sprouted buckwheat flour

65g sprouted spelt flour

2 large eggs from pastured hens

30g unsalted butter, preferably raw, melted

1 teaspoon fine sea salt

Ghee (pages 36–39) or butter, for sautéing

To serve

Wild smoked salmon

Raw soured cream (pages 33–35)

Freshly ground black pepper

Lemon wedges

Savoury – with cheese - cover blinis with strongly flavoured grated mature Cheddar or Gruyère. This follows the Jewish tradition of cheese-stuffed blinis served at Hannukah and Shavuot.

Sweet – spread with raw honey, almond butter (see page 92), apple or apricot butter (see page 90) or serve with butter and a drizzle of maple syrup.

LIGHT, BUBBLY AND WONDERFULLY FRESH-TASTING, these buckwheat pancakes are a perfect weekend treat, even more so when served warm from the pan topped with slices of wild smoked salmon and raw soured cream refreshingly paired with a glass of natural sparkling wine (see page 301).

Originally from Eastern Europe, and also known as blintz or blintchiki, in pre-Christian times blinis were served at the end of winter to commemorate the rebirth of the new sun and its warmth.

Made with sprouted flour, your batter will be ready to use within no more than 3–4 hours. If, however, you opt for conventional flour your blinis will not only taste better when the batter is fermented for longer, say overnight, creating a slightly savoury sour character, but also you will make available more nourishment. Sprouting, like fermentation, neutralises the phytic acid and enzyme inhibitors present in all grains that reduce our ability to absorb nutrients and minerals.

–

Combine the milk and cream in a large glass bowl and warm to just above room temperature using a double boiler. Remove the bowl from the heat and add the yeast, and then stir well.

Combine the flours, add to the yeast mixture and stir to mix completely. Cover the bowl with a cloth and leave it to rest and lightly ferment for 3–4 hours at room temperature. (For conventional flours leave to rest and ferment overnight or for 8–12 hours.)

Separate the egg yolks from the whites. Whisk the whites until stiff. Beat the egg yolks lightly. Stir in the egg yolks, melted butter and salt into the batter, and beat or mix thoroughly for 3–4 minutes. You're looking for a consistency that's thick but pourable. Now gently fold in the stiff egg whites.

Heat a heavy iron frying pan until it smokes. Swipe with a smear of ghee or butter and then ladle a dollop of batter onto the pan. The size of the blini is your call. Wait a few moments as it spreads and sets, and when little bubbles begin to appear, flip the blini over. Press down lightly before scooping out of the pan onto the warmed plate. It may take a few blinis for the pan to settle down, but with a little practice and confidence you will be able to cook many at a time.

Serve freshly made – you're liable to be a slave to the stove as you please your guests – with a slice of wild smoked salmon and a scoop of soured cream, freshly ground black pepper and a squeeze of fresh lemon juice.

Gluten-free sprouted buckwheat blinis

Serves 4 (makes lots)

400ml raw milk

200ml double cream, preferably raw, otherwise Guernsey or Jersey

2 teaspoons active dried yeast

295g sprouted buckwheat flour

2 large eggs, from pastured hens

30g unsalted butter, preferably raw, melted

1 teaspoon fine sea salt

Ghee (pages 36–39), for sautéing

YOU CAN ALSO MAKE THESE BLINIS GLUTEN-FREE. Just be sure to check that the buckwheat flour is certified gluten-free. They will cook really fast and are extremely moreish, being light and full of flavour.

Follow the recipe on page 126, but let the batter sit and ferment for only 2½ hours.

Corn blinis? A Southern USA twist

Follow the main recipe but substitute sprouted wheat flour for the buckwheat and sprouted corn flour for the spelt.

Serve warm with pulled pork and a drizzle of barbecue sauce.

Leftovers

Dried blini biscuits – spread blinis on a baking tray and slow-bake in the oven at 40°C (or as low as your oven will go) for 8–12 hours, or overnight. Crispy and moreish, especially with butter and nut butter, or raw honey. They'll also keep for ages in an airtight jar or tin.

Frozen – Blinis freeze beautifully. Defrost and reheat carefully in a warm frying pan.

Gluten-free

Never before in human history have so many people based a significant part of their diet on grains. Empires and fortunes have been built and lost feeding citizens and customers with ground-up seeds. It's a seemingly efficient, but environmentally stressful and often destructive annual agricultural practice, as it inevitably leads to monoculture and a completely unbalanced ecosystem. Humans are naturally omnivores and the modern diet is skewed out of all recognition from the predominantly vegetable-, fruit- nut- and occasional meat- and fish-based diets that nourished our ancestors.

On the face of it, intensive arable farming makes it possible to produce a lot of cheap food that historically has been the staple of the masses, whether wheat for bread, or rice, or maize meal. In more recent times, industrial food manufacturers crave cheap and consistent ingredients to maximise profit, and so grains have been genetically and intensively bred for about 150 years and, more recently, genetically modified to maximise yield and homogeneity. Not long ago, every country, every region, every locale, possessed an assortment of grain varieties all suited to their local farming environment and practices. China alone once grew thousands of wheat varieties. Now the world's wheat supplies are dependent on fewer than five varieties.

All grains contain protein, but of the three most commonly grown grains, wheat alone contains a protein called gluten, which gives wheat flour dough its texture and elasticity. Other less well-known grains containing gluten include spelt, rye and barley. Most people can digest gluten, but typically about 1 per cent of the population cannot, and they are diagnosed as coeliac. Anyone with coeliac disease seeks to avoid all food and drinks with gluten, which is rarely straightforward as manufacturers use gluten to stabilise and improve the texture of many processed foods. Gluten is often found in ice cream, tomato sauce, soy sauce, hot dogs, strongly -flavoured crisps and very commonly in imitation meats, particularly in Asia. In principle, coeliacs ought to be able to safely enjoy naturally gluten-free grains such as rice or corn, or the pseudo-grain buckwheat. In a bid to create safe food for coeliacs, many governments now provide a regulatory framework to control the production of gluten-free foods. To be labelled gluten-free the accepted level of gluten is less than 20 parts per million.

Now that recognition of the condition is well established, it's clear that the percentage of diagnosed coeliacs is growing somewhat but not exponentially, so why has the gluten-free food and drink sector grown substantially? The key driver is the new obsession against wheat. Many doctors have a new easy-care mantra for the growing numbers who seek medical solutions for such lifestyle complaints as bloating, listlessness, uncomfortable digestion: try a gluten-free diet. This is all well and good, but does not address the fundamental issue. Their patients may well have become sensitive to gluten because of the nature of their diet and the way the food is processed, not because of gluten itself. The modern Western diet includes a lot of highly refined foods and a lot of wheat: how often do you eat a bowl of cereal in the morning, a sandwich or wrap at lunchtime and a plate of pasta in the evening? Congratulations, that's three meals of industrial wheat products, full of gluten. So, not only do we eat a lot of wheat, but we no longer, for the most part, prepare the grain to make it more easily digestible.

For millennia bread has been made with love and patience, and the miller, the baker and his bakery were at the centre of every community. Bread was digestible because the grain had often sprouted, and/or had been milled locally so it was very fresh, then proved and fermented to pre-digest the gluten. Now, for the most part, we rely on industrial bakeries, where refined bread is made as fast as possible, using a lot of yeast, with ingredients that are mind-bogglingly complex. Good bread can be made with three or four ingredients not twenty-three.

Coeliacs must be delighted by the increase in gluten sensitive consumers, because at last manufacturers are waking up to the reality that gluten-free food is not just for a minority but for a new health-obsessed community desperate for dietary solutions. Remember when gluten-free was a poor relation to the rest of the foods on offer? Take out gluten and you lose flavour. The industry's answer? Add cheap and addictive flavour-rich ingredients, namely refined sugars and refined fats, which are scarcely a healthy option. Thankfully this practice is more or less over, although you must check the ingredients even more carefully than usual before you buy any gluten-free foods or drinks or, better still, make your own.

SOUPS

Bubur ayam
Rice and chicken porridge

Serves 4

375g white rice

2 litres chicken stock (see page pages 78–81)

2 bay leaves

Sea salt

Eggs (optional), from pastured hens

Some cooked chicken meat, diced

To serve

Some spring onions, finely sliced

Some shallots, finely diced

Some celery, finely diced or chopped

Some chopped coriander leaves

Soy sauce

THIS SIMPLE DISH of boiled rice and chicken is extremely popular throughout Indonesia and Malaysia. Burbur ayam is probably a derivative of chicken congee and is much enjoyed for breakfast, served up by street vendors and smart restaurants alike, and as a soothing late-night small meal. It is a comfort food, soft and easy to digest – which also makes it entirely suitable for anyone in need of a dose of gentle energy, whether during illness, tiring in old age, or when young and fast growing.

Bubur, which means porridge, is usually cooked in chicken stock, and forms a porridge-like soup, and as bubur ayam, is served with diced cooked chicken, often an egg, and vegetables and condiments such as chopped shallots, spring onions, celery and soy sauce.

Wash the rice until the water runs clear and then drain.

Bring the stock to a gentle simmer, and then add the rice and bay leaves. Cook, uncovered and at a gentle simmer, for about 30 minutes, or until the grains begin to disintegrate. Taste for salt.

If you would like an egg with your bubur ayam, poach it in the soup.

Just before serving, add the chopped cooked chicken to warm it through. Put out an array of condiments in little dishes for people to scatter on top of their bubur and serve with soy sauce.

Burbur is a comfort food, soft and easy to digest.

Sprouted garden pea soup

Serves 4

Butter, preferably raw, or ghee (see pages 36–39)

2 medium or 1 large onion, chopped medium-fine

1 litre chicken stock (see pages 78–81)

500g freshly sprouted garden peas (see pages 98–101)

Sea salt or shio-koji (see page 67) and freshly ground black pepper

To serve

Croutons made with sprouted spelt sourdough (see pages 278–280), fried in lard

Crème fraîche or soured cream

GARDEN OR GREEN PEA SOUP made with freshly picked immature peas, simmered in a meat stock and puréed, is a relatively modern food, and one of the pioneers of French cuisine. Prior to the invention of this rather refined and fresh dish, pea soup, pease pudding, porridge or pottage, was a simple peasant food enjoyed since ancient times and made with dried split peas, now known as field peas.

You can make this soup with freshly podded or frozen garden peas or, more innovatively, and year-round too, with freshly sprouted garden peas. See pages 98–101 for how to sprout your own.

–

Melt a large wedge of butter (say about 50g) in a heavy casserole over a low–medium heat. Sauté the onions gently, until they are tender but not coloured.

Pour in the chicken stock, and throw in the peas. Turn up the heat and bring to the boil. Skim off any foam, if necessary, then reduce the heat to a gentle simmer. Cook for 10–15 minutes, or until the peas are softish to the bite.

Meanwhile, fry up some croutons in some lard, and put to one side.

Purée the soup in the pot using a hand-held blender. Taste for salt and add cracked black pepper as you like.

Serve with the croutons, a swirl of crème fraiche or soured cream, or keep the cream on the side and dip your spoonful of hot soup into the cold cream.

Mishoshiru
Miso soup

Makes 1 litre stock or soup

For the kombu dashi

Dried kombu – a piece about 10–15cm square, or about 10g

1 litre water

For the miso soup

1 litre kombu dashi

2–4 tablespoons red miso paste, or combinations of, such as white, brown and dark – it's really to your taste

2 spring onions, thinly sliced

MISO SOUP WITH A BOWL OF PLAIN RICE is the staple breakfast in Japan and is typically made from very simple ingredients: some miso paste and some flavoured stock, or dashi. From such a simple recipe comes a galaxy of miso soup recipes, usually with subtle and very personal preferences that make this one of the most intriguing and exciting foods that you think you can master.

It's not just what you add to the soup, but the choice of miso and the style of dashi that makes the soup so delectable. In Japan, there's a bewildering assortment of miso available beyond the major categories of white, yellow and red, influenced by regional, seasonal and personal factors. The dashi can be flavoured with fish, seaweed or mushrooms, or a combination of these. Finally, the other ingredients that are added to the miso soup – tofu, daikon, mushrooms or shrimp, for instance – again reflect seasonality and provide a visual theatre of flavours, textures and layers of discovery within a bowl. A simple soup indeed. It's time to become a miso soup devotee; and that's not hard as it's so delicious, sweetly sour, and full of complex and mysterious umami.

There's not only pleasure, but deep nourishment too. Miso paste is very much a ubiquitous seasoning in Japan. In principle it's made by fermenting cooked soya beans with the fungus *Aspergillus oryzae* (see also shio-koji, page 67) and salt. The plethora of miso varieties reflects the length of fermentation, temperature, quantities of salt, the addition of other grains or some aged miso, even the type and shape of the fermentation vessel. As for nourishment, yes, it can be salty, depending on the variety of miso, but the paste is also rich in protein, vitamins, minerals and fibre, as well as the enzymes and microorganisms encouraged by the fermentation process. Miso is a relatively delicate seasoning and both its flavour and nutrients will be spoiled by fierce heating and boiling. Always add the koji paste when the pan is off the heat and warm very gently.

This recipe calls for red miso and kombu (dried kelp) flavoured dashi; it's wise to begin with such a humble combination in your pursuit of miso soup perfection.

Wipe the kombu with a damp cloth to clean it, but don't wash the kombu or wipe off the traces of white powder. Make some slits around the sides of the kombu with a pair of scissors. If you have time, soak the kombu in the water for 30 minutes or so in a heavy saucepan, or you can leave soaking overnight.

The plethora of miso varieties reflects the length of fermentation, temperature, quantities of salt, the addition of other grains or some aged miso, even the type and shape of the fermentation vessel.

Bring to a simmer gradually over a low–medium heat, and skim off any residues from the surface, but be sure to remove the kombu before the water boils or your dashi will be bitter and slimy. Your kombu dashi is now ready for use, or, once cooled, it will keep in the fridge for up to a week, or can be frozen.

Bring the kombu dashi to a simmer. Pour some of the dashi into a small bowl and add the miso. Stir into the liquid so that it dissolves, ideally with your new small miso whisk, specially selected and purchased because you will soon be hooked and making miso soup very often.

Remove the dashi from the heat. Return the miso-enriched liquid to the pan, stir to combine and taste. Add more miso in the same way if you need to.

If you want to heat the soup, do so gently, and don't allow it to simmer or boil. Serve with a scattering of sliced spring onions. If you leave the miso soup to sit, the miso will tend to settle to the bottom; stir to mix again.

Once you have mastered this simple miso soup, you will be up for developing your dashi and also adding other ingredients.

Everyday kombu dashi with bonito (niban dashi)

Follow the kombu dashi instructions and once you have removed the kombu, let the stock cool a little and then add about 30g bonito (dried, smoked tuna) flakes (katsuobushi). Bring to the boil, skimming if necessary, then reduce the heat and simmer for no more than 30 seconds. Turn off the heat and let the pan sit for 10 minutes, until the katsuobushi settles at the bottom. Lay a piece of muslin over a sieve and pour the dashi through the sieve. Gather up the muslin and twist, making a ball of the katsuobushi, and gently squeeze out any of the remaining liquid into the bowl. Taste for salt and adjust. Niban dashi will keep for about a week in the fridge and also freezes well.

Tofu and spring onions with the soup

Once you've combined the miso with the dashi, add about 200g of silken tofu, cut into small cubes, and simmer gently for no more than 2 minutes, or until the tofu has been heated through. As before, scatter with 2 or 3 thinly sliced spring onions.

Grated fresh ginger

Good-quality powdered miso soup is not bad really, but is much improved with a grating of fresh ginger.

Miso chicken broth

For a quick cup of miso broth, add 1 tablespoon of miso and stir to combine.

Leek, cavolo nero and watercress soup

Makes plenty for 4

About 1kg leeks

A good handful of cavolo nero

Butter, preferably raw

Some thyme sprigs

About 1.5 litres hot chicken stock (see page 78–81), or use ½ stock, ½ water

Flaked sea salt

To serve

A bunch of watercress

Parmesan cheese, preferably from brown or red cows, coarsely grated

ONCE YOU ARE REGULARLY CREATING MEAT STOCKS AS PART OF YOUR NOURISHING RITUAL – better understood as a richly rewarding investment in your well-being – you have a convenient yet nutrient-dense base for simple soups and stews. So, always have frozen meat stock available; it's quick to defrost – sit the stock container in a bowl or sink of hot water for half an hour or so, then slide the partially frozen stock into a saucepan and warm gently.

–

Trim the leek root ends and the very coarse green upper parts. Use as much of the green stem as you can, unless it is tough. Slice lengthways into halves, and then turn the flat side onto the board and chop crossways into roughly 5mm strips. Place the leek strips in a colander or sieve and immerse in a bowl of water. Rinse thoroughly and drain.

Cut away only the very coarse parts of the cavolo nero stems, before cutting across the bunch into roughly 5–10mm strips. Rinse and drain. Remove all of the thick stems, wash, drain and chop coarsely, or leave as tender sprigs.

Melt a good-sized wedge of butter, say 50g, in a medium-sized saucepan over a medium heat. Throw in the drained leeks, cavolo nero, thyme sprigs and a couple of generous pinches of salt. It will be a very full pan, but the vegetables will sweat down in volume. Stir and sweat the vegetables for 8–12 minutes, until they soften without browning.

Add the stock and bring to the boil. Reduce the heat to a simmer and leave to cook, bubbling gently, stirring occasionally, for 20–25 minutes, or until cooked to the bite you prefer.

Taste and adjust the seasoning, and then serve with a generous handful of both the watercress and the grated Parmesan.

This soup also goes well with a sprinkle of sesame seeds or gomashio (see page 72).

Hungry? Add some leftover roast chicken

For less of a soup and more of a meal, dice some leftover roast chicken and add to the soup in the last 5 minutes of cooking.

With potatoes?

This sweating in butter and simmering in broth is a very versatile soup-making technique. For leek and potato soup, replace the cavolo nero with about 500g yellow potatoes, such as Mayan Gold, Yukon Gold or Charlotte, peeled, quartered and thinly sliced. Add a bay leaf alongside the thyme. You will need to simmer for longer, about 30 minutes. Once served, garnish with a big spoonful of thick raw cream, or crème fraîche and some chopped chives.

Potato knowledge

The pigment in these yellow potato varieties comes from the presence of anthoxanthins, which are loaded with antioxidants. Yellow potatoes are often sweeter and more waxy than starchy.

Smooth or coarse texture?

Leave your soup rough, or purée to whatever texture you prefer with a blender. Remove the thyme and bay leaf before you do.

Parmesan from red cows

Parmesan cheese is nutty, savoury–sweet, crumbly and sometimes rather granular and crunchy. The very best is extremely moreish when broken off the round and nibbled on its own. All certified Parmesan is made from the raw milk of cows that have traditionally been fed hay or grass, and the only non-dairy additive permitted is sea salt. Parmesan is aged for 12–36 months, it is very rich in glutamate and is therefore a terrific source of umami.

It's worth tasting different ages and producers, and also to ask what sort of cows produced the milk. There are two particularly delicious artisan varieties of aged Parmesan to look out for, made with milk from red, and also brown cows. Milk from brown Swiss cows is suitably rich and creamy for Parmesan. This sold marked as DiSola Bruna (only brown), or stamped Vacche Brune.

The traditional Italian breed for Parmesan-making was the Reggiana, a statuesquely beautiful red to yellow-brown animal. Its luxurious milk is absolutely ideal for making Parmesan, as it is rich in casein (cow's milk protein) and high in butterfat – the perfect combination for aged, sophisticated Parmesan. Look for the Vacche Rosse stamp on the rind. This cheese is aged for at least 30 months, and yet remains fresh tasting, so that you're enjoying grassy as well as complex nutty flavours all at once. Magnificent.

Support this cow, as it's making a fight back after years of decline in popularity for all the wrong reasons. Reggiana numbers fell from over 100,000 in the 1950s to under 1,000 by 1980, replaced for the most part by the ubiquitous, high-yielding black and white Friesian/Holstein, all in the pursuit of standardisation and efficiency rather than milk characteristics and suitability for making the best Parmesan. The respect and deserved acclaim for the Vacche Rosse Parmesan has ensured that the Reggiana breed numbers are on the increase, numbering some 2,500 head of cattle in Italy today.

Coconut Chicken Soup

1 litre chicken stock
(see pages 78–81)

350g whole coconut milk or
225g creamed coconut

Juice of 1 lemon

1 teaspoon freshly grated ginger

Flaked or grey sea salt

Flat-leaf parsley, finely chopped,
to serve

Variations

Use fish sauce instead of sea salt.

Finish with a combination of
finely chopped coriander leaves
and spring onions.

Add heat by cooking with some
very finely chopped red chillies.

Make the soup with venison
or fish stock.

THERE'S SOMETHING UNIQUELY COMFORTING ABOUT
A BOWL OF SIMPLE HOMEMADE SOUP. This flavoursome recipe
is quick, easy to make and combines the therapeutic powers of chicken
stock with the nutrient-dense wonders of coconut. In the tropics coconut
has been an everyday food and ingredient for millennia. Only recently
has it acquired superfood status among the health and fitness fraternity
in the West.

Make sure your coconut milk is whole and contains no additives.
Creamed coconut is finely ground fresh coconut meat formed into a
block. You will find it in the chilled section of Asian/Indian food stores
and many health shops. Its creamy, rich texture, taste and satiety
comes from its high fat content – it's 60 per cent fat, of which 92 per
cent is saturated fat. Don't let that put you off: these medium-chain
fatty acids are extremely nourishing. In combination with the chicken
stock – widely known as Jewish penicillin – it's a delicious, easy to digest
comforter for colds and a sore throat.

–

Bring the chicken stock to a simmer and if necessary skim off any foam.
Add the coconut, lemon juice and ginger. Continue to simmer for 15–20
minutes and taste for salt before serving with some flat-leaf parsley.

Kasha
A hearty Russian soup

Serves 4

175g sprouted, dried
buckwheat groats

1 egg, from pastured hens

2 tablespoons butter, preferably
raw, plus extra to serve

500ml hot chicken stock
(see pages 78–81)

Sea salt and freshly ground
black pepper

KASHA IS THE GENERIC TERM IN EASTERN EUROPE FOR
GRUEL OR PORRIDGE. Cooking up a thick soupy mush of grains is one
of the least challenging ways to prepare grains. However, our ancestors
knew full well that the grains had to be sprouted or fermented (or both)
before cooking, to ensure that as much of their nutrients were bio-
available, and indeed, not harmful.

Kasha is also the name given to sprouted (cracked) buckwheat,
which, alongside barley, is a staple source of carbohydrate in Eastern
European cuisine; it is also a popular ingredient in Jewish food. Sprouted
buckwheat is the northern climes' equivalent of bulgur or cracked
wheat. Unlike wheat, buckwheat is gluten free and in fact it is not a grain
(a grass) but the seeds of a herb, so it's a false or pseudocereal. Prepared
properly, buckwheat is full of valuable nutrients, including all the amino
acids, especially lysine, as well as iron, zinc and selenium.

Sprouted buckwheat does not need soaking before cooking. Start by
toasting it in a heavy cast-iron frying pan over a medium heat, stirring,
until nicely golden. Set aside to cool.

Beat the egg in a bowl large enough to take the toasted buckwheat as well.
Mix the two together, then put the frying pan back on the heat and cook,
stirring, so that the egg cooks through and the buckwheat is not clumped.

In a heavy soup or casserole pot, add the butter and stock and bring to
a simmer. Taste and season with salt, if necessary, and also black pepper.

Tip the buckwheat and egg mixture into the stock, bring to a simmer,
cover and turn the heat down so that it cooks at a bare simmer for
30 minutes.

Serve, and, if suffering the rigours of an Arctic ice storm, or you're
extremely sporty, add a knob of butter to each bowl.

Chicken and egg

Bird's eggs are a true wonder of nature. That beautiful ovoid case contains enough nutrients to sustain the development of a chick, and once hatched, the little bird will peck at the shell for additional minerals. Nothing is wasted. Just think of all that concentrated nourishment, and stored in such a convenient way. No wonder our ancestors prized domestic and wild bird's eggs as an essential part of their diet.

Chicken eggs, from happy, naturally reared and fed hens are the source of complete and high-quality proteins, the vitamins A, B and D as well as bioavailable iron, calcium, phosphorus and other trace minerals. Fatty acids? When from pastured chickens, the eggs contain an equal and ideal balance of omega-3 and -6 as well as other long-chain fatty acids that are known to be beneficial to the nervous system. In Asia, eggs are esteemed as brain food.

As ever, in the pursuit of cheap food all year round, we have messed up our relationship with the provider of eggs, the chicken. Domestic chickens were originally woodland birds from Asia. They are, and always were, omnivores, foraging, scratching and pecking, not only at green sprouts, plants and seeds, but also seeking out grubs, worms and insects. Our ancestors understood this completely and let their chickens roam daily in their pastures, woodlands and yards, supplementing their natural diet with some grain and kitchen scraps. Children were tasked with finding extra bugs and grubs to hand-feed the birds.

Contrast the time-honoured, natural life and diet of pastured chickens with the intensive world of industrial egg production. Their big sheds are nothing more than slave dormitories for laying birds, and they are now, after the animal-waste feed scandal, usually fed a vegetarian diet of grains, more grains, and yet more grains. They are fooled, by clever lighting, into laying eggs all year round. Free range? Leaving the shed door open as a token gesture is not the same as keeping birds in moveable small huts and flocks, surrounded by pasture and woodland.

Organic? As long as they are fed organic grade feed and given the chance to go out, the birds qualify. But eggs from pastured hens are in a different league, and these are the eggs you should seek out. One study shows that eggs from pastured birds contain two-thirds more vitamin A, three times more vitamin E, twice the omega-3 fatty acids and seven times more beta carotene than eggs from what are called conventionally reared hens. It is logical and self-evident that chicken eggs can only be as nourishing as the natural and beneficial quality of the birds' diet and lifestyle.

The everyday evidence is in the appearance, and then the eating of an egg. Eggs from pastured hens have an almost shockingly vivacious deep yellow to orange yolk, sitting firm in a pool of clear egg white, complete with a fresh and pert lustre. To taste the difference, try one lightly cooked, by either soft boiling or poaching. It will take you to a different and new dimension; pastured eggs are so flavoursome and nutritious that you will be a convert for the right reasons: there is pleasure and deep nourishment in the eating, and a better life for the chickens.

Contrast the time-honoured, natural life and diet of pastured chickens with the intensive world of industrial egg production.

Kimchi jigae
Pork and tofu soup with kimchi

Makes plenty for 4

For the pork stock

2kg pork bones from a pastured heritage pig

Fresh filtered water

2 medium onions

1 large leek

2 carrots

1 bay leaf

2 tablespoons apple cider vinegar with the mother (see pages 62–66)

For the soup

250g kimchi, roughly chopped – strong/fully fermented (see pages 52–55)

1 onion, diced medium-fine

200g thick-sliced pork belly from a pastured heritage pig, cut into soup spoon-sized pieces

1 tablespoon Korean hot chilli paste (Gochujang)

150g freshly made, firm silky organic tofu (see page 144)

1 teaspoon toasted sesame oil

SOUPS AND BROTHS ARE A STAPLE OF EAST ASIAN CUISINE, and provide not only spicy satisfaction but also all the deep nutritional richness from a well-made stock, and the soothing digestibility of fermented foods. This simple, ancestral family recipe from Korea is an inspirational example of just how nourishment and food pleasure can go hand in hand, naturally.

Traditionally eaten on a cold winter's evening, the piping hot soup would be served from a pot warming on a portable cooker or brazier placed in the middle of the table. This is but one of the typical and numerous hotpots of East Asia.

Tofu is the perfect companion for such a strongly flavoured soup; it's largely bland and also cooling in nature, and so provides a soft respite from the heat and power of the broth.

Make the stock

Place the pork bones in a stockpot and fill with filtered water until the bones are immersed. Bring to the boil and boil rapidly for 3 minutes. Remove from the heat and discard the water. Rinse the bones with running filtered water until all the froth and residues from the cooking have been removed.

Clean the stockpot. Put the pork bones back into the stockpot, immerse in filtered water again and bring to the boil.

While the stockpot heats, prepare and add your vegetables to the stockpot as follows:

Onions – remove any dirt but keep the outer skin intact, halve.

Leek – wash to remove any dirt, cut in half and then slice the two halves along their length.

Carrots – top and tail, peel and cut in half.

Throw in the bay leaf, and add a generous splash of apple cider vinegar. Bring to a rolling boil, then simmer, uncovered, for 2–3 hours.

Make the soup

Strain the stock through a sieve into a saucepan, add the kimchi and onion, cook at a rolling boil for 10 minutes, then simmer for 15 minutes.

Taste to check the kimchi and onion are cooked before adding the pieces of pork, hot chilli paste and tofu, and then bring to the boil again. Cover and simmer for no longer than 5 minutes, so that the pork remains tender and the tofu does not fall apart.

Sprinkle with sesame oil before serving.

Less well-cooked tofu

If you prefer your tofu very lightly cooked, place some sliced tofu in each bowl and then ladle the hot soup onto it.

Buying tofu

There's tofu and there's tofu. In fact there's as much choice of tofu as there are varieties of bread, from the indigestible highly refined industrial commodity to the local, traditional and fresh tofu made in small batches by artisan producers. The key criteria are:

Always buy organic – you will avoid GM soya this way.

Buy from a small producer who soaks the soya beans overnight before making fresh soya milk, and hand-makes the tofu, using a traditional coagulant, such as nigari, a magnesium salt, extracted from sea water.

Handle and taste the tofu – it should have a tearable texture and a rounded, fresh and appealingly pleasant sweet savoury flavour.

Keep chilled, and use within 3–5 days.

Tofu

Tofu is the pressed curds of coagulated soya milk. Soya is a legume, and although in theory full of protein, it is tightly protected in the seed, resisting digestion with its powerful combination of enzyme inhibitors and phytic acid. The Chinese and Japanese have known this for thousands of years, and have developed a happy relationship with soya, using it as a nitrogen-fixing crop, and by feeding it to their cows and buffalo. Such ruminants, with their four-part stomach, can digest soya by fermentation, in league with their cudding.

By contrast, the simple human digestive system cannot digest soya and release the nutrients available without help, which, as ever, involves fermentation. The East Asians were fully aware of this need and, about two thousand years ago, developed a range of fermented soya foods and condiments, such as soy sauce, fermented bean curd, natto, miso (often with other grains) and tempeh. Made well, using wholly natural and nutrient-rich ingredients, these are all full-flavoured foods, brimming with umami, and all are extremely nourishing and should be eaten as often as possible.

Tofu is less nourishing as it is not fully pre-digested by a complete fermentation process. Soaking soya beans overnight before making soya milk helps, but even this, when combined with the coagulation process, neutralises and removes (in the whey) only some of the enzyme inhibitors and phytates. This is why, in East Asia, tofu is most commonly combined with other foods, especially soups, and eaten with meat and fish, as well as seaweed and other condiments to make it more digestible. Tofu is not a primary source of protein but a small part of a panoply of diverse, seasonal, time-honoured, nutrient-dense ingredients used and understood by people in all the countries of East Asia. Such understanding is part of the embedded respect they hold for their ancestral foods that are the historic, yet living connection between the nurturing of health and the wonderful pleasures of eating.

Haricot bean soup with sauerkraut and chorizo

Serves 4

For the haricot beans

425g dried haricot beans

Sea salt or shio-koji (see page 67)

For the soup

1 litre chicken stock (see pages 78–81)

4 garlic cloves, mashed

500g cooked haricot beans

450g cooking chorizo, chopped small if necessary

300g sauerkraut (see pages 44–49)

Sea salt or shio-koji (see page 67)

THIS IS A HEARTY SOUP, and a perfect food in wintertime. Haricot beans, whether disguised as baked beans or not, are a beguiling comfort food and an excellent source of protein and fibre, as well as a source of selenium and potassium. Most cuisines marry a little meat and a lot of beans, especially historically, when meat was less available, and the beans were the most filling part of the dish. Enhanced with the spiciness of chorizo, the rich sustenance of the broth and the fermented powers of the sauerkraut, they give you a complete meal in a bowl.

Prepare the beans

Cover the beans in warm water and soak overnight.

Drain and rinse well, then cover with water, add a big pinch of salt, and bring to the boil in a large saucepan. Skim off any froth, then cover and reduce to a simmer. Cook at a gentle simmer for 4 hours, checking from time to time to see if you need to add more water. Taste for salt, and adjust to your liking.

Make the soup

Heat the chicken stock until it simmers and then add the garlic, beans and chorizo. After 10–15 minutes the chorizo should be cooked through. Taste for salt and adjust.

Ladle into bowls, and then add and stir in the sauerkraut.

Haricot beans are a beguiling comfort food and an excellent source of protein and fibre, as well as a source of selenium and potassium.

Onion soup

Makes plenty for 4

Large wedge of unsalted butter, preferably raw, or about 4 tablespoons olive oil, or a mix of the two, or a wedge of ghee (see page 36–39)

700g onions, thinly sliced

3 thyme sprigs (remove the twiggy stems before serving)

1 litre warm chicken stock (see pages 78–81)

Sea salt

THIS IS THE PERFECT SOUP for a light supper. It's made with chicken stock, full of excellent-quality fat and gelatine, so it's enriching, tasty and quick to digest. And that's really important at the end of the day – you really don't want to be struggling to digest a large or heavy meal before bed. A carefully made onion soup is sustaining, tasty and nutritious, perfect for a good night's sleep.

Melt the butter and/or heat the oil in a large, heavy, cast-iron saucepan. Add the onions and thyme, and cook over a medium-low heat for about 30 minutes. The onion slices will soften, reduce and colour. You will need to stir from time to time, and whatever you do, make sure the onions don't catch and burn. The aromas filling the kitchen should be sweet, not burnt and smoky. When quite soft, turn up the heat slightly, and cook for a further 15 minutes, stirring occasionally, until the onions cook to a medium golden brown – again don't let them burn. Add salt to taste. This will also encourage the onions to caramelise.

Add the warmed stock and simmer for about 15 minutes. Taste for seasoning, and serve.

You could also garnish with:

Lightly toasted sprouted sourdough bread with melted Gruyère Alpage – as it sounds, one from the mountain pastures of the Alps (see page 159) – cut into little squares.

A heap of coarsely grated Vacche Rosse Parmesan (see page 138).

In praise of onions

Onions worldwide

Onions are found worldwide in the oldest recipes, particularly in the northern hemisphere, and appreciated not only for their flavour-enhancing qualities but also as the foundation of a hearty soup, stew, casserole or sauce.

Onions for health

Onions contain carotenoids, B complex vitamins (including the very important vitamin B6) and vitamin C, calcium, magnesium, potassium and sulphur compounds. Onions are valued for their medicinal qualities too, including fighting off colds and flu, thwarting the plague, improving kidney function, and for their antibacterial qualities. When you make stock, don't peel the onions; onion skin is rich in antioxidants, quercetin and fibre.

Onions summer and winter

Fresh harvested summer onions are very wet and will take longer to caramelise. Old onions in the late winter and spring will tend to sprout and are not worth cooking with – like that they are more suitable for composting.

Onions are very good with:

- Cream – pour a swirl of raw cream on some caramelised onions, add a little Dijon mustard, and you'll have a quick and rich sauce for pork chops or beef steak.
- Woody herbs – rosemary, thyme and bay
- White wine
- Butter – cook onions with butter only and you'll make them even sweeter... but because butter burns readily you can prevent this by adding some olive oil, lard, goose or bacon fat and, as a bonus, create more flavours too. Or, cook them in ghee.
- Good-hearted homemade stock – chicken, beef or fish.
- Strong raw cheeses – Parmesan, Gruyère, Cheddar.

Onions demand:

- Precision cutting – with a super-sharp knife.
- A heavy pan – how else could you cook them slowly?
- A slow start – don't heat your fat too much before adding the onions or the smaller pieces tend to burn. Apply just enough heat to melt the fat.
- Slow cooking – you'll create a unique warmth, sweetness, body and softness...
- Touch, timing and patience – never ever add garlic, celery, tomato, spices or herbs until the onions are glossy, softening fast and honey coloured – they take much longer to cook than you expect.
- Control and practice – vary the character of the onions you cook by playing with the thickness of the onion slices and chop size – from a bulky tangle of thicker strands, to a more delicate mesh of fine filaments.

Decisions

- White onions versus red onions? Red onions are sweeter but they look pretty murky and dull when slow fried.
- Darker or lighter caramelised onions? It's up to you. Cooking slowly without much colouring makes the onion less sweet and more aromatic. You'll need to prepare carefully, be observant and sensitive, and also to stir as much as necessary so they don't stick – and it may well take at least 30 minutes before the onions begin their transformation from hard white rings to a soft, pale, transparent hue, more gold than brown.

Onions are valued for their medicinal qualities too.

Oxtail and whole barley soup

**Serves 4 with lots left over
to freeze for another day**

200g whole barley, hulled

Freshly filtered water

1.75kg oxtails

120ml dry white wine

60ml apple cider vinegar
(see pages 62-66)

2 medium onions, cut into
medium dice

2 celery sticks, peeled and cut
into medium dice

4 medium carrots, peeled and
cut into medium dice

A bunch of fresh thyme sprigs

2 teaspoons green peppercorns,
cracked using a pestle and mortar

Sea salt or shio-koji (see page 67)
and freshly ground black pepper

Flat-leaf parsley

BARLEY IS AN ANCIENT GRAIN, popular in antiquity for beer, bread, and gruels or porridges, but not much appreciated in modern times. Like oats, barley contains soluble fibre, known as beta-glucan, and also fat-soluble antioxidants. The former is known to help reduce cholesterol levels; the latter, to help liver function. For the best available nourishment from barley, prepare this soup with properly prepared hulled whole barley. Properly prepared? As ever, this involves soaking the whole grains for at least 7–8 hours or, conveniently, overnight. All barley must be hulled before eating. Dehulling removes the outer fibrous hull. Pearl barley is dehulled barley that, like white rice, is polished, which removes the layer of bran. Pearl barley cooks more quickly than whole barley. You can use pearl barley for this recipe. There's no need to soak pearl barley before cooking, and it will cook in about half the time.

Oxtails are no longer exclusively from castrated male cattle, known as an ox or a steer, but come from both sexes. This inexpensive cut may be meat poor, but it certainly is gelatine- and flavour-rich. For maximum extraction of goodness and flavours, it pays to cook oxtail slowly. Very slowly.

—

Immerse the barley in warm water, cover and leave to soak overnight. The next day, drain and wash the barley and drain again. It is now ready for cooking in the oxtail stock.

Put the oxtails in a roasting pan and cook in the oven at 180°C/gas 4 for 1 hour.

Transfer the browned oxtails to a cast-iron casserole. Put the roasting pan on the hob and deglaze by pouring in the wine. Bring to the boil while stirring and scraping the pan base to combine with the meat juices and residues. Pour the juice and wine reduction over the oxtails in the casserole pot, then add enough water to submerge the oxtails.

Pour in the apple cider vinegar and bring to the boil, skim off any scum, then add the diced vegetables, thyme and cracked green peppercorns. Cover and simmer gently for at least 18 hours, ideally for 24 hours, on the hob or in the oven at 120°C/gas ½.

Transfer the oxtails to a dish to cool. When cool enough to handle, remove the meat from the oxtails and chop it medium to fine.

Strain the oxtail stock through a sieve into a saucepan and discard the vegetables. Bring to the boil and add the soaked barley. Reduce to a simmer and cook for 45 minutes to 1 hour, or until the barley is tender. Add the chopped oxtail meat. Check for seasoning and adjust.

Serve with a scattering of parsley.

MEATS, EGGS & CHEESE

Frittata with wild garlic and shiitake mushrooms

Serves 4

A combination of seasonal vegetables, such as a big handful of wild garlic and a small handful of shiitake mushrooms

Ghee (see pages 36–39) or olive oil

1 onion, sliced

6 eggs, from pastured hens

5 garlic cloves, sliced thinly across the length

Sea salt and freshly ground black pepper

Frittata makes the perfect backdrop for the freshest seasonal vegetables.

A FRITTATA IS AN OPEN OMELETTE and makes the perfect backdrop for the freshest seasonal vegetables, mushrooms and herbs, as well as presenting the ideal opportunity to eat lots of pastured eggs. The principle is simple: gather together and lightly cook a combination of the very freshest seasonal fare, whether wild garlic and shiitake mushrooms, or spinach and leeks, or broad beans and parsley, or new potatoes and lots of spring onions, and stir them into the eggs before pouring into a frying pan and sautéing.

Trim most of the stems from the wild garlic, gather the leaves into a bunch then slice very coarsely with a very sharp knife. Keep the florets.

Dice the shiitake mushrooms quite small as they hold their shape well when cooked.

Melt some wedges of ghee, or 2–3 tablespoons, in a large, well-seasoned cast-iron frying pan and begin by sautéing the onion over a medium heat until it softens. Now add the mushrooms and cook for about 5 minutes, stirring from time to time.

Cook the wild garlic in the pan, stir to coat in the ghee, and let it wilt, which will take 2–3 minutes. Remove from the heat and allow to cool.

Lightly beat the eggs in a large bowl so that they are incorporated, no more, then season with salt and black pepper. Stir in the cooled wild garlic and mushrooms, and the sliced garlic.

Wipe out the frying pan with kitchen paper and place back on a medium heat. Melt another big piece of ghee, or about 2 tablespoons, and once melted and hot, pour the egg mixture into the pan. Let it cook and set for a few minutes then, lifting the pan at a slight angle, use a spatula to raise the edge of the frittata to allow the liquid to run under it. Keep doing this around the pan, so that the frittata has a raised rim and very little liquid remains in the centre.

Place an oversize plate over the pan, and carefully and quickly invert the two. Drop a little more ghee into the pan, let it melt and then slide the frittata off the plate and back into the pan to complete the cooking of the underside, which will take 2 minutes or so.

Alternatively, you can finish cooking the topside of the frittata in the oven, if you use an ovenproof frying pan. Sauté the frittata on the hob, then transfer the pan to a hot oven or under the grill to complete the cooking.

Sprinkle with the garlic florets and serve with some just-picked tomatoes, sliced or quartered, salted and swimming in good olive oil, or a tomato sauce with garlic (see page 76). Frittata is extremely good eaten cold too.

Kimchi omelette

Serves 4

150g kimchi (see pages 52–55)

Olive oil, lard (see pages 82–85) or ghee (see pages 36–39) or coconut oil

6 eggs, from pastured hens

Flaked or grey sea salt

Freshly ground organic pepper

FERMENTED VEGETABLES, particularly cabbage, are a truly wise food, one consumed in China for over 6,000 years, and known in Ancient Rome as easily digestible and immune-system boosting. Sauerkraut (see pages 44–49) is the European style of fermented cabbage, and kimchi is the highly aromatic daily condiment and national dish of Korea. Traditionally – as with sauerkraut and most fermented foods – kimchi (see pages 52–55) is homemade and buried in the ground for months in earthenware pots. Unlike sauerkraut, kimchi is made from a variety of vegetables, including cabbage, radish, cucumber and spring onions. The most common seasoning is garlic, making for a potent brew.

Kimchi is low in calories and high in fibre, rich in vitamin C and carotene, vitamins A, B1 and B2, and calcium and, of course, alive with highly beneficial lactic acid bacteria. It's no wonder that kimchi has been lauded as Korea's superfood.

–

Drain the kimchi in a colander and chop coarsely. Add a tablespoon of your fat to the eggs, season with salt and black pepper, and beat lightly. Stir in the chopped kimchi.

Heat a cast-iron frying pan over a medium heat, add a tablespoon of the fat, and once melted, add the eggs and kimchi mixture.

As soon as the eggs start to set at the edges, tilt the pan and use a spatula to lift and let the liquid egg run under the omelette. Do this all round the pan to make a thick rim. Continue cooking over a medium heat until the centre has nearly set. Place a large plate on top of the frying pan and quickly and carefully invert both so that the omelette is on the plate.

Add a little more fat and slide the omelette back into the pan to continue cooking for a further 2–3 minutes.

Slide onto a board and serve warm or at room temperature. Enjoy with a simple green salad of mild lettuce leaves, with a dressing of extra virgin olive oil.

Korean supermarkets will offer a variety of kimchi – not only varying in the types of vegetables used, but also in impact: some are fiery hot, some mild, some very sour – all are fermented.

The wonder of our microbiome

The microbiome is a newly popular word that describes more clearly and accurately what used to be known as our gut flora and fauna. In western lifestyle and medicine, for many generations, the digestive system has been treated as a useful device for dealing with whatever food we care to eat and it, along with any imbalance in its flora and fauna, was targeted and treated in isolation on the assumption that the gut is largely a vehicle for digestion only. We completely ignored the ancient wisdom of Hippocrates: 'all disease begins in the gut'. Now, belatedly, research is revealing just how complex, wonderful and crucial the health, diversity and vitality of the microbiome is to our entire well-being.

The digestive system is an extraordinary creation, and is linked dynamically, richly and intimately with the brain, so much so that the gut is often referred to as our second brain. It's also home to the greatest concentration of microbiotic life in our bodies, largely bacteria, but also fungi and viruses, that outnumber our own cells 10 to 1 and whose genetic diversity outnumbers our own some 100 times. We are now beginning to understand (or perhaps reawaken our understanding as to) just how important it is to live in harmony with our microbiome because its health and well-being are absolutely critical for a dynamic and robust immune system. Hippocrates was right – a healthy gut protects us from illness.

For over a hundred years, since western medicine embraced Pasteur's germ theory (all germs are bad and should be wiped out), and, crucially, since the advent of antibiotics and the subsequent emergence of the powerful pharmaceutical corporations, we've been waging an all-out war against microbiotic life within and around us. We have embraced the sense that we are hapless victims of deadly microbiotic onslaughts that can only be dealt with by sophisticated medicines and chemicals. This dependency culture is self-reinforcing, feeding a human craving and addiction for immediate cures and magic bullets, that drug manufacturers and their advisers are only too willing to encourage. And yet as Hippocrates also said, the freedom from this cycle of dependency is in our own hands: 'let food be thy medicine, and medicine be thy food'. We have all heard this quote, but how many of us truly understand the significance of these words? What we eat not only gives us pleasure and feeds us, it also feeds our microbiome, which in turn, when correctly fed, respected and nurtured, provides us with a strong immune system.

It's time to stop the assault on our microbiome; years of antibiotic dependency in humans and in the farming world, antibacterial obsessiveness, harsh environmental chemicals and pollution, and an addiction to dead processed foods and drinks have left our microbiome depleted, and our ability to fight off illnesses and diseases severely compromised. Research has shown that whereas the total quantity of microbes in our microbiome remains relatively constant no matter how badly we treat it, what suffers is microbe diversity. Without microbe diversity we cannot thrive.

A call to action? A chance to break free from dependency? Absolutely. Moreover, it will be a pleasure to find, create and enjoy nutrient-dense foods and drinks while rebuilding your microbiome. So, don't hold back: make and consume lots of fermented, living, microbe-rich foods and drinks; make, cook and eat more fresh, seasonal foods sourced from trusted farms; grow your own vegetables instead of a lawn, get outside more and sit down less, and, as a reward, discover natural wines. Your microbiome will thank you and keep you in rude health.

We are now beginning to understand just how important it is to live in harmony with our microbiome.

Spelt or barley risotto
Made with goat or mutton stock, with broad beans and coppa

For the stock

About 2kg raw mutton or goat bones, such as shoulder pieces, small legs, breast, ribs and neck, and feet too. Have the feet cut into pieces

Filtered water

Apple cider vinegar with the mother (see pages 62 66)

2 white onions, unpeeled and halved

2 carrots, trimmed, peeled and halved diagonally

1 celery stick and leaves, halved

1 leek, trimmed and halved

1 head of garlic, halved widthways

About 9 peppercorns

Some thyme sprigs, 1–2 bay leaves and a big sprig of parsley

For the risotto

1.5kg broad beans in their pods

Butter, preferably raw

150g thick slice of coppa, diced small or chunky

1 medium onion, finely diced

375g pearled spelt or barley

About 175ml white wine – leftover is fine

1.5 litres warm mutton stock (if you run out of stock, use water)

Butter, preferably raw

A hunk of Parmesan cheese, preferably from brown or red cows (see page 138), freshly grated when ready to serve

SHEEP AND GOATS ARE LESS INTENSIVELY REARED than the majority of farm animals. They will have spent most of their lives on pasture, often heath or open land, with access to a variety of nourishing wild grasses and herbs. Meat from sheep that graze on marshlands is particularly renowned for its sweet saltiness. More gamey and characterful meat than beef, chicken or pork, the most popular sheep meat is lamb. This is surprising, as the meat from older animals, such as mutton and hogget – and, for that matter, goat – has so much more character and tastes more rounded than lamb (which is less than a year old), and the fat from a more mature animal is absolutely meltingly delicious. This fat is rich in fat-soluble vitamins, which is what we need to be able to utilise the minerals found in food. Fat from pasture-reared animals is a particularly good source of many beneficial fatty acids, such as conjugated linoleic acid (some research shows anti-cancer benefits) and palmitoleic, an omega-7 monunsaturated acid.

Mutton and goat bones? Try a halal butcher. Otherwise lamb, the older the better, will suffice.

Spelt or barley? Both are perfect companions for this robust stock. Barley risotto (orzotti) is common in Italy, and takes about 40 minutes to cook. Spelt will cook in less time, about 25 minutes.

–

Put all the bones in a large, ovenproof stockpot, immerse in filtered water and add a splash of apple cider vinegar (with the mother). Leave to sit for about 1 hour.

Place the stockpot over a medium heat, bring to a simmer, not a boil. Skim off any scum, then add all the prepared vegetables, the peppercorns, thyme and bay leaves, and continue to cook at the barest simmer for about 12–24 hours either with the lid removed or ajar. From time to time check that the water covers the bones add more if needed. Keep the heat low: if you boil a stock it will go cloudy.

You can also put the stockpot, covered, in a low oven (say 110°C/gas ¼). Make sure it is barely simmering. Provided the pan is covered and simmering there is no need to check the water level.

In the last hour or so, press down on the bones in the pan to make sure you extract all their goodness, and then add the parsley.

Remove the bones and vegetables, then strain your stock through a sieve into a big bowl and let cool. If it's a warm day, cool the bowl of stock in a sink of iced water until it is tepid.

For an hour or so refrigerate in open glass jars and remove the fat that rises to the surface (this is sheep's tallow – perfect for frying). Seal and store in the fridge for 5 days or freeze – it will keep for many months.

Meat from sheep that graze on marshlands is particularly renowned for its sweet saltiness.

When you are ready to eat, pod the beans and blanch in boiling water for about 1 minute. Drain, cool and peel off the grey skins. Set aside.

Melt about 30g butter in a heavy saucepan or high-sided heavy sauté pan over a low–medium heat and add the coppa. Cook gently so that the fat in the coppa renders nicely and begins to colour. Add the onion and sweat until it softens and becomes translucent. Throw in the barley or spelt and stir so that the grains glisten with the fat. Turn up the heat a little and add the wine. Stir and allow it mostly to evaporate.

Now add some of the warm stock using a ladle, stir and allow to simmer. Continue to simmer and add stock as the grains absorb the liquid. Don't let the grains dry out.

After about 15 minutes (for spelt) or 25 minutes (for barley) add the broad beans.

Start tasting your risotto. You should to be able to bite into the grains, but they should remain firm. In all, the simmering, stirring and adding stock routine will take about 25 minutes for spelt or 35–40 minutes for barley, before the risotto is ready.

Keep the risotto quite moist and if you begin to run out of stock, add some warm water.

Remove from the heat, add 30g cubed butter and 50g freshly grated Parmesan, stir to combine and leave the risotto to rest for a minute or two before serving.

Cubed pancetta or cured raw ham, Italian or Iberian, is a good alternative to coppa.

Sprouted wholegrain spelt or barley risotto
If you want to use wholegrain spelt or barley for this recipe, then sprout the grains (see pages 98–101). Both grains will sprout within 3–4 days. As soon as you see a tiny white sprout, they are ready to cook. Rinse, drain thoroughly, then cook as above.

Gruyère Alpage toasted sandwiches

Serves 4

Loaf of spelt sourdough, preferably sprouted (see pages 278–280)

Raw butter, warmed a little to make it easy to spread

A large slab of Gruyère Alpage cheese, thinly sliced

Condiments and sides

Fermented tomato ketchup (see page 57)

Mayonnaise (see pages 70–71)

Sauerkraut (see pages 44–49)

Cornichons and other cucumber pickles

Variations

Ham Add a slim slice of cured or cooked ham between the layers of cheese.

Garlic Rub the bread with a cut clove of juicy garlic before you butter it.

ONE OF THE MOST SIGNIFICANT RITUALS IN THE ALPS is largely unknown to the outside world. It takes place in late spring, when the cows are led from their winter quarters in the valleys, up to the lush pastures of the high Alps. The mountains echo again to the sound of cowbells as the magnificent cattle ramble up the mountain tracks to their familiar summer quarters, close to glaciers and the highest snowfields. There the streams are running with snow and ice melt, rich in minerals and energy, and the mountain pastures are full of the nutrient-dense grasses and wild flowers of the short summer season. The cows produce the richest milk at this time, and so the butter is highly prized as a special food for expectant mothers and young children. Far away from the market, most of the milk goes to make cheese, which is of course also a storehouse of nutrients for the winter months. Some of the high Alps pastures are so remote that these summer cheeses have to be helicoptered down at the end of the season to be stored and matured. These pastures are known as the Alpage.

Gruyère is one of the great hard cheeses of the Alps and the Jura, along with Beaufort. Both share a protected status as raw milk cheeses and those that are handmade in huts in the high Alps from the rich summer milk are also given the title Alpage. They are well worth seeking out.

You can buy Gruyère of different strengths, dependent on the length of maturation, from between 3 and 10 months. Gruyère is a robust cooking cheese, sweet and also slightly salty, and historically associated as a garnish for French onion soup (see page 146) and as a filling for the ever-popular, now mostly debased, toasted cheese and ham sandwich, the croque-monsieur. This recipe restores the reputation of the humble toasted cheese sandwich.

—

Cut 8 slices of bread thinly, 8–10mm, and then cut into pairs to fit the pan, if necessary, and the appetite. Spread the outside of the pieces thickly with butter.

Place a medium-sized, well-seasoned cast-iron griddle pan over a medium–high heat. Just as the pan begins to smoke, turn the heat down to medium and lay one of the slices, butter-side down into the pan. Place some slices of Gruyère on the bread in the pan, covering it in 2–3 layers. Place the second piece of buttered bread, butter-side up, on the first, and press down with a spatula.

Let the sandwich sizzle and settle, but make sure it does not burn. When it is nicely marked by the pan ridges, carefully turn it over and press down again. Once the cheese starts to ooze out of the sides and holes in the bread and the second side is nicely fried, your sandwich is ready.

With practice you will be able to cook 2 sandwiches at once.

Sausage, chickpea and spinach stew

Serves 4

About 3 tablespoons lard
(see pages 82–85)

2 medium onions, finely sliced

5 garlic cloves, smashed and
chopped medium–small

400–600g pork or venison
sausages, or 6 fat ones – not
chipolatas – chopped into 2cm
lengths (and split in half if you're
feeding young children)

400g tin chopped tomatoes

400g tin chickpeas or 350g
dried chickpeas soaked overnight

A good-sized bunch of fresh
spinach leaves or wild garlic,
cavolo nero or ruby chard

Sea salt and freshly ground
black pepper

ANY SIMPLE AND QUICK-TO-MAKE RECIPE that includes fresh, nutrient-rich greens and ever-popular sausages in a moreish sloppy sauce is perfect for all the family, especially fussy children and their parents, anxious about a balanced diet. This takes almost the same time to make as a bowl of pasta, so now is the time to switch.

When you buy sausages, artisan or not, check the ingredients carefully. You are looking for about 80 per cent meat or more, within a natural casing, and as ever, no ingredients you can't spell or pronounce.

Melt the lard in a medium-sized cast-iron casserole pot over a medium heat. Sauté the onions until soft and golden, about 2–3 minutes. Add the garlic and chopped-up sausages, and cook for about 2 minutes, stirring frequently so that the garlic does not catch and burn. Chuck in the chopped tomatoes with two big pinches of salt and the chickpeas. Cover and simmer for 15–20 minutes.

Remove any fibrous stems from the greens. Wash, drain and chop into medium slices. Drop the greens into the stew and stir. They will wilt within a minute or two. Taste for salt and adjust, and add some freshly ground black pepper.

This stew is good with a hunk of freshly baked crusty bread and lashings of butter.

Add 2 finely chopped small red chillies or some harissa or some paté di peperoncini to taste, when you cook the onions.

This takes almost the same time to make as a bowl of pasta, so now is the time to switch.

Slow-cooked pork belly with warm lentil salad

Serves 4, with plenty for cold cuts

About 1.5kg pork belly complete with skin, from a heritage breed pastured pig

Sea salt and freshly ground black pepper

For the warm lentil salad

210g Puy lentils

1 tablespoon red wine vinegar

1 red pepper, finely diced

A small bunch of spring onions, trimmed and thinly sliced

3 tablespoons olive oil

A bunch of flat-leaf parsley, leaves chopped

WHEN IT'S WINTER TIME and you're yearning for comforting, warming, energy-rich food, a very slow-roasted belly of pork not only satisfies, but will provide cold cuts as well as lots of practical fat (lard) and delicious dripping.

Pigs have always been the most versatile of farm animals, not only in their rearing – they'll guzzle almost anything – but because they are so useful to the cook. A pig provides nose-to-tail dining and more. This recipe is disarmingly simple, and will introduce you to the wonder and generosity of the pig in one dish.

Homemade or unrefined lard from heritage-breed pigs is inexpensive, health-giving, nourishing, useful and local – qualities our ancestors well understood. For all you need to know about good and bad animal and other fats, see pages 82–89.

–

Preheat the oven to 110°C/gas ¼.

Lay the pork belly skin-side up in a roasting pan, rub the skin with some salt and slash with a very sharp blade if you want to create the best crackling later. Cook for 7–8 hours – the pork belly is kept moist and tender in its pool of rendered fat and juices (dripping).

To crisp the crackling, finish the pork belly at about 200°C/gas 6 for 5–10 minutes, or slide under a hot grill for a few minutes, not too close to the heat, and keep a close watch to make sure you don't cinder the skin.

Pour off the rendered fat and meat juices into a pot or jar and leave to cool. This is dripping at its finest. Pull away the crackling and fight over who gets the biggest piece.

Serve the pork belly in thick slices. It does not need to be piping hot.

Rinse the lentils and check there are no stones in their midst. Put the lentils into a heavy pan and immerse in water so that the water level is about 7.5cm above the lentils. Bring to the boil, reduce the heat and simmer for about 30 minutes – adding more water if necessary – until the lentils are tender. Drain, reserving about 100ml of the lentil water.

Tip the lentils into a serving bowl, toss with the vinegar, and some salt and black pepper. Leave the lentils to rest for a few minutes, and then taste for salt and vinegar, adjusting as you like.

Salt the red pepper to soften, leaving it stand for a few minutes before adding as much as you like to the lentils along with the spring onions. Pour the olive oil over the lentils and stir. If you need more moisture, add some of the reserved cooking liquid.

Sprinkle the warm lentils with the parsley and serve with the pork.

Lardy ideas

Puy lentils also have a natural affinity for lard. Boiled lentils drained and then mixed with melted lard and some pieces of fried (in lard) crispy bacon (preferably streaky – from the belly) make an energy-rich meal. Mix in some finely chopped parsley if you want two vegetables with your meat. It's also worth remembering the ancestral understanding about eating lentils with meat, in this case, pork. Such food combining drastically improves the absorption of iron from the lentils. Along with the iron in the pork, this makes for a high-iron meal.

Any cold pork belly left over makes a perfect scratch meal, alongside a crispy-skinned baked potato with plenty of butter, and a pile of sauerkraut (see pages 44–49) or kimchi (see pages (52–55). Naturally rendered fat from a pastured pig is about as good as it gets when it comes to lard, so once the fat has cooled and set,

the belly fat will have separated from the brown jellied meat juices below. Carefully spoon out the fat and store it in a jar, or your new lard pot (crock) by the cooker for roasting potatoes and for the very best breakfast fry-ups, and especially for fried bread. This fat will keep in the fridge for a good 3 months, and pretty much indefinitely if you reheat it every now and again and add a little salt before pouring back into your pot.

There's no clear definition of dripping – it's really a concoction of some of the rendered fat (called lard if from pig meat or tallow if from sheep or beef) and the meat juices that have seeped out or dripped down from the cooking meat. Regardless, freshly made dripping is divine – a mouth-watering combination of the savoury jellied meat juices and the deeply satisfying fat. Carefully remove the jellied juice along with as much fat as you like and the fat that has a hint of meat or brown

residue. Set this aside to enjoy as a spread in a cold pork belly sandwich, with a handful of rocket leaves.

The fat mixed with the jellied juices is also the perfect savoury butter – it is dripping after all. Spread it extra thick on toast for a snack with a sprinkling of chopped parsley and freshly ground flaked sea salt and black pepper, or use it in place of butter or mayonnaise for the ultimate BLT.

Pig fat is wonderful

Until about 100 years ago pigs were reared not only for their meat, but, just as importantly, for their fat, and pigs were specifically bred for their bountiful and tasty fat, such as the lovely and hairy Mangalitza from Hungary. Lard was the cooking fat of choice not only in chilly northern Europe and the Americas, but China too. This happy co-existence with pigs as an integral part of our food culture and the farming landscape (pigs to plough and turn over the soil, and to recycle food waste and scraps) was derailed by two factors. First, the arrival of cheap vegetable-based cooking oils, and secondly by the association between animal fats and poor health. This was a double blow from the left and the right; the positive aspects of convenience and cheapness in vegetable oils, combined with a fear of death. A winning marketing formula for mankind, played out so many times in the last century when new science-based refined convenience foods, that are on the face of it cheap, meet traditional foods and practices. Sweetened fizzy drinks versus fermented refreshments, margarine versus butter, breakfast cereals versus porridge, hydrogenated or low-fat foods versus real foods ... and the result? We are fatter, less well and probably more anxious than before. We're certainly more anxious and confused about what constitutes health-giving and nourishing food than ever before.

And the pigs? They have become, or rather, been bred to be, more lean. The same situation applies in our attitude to beef. Over the four decades from 1950, the amount of fat from a typical pig fell from 15kg to 4.6kg, and our per capita annual consumption of lard collapsed from 5.7kg to 180g. Quick-reared lean pork has become, alongside mass-produced chicken, a bland and convenient source of white animal protein. Compare succulent rosy or darkish pinkish pork chops edged and marbled with fat from a well-grown traditional breed of pig, especially an acorn-fed black Iberian porker common in Spain and Portugal, to a flabby, damp, lean, off-white chop from an intensively reared animal, and then cook and taste them. You'll never eat mass-produced pork again. It's all down to the breed, the food they eat, their welfare, their age and, crucially, the natural fattiness of the meat that gives pork its sweet flavours and a succulent texture.

So, let's remind ourselves; good lard from pastured happy pigs, like good butter from pastured contented cows, is in reality more of a health food when reintegrated into our cooking and our eating habits in the style of our ancestors. Pork fat is a stable fat, predominantly composed of saturated and monounsaturated fatty acids, so that it is resistant to rancidity, and also has a smoke point around 190–200°C. This makes it brilliant for all types of frying. These fatty acids are short- and medium-chain fatty acids, crucial sources of energy for the brain, heart and other muscles. Pastured pig fat contains conjugated linoleic acid and good amounts of omega-3 fatty acids, and the fat from a happy pig that has lived outside, especially the back fat most exposed to the sun, is a good source of vitamin D. We're being made anxious about taking omega-3 and vitamin supplements; our ancestors found all they needed in pastured animal fats.

Quick-reared lean pork has become, alongside mass-produced chicken, a bland and convenient source of white animal protein.

Risotto with chorizo *and peas and butternut squash in season*

Serves 4

Raw butter

1 medium onion, finely diced

150–175g cooking chorizo or chorizo, as spicy as you like, skinned if need be and diced

1 small or ½ large organic butternut squash (when in season), peeled and cut into medium dice

375g risotto rice (Arborio or Carnaroli) – about 4 or 5 spilling handfuls

About 175ml white wine – leftover is fine

About 1 litre warm chicken stock (see pages 78–81)

50–60g fresh or frozen peas, or sprouted peas

30g raw butter

50g Parmesan cheese, preferably from brown or red cows (see page 138), freshly grated when ready to serve

RICE MAY WELL BE A STAPLE FOOD FOR MILLIONS, if not billions, of people and whereas it is a good source of protein, it is not a complete source of protein, which is why so many cuisines the world over pair rice with nuts, seeds, beans, and meat or fish. Asia is the biggest consumer of rice, with inhabitants typically consuming ten times more per head than westerners. Eating a grain-based diet for millennia has been possible, not only because Asian peoples draw on ancestral knowledge of food combining, but also because of physiological adaptations – in proportion to their body weight Asians typically have larger saliva glands and pancreas than westerners to cope with this diet.

Rice is of course gluten-free, and is also comparatively low in phytic acid. When brown, complete with the bran, it is one of the richest of grains in vitamin B and is also a good source of phosphorus, selenium, manganese and magnesium. During autumn and winter, soften the spiciness of this dish with some sweet-tasting butternut squash. You will also be adding more fibre and vitamins A, C and E, as well as potassium.

–

Peel, and dice the root vegetables and chorizo before you start and keep the stock warm throughout.

Melt about 30g of butter in a heavy saucepan or high-sided sauté pan over a low–medium heat and sweat the onion until it softens and becomes translucent.

Now add the chorizo and continue to cook over a medium heat. The fat and colour will render from the chorizo and infuse the onion. If you are using seasonal butternut squash, sauté it in the fat for about 1 minute.

Throw in the rice and stir so that the grains glisten with the fat. Turn up the heat a little and add the wine. Stir and allow it mostly to evaporate.

Now add some of the warm stock using a ladle, stir and allow to simmer. Continue to simmer and add stock as the rice absorbs the liquid. Don't let the rice dry out.

Time to add the peas? For sprouted: after about 6 minutes. For frozen: after about 8 minutes. For fresh: after about 9–10 minutes.
About 10 minutes after adding the rice, start tasting your risotto.
You should to be able to bite into the rice, but it should remain firm.
The squash should be slightly softish. The simmering, stirring and adding stock routines take about 12–15 minutes in all, before the rice is ready.
Keep the risotto quite moist and if you begin to run out of stock, add some filtered water.
Remove from the heat, add 30g cubed butter and 50g freshly grated Parmesan, stir to combine and leave the risotto to rest for a minute or two before serving.

During autumn and winter, soften the spiciness of this dish with some sweet-tasting butternut squash.

Brown risotto rice

Brown risotto rice is a much nuttier, more intensely flavoured rice, which the piquant chorizo stands up to well. However, don't try to cook brown risotto rice without either soaking or sprouting it first. If you don't you will be cooking your risotto for about 45 minutes, and needing a bottomless vat of stock. As with all grains, and especially whole grains, soaking or sprouting will speed the cooking time, unlock flavours and nutrients, and become more easily digestible. Wash and then submerge the brown rice completely in warmed filtered water with a splash of organic apple cider vinegar with the mother. Leave to soak for about 8–24 hours. Rinse and then allow to drain well before cooking.

You can also sprout the rice, and cook just as soon as you see the buds emerging. See pages 98–101.

No chorizo?

Fry some streaky bacon in lard until crisped and then let cool. Break up the crispy bacon and scatter over the cooked risotto.

Quick chicken stew

Serves 4

4–6 chicken thighs or legs, or some of each (from pastured birds)

3 tablespoons rendered chicken fat (see page 89) or ghee (see pages 36–39) or olive oil

2 onions, roughly diced or sliced

5 garlic cloves, thinly sliced lengthways

Some fresh thyme sprigs, or fresh oregano

1 fresh bay leaf

300–400ml chicken stock (see pages 78–81)

400g tin chopped tomatoes

Sea salt and freshly ground black pepper

THE UNIVERSAL and, in reality, bizarre obsession with the breast meat from a chicken ensures that some of the tastiest cuts – the legs and the thighs – are inexpensive. This is entirely contrary to the nutrient value, as the best nourishment is to be found in the combination of the brown muscle meat, the bones, the marrow and the connective tissues – in the limbs of the bird. Many traditional food cultures shun the breast meat almost entirely and relish the succulent brown meat, and enjoy in particular cracking open the bones to slurp and suck out the marrow, chew on the gristle and gnaw at the joints.

This recipe takes about 1 hour to complete from start to finish. Serve with mashed or boiled potatoes to mop up the simple and delicious sauce. Any leftover sauce will make another meal with pasta.

As soon as you get your chicken home, if it's in a plastic bag or tray, repack it in some greaseproof paper, loosely, and refrigerate. The night before you cook the chicken, season it with salt and black pepper.

Heat the chicken fat, ghee or olive oil over a medium-high heat in a heavy casserole pan – big enough to take all the chicken in a single layer.

When hot but not smoking, place 2 or 3 pieces of the chicken skin-side down into the pan. Reduce the heat a little and leave them alone to sear and brown for 8–10 minutes before turning them over to sear for about a further 5 minutes. Remove with a slotted spoon to a dish to catch any juices and repeat with the remaining chicken pieces.

Keep the pan on the heat and fry the onions until they soften a little, which will take 4–5 minutes, and then add the garlic, thyme and bay leaf, cooking these for 1–2 minutes.

Warm the chicken stock in a separate pan.

Pour in the tomatoes and stir them around the pan, scraping off any bits of meat or onion from the bottom of the pan. Add a big pinch of salt. Let the tomatoes bubble and simmer for about 5 minutes, then, one at a time, put the chicken pieces into the pan, browned skin-side up, so that they fit in one layer. Pour in any juices.

Add enough chicken stock to the pan so that the chicken is partially submerged but not immersed. Bring to a simmer, cover and cook at a gentle simmer for 45–50 minutes, or transfer to the oven at 160°C/gas 3. The stew is ready to serve.

Some of the tastiest cuts – the legs and the thighs – are inexpensive.

Roast chicken, Danish style

Serves 4 with some left over for cold cuts, and the carcass for stock

1.3–1.5kg fresh chicken

Some fresh garlic cloves, thinly sliced

Lots of fresh herbs, such as thyme, marjoram, oregano, flat-leaf parsley, French tarragon and rosemary

Sea salt and freshly ground black pepper

Butter, preferably raw

250ml cream, preferably raw, otherwise Guernsey or Jersey (optional)

OUR ANCESTORS WOULD RARELY EAT THEIR CHICKENS; for one a chicken is not a particularly fatty or meaty animal – unlike a pig – and of course, they were simply too valuable: their crucial role was as providers of eggs. If people did eat a chicken, it would be for a celebration, and they prepared a nice fat hen for the occasion.

In our time, the greater majority of chickens for slaughter (known as broilers) are not farmed but enslaved in high-density, high-turnover industrial gulags, taken from day-old chicks to the packing line in less than 6 weeks. The result of this, and the breeding of birds for fast muscle growth, is a miserable, unnatural life for the chicken, and flavour-compromised chicken for us, complete with reduced nutrient density, poor bone structure and reduced fat content. Just as for their eggs (see page 141), so for their meat; how the birds live and what they are fed makes the chicken we eat.

Look out for traditional breeds of birds in small flocks, kept in pastures and around the farmyard by farmers who understand that chickens are omnivores and curious roaming birds, that like a dust bath, want to peck at and forage for bugs, grubs, seeds, buds and scraps. The difference is in the eating. Pastured chicken is an entirely different food from the broiler bird. The carcass will make better, more nourishing stock too. And don't forget to ask for the cavity fat; that is where the majority of the bird's fat resides, and it is often discarded when the bird is gutted. Chicken fat is precious and should be rendered immediately to preserve it (see page 89).

As soon as you get your chicken home, unwrap or remove it from any plastic, as well as the plastic strings, and then season and flavour the bird. Do this by sliding slices of garlic into incisions made in the skin, between the skin and the flesh, all over the bird. Stuff the cavity with a generous mixture of fresh herbs (note that rosemary is good, if somewhat overpowering, so use sparingly). Now rub the skin all over with sea salt, and sprinkle with some freshly ground black pepper. Wrap in greaseproof paper and return the chicken to the fridge.

Remove the chicken from the fridge 1 hour before you want to start cooking. Set the oven to 140°C/gas 1.

Rub the chicken with some butter, generously on the upper surfaces. Lay the bird in a roasting dish and pour about 150ml of water into the pan – it should be about 1cm deep. Check the amount of water in the pan after 45 minutes' cooking; top up if necessary as this will be your gravy as well as the steam bath for the bird, ensuring that the meat is moist and tender.

Roast the chicken for about 1 hour 15 minutes at this temperature. It will, in effect, steam and roast at the same time. For the last 15 minutes

increase the temperature to 180°C/gas 4 to crisp the skin, or for 2 minutes under the grill. If you are concerned as to whether the chicken is cooked, slice into the thigh area, which is ready last, and if the juices run clear, it's ready.

Remove the chicken from the roasting dish to rest for about 10 minutes and transfer the gravy to a saucepan, to reduce if necessary, or merely to keep warm.

Make a rich gravy by adding the cream (if using) over a low heat, and stir to combine and reduce a little, seasoning generously with salt and pepper.

In Denmark roast chicken is typically served with cucumber salad and new potatoes, roasted or boiled, with lots of freshly chopped parsley.

For a cucumber salad
Slice a cucumber thickly. Make a dressing with 100ml of apple cider vinegar, 50ml of water and 2 tablespoons of honey, seasoned with salt and black pepper. Pour over the sliced cucumber and let it rest for 1 hour before serving.

During early summer, rhubarb compote, lightly sweetened with sugar and also with a little vanilla, is offered instead of cucumber salad.

Breadcrumbed chicken livers or sweetbreads, sautéed

Serves 4 (chicken livers as a starter, sweetbreads as a main)

4 lamb's or 2 calf's sweetbreads, or 300g prepared chicken livers

Apple cider vinegar (see pages 62–66) and chicken stock (see pages 78–81) if using sweetbreads, or milk if using chicken livers

2 eggs, from pastured hens

Plain flour

100g breadcrumbs

Lard (see pages 82–85) or ghee (see pages 36–39), or butter and olive oil

Sea salt and freshly ground black pepper

1 unwaxed lemon or lime, quartered

WE SHOULD ALL FOLLOW OUR ANCESTORS AND EAT MORE OFFAL. They knew full well the benefits of the nutrient-dense organ meats, fat and fatty cuts, prizing these over lean muscle meat. In reality, the goal is to create offal recipes that are moreish for even the most squeamish. Offal is inexpensive but not widely available or in much variety, so it's best to order what you want from your trusted butcher.

Chicken livers benefit from a marinade in milk and, once breadcrumbed and shallow fried, they become crispy tidbits. Sweetbreads, which are the glands or glandular organs, such as the pancreas and thymus, are also ideal for breadcrumbing and frying because they taste rather neutral. Sweetbreads are best sourced from milk-fed calves and lambs, and do not keep well, so buy super fresh and prepare and cook immediately. Both types of offal go well with a watercress salad and a vinaigrette dressing (see page 77) or a simple tomato sauce (see page 76).

–

To prepare the sweetbreads

Wash and soak in a bowl of water with some apple cider vinegar for 2–3 hours. Change the water every hour. Washing and soaking will rinse away any blood and helps to cleanse the sweetbreads. Remove from the water, examine closely and cut away any strangely coloured parts.

Put the sweetbreads in a cast-iron saucepan, submerge in chicken stock, bring to the boil, then simmer for 3–5 minutes (for lamb) or 5–7 minutes (for calf). Remove from the heat and allow to cool.

Once cooked and cooled, examine the now quite delicate sweetbreads closely again then, using a very sharp knife, carefully cut away any loose surface tissue, fat or membrane.

Lay the sweetbreads on a large plate, cover with parchment paper and then lay another plate on top. Put sufficient weight or weights on this plate to flatten the sweetbreads, but not too much or they will disintegrate – about 750g is fine. When you are ready to cook the sweetbreads, remove and slice them medium thin.

To prepare the chicken livers

Chicken livers are much more widely available, as well as being quick and simple to prepare. All you need to do is wash them and then trim them with a very sharp knife to remove the veins, membrane and anything of an odd colour and then cut each into 2 or 3 pieces. Cover with milk and leave to soak for at least 15 minutes. When you're ready to sauté, remove and drain the livers.

Beat the eggs in a bowl. Prepare a production line of three platters and one bowl; starting with a platter of flour seasoned with lots of salt and black pepper, the bowl of eggs, a platter of breadcrumbs and finally an empty platter by the hob.

Warm the fat in a cast-iron frying pan while you breadcrumb the offal. Start by rolling the pieces lightly in flour, then dipping in the beaten eggs and finally into the breadcrumbs, coating them as completely as you can.

Once you have them all breadcrumbed, increase the heat to medium-high, and then sauté them quickly, not crowding the pan, turning once, until nicely golden. Serve immediately with a wedge of lemon or lime.

We should all follow our ancestors and eat more offal. They knew full well the benefits of nutrient-dense offal meat.

Sautéed venison tenderloin

Serves 4 as a real treat

2 large or 4 small venison
tenderloins

Some Ghee (see pages 36–39)
or lard (see pages 82–85)

2 garlic cloves, smashed and
coarsely chopped

A small bunch of flat-leaf parsley,
leaves roughly chopped

Sea salt (or some Shio-koji, see
page 67) and freshly ground
black pepper

CURIOUSLY, GAME DOES NOT POSSESS A POPULAR ASSOCIATION WITH HEALTH. This is completely contrary to its value historically and to its extraordinarily nourishing, natural qualities. In many ways game should be as appreciated as much, if not more, than fish from the wild, that has not been farmed – after all, fish is game from the sea, and a fisherman is a hunter too. All wild animals and birds from unspoilt habitats – elk, duck, buffalo, ostrich, deer or pheasant, for instance – are particularly rich in good proteins and fats, as well as minerals and vitamins.

Game meat may be more lean than meat from domesticated breeds, but traditional peoples valued the nutrient-rich fat from mature game very highly, and sought out the older male animals because they possessed the greatest deposits of back and cavity fat, the largest vital organs, and the greatest amounts of bone marrow. Trapping or hunting such a beast would be a cause for celebration, but not as a victory; rather to show respect for their good fortune and the gracious bounty of nature.

Lean game meat can be tough so it should be tenderised by time-honoured methods of preparation and cooking. Hanging game birds and meat in a cool dry place for as long as possible allows cathepsin, an enzyme naturally present in the meat, to break down muscle fibre. Marinating game meat – for up to 48 hours – has the same effect.

You can marinate the tenderloins, the most succulent cuts of venison, in some red wine, apple cider vinegar or lemon juice, complete with salt, pepper and herbs, but simply flash-frying them as here is very effective. If the venison is really really fresh, you might be inspired to try it raw.

–

Season the tenderloins with some salt and black pepper, preferably the night before. If you have shio-koji, brush some over the tenderloins instead of the salt. Keep refrigerated until you are about to cook the meat, which will help to ensure that you don't overcook the centre of the meat.

Melt a good wedge of ghee in a well-used and seasoned cast-iron frying pan over a medium–high heat. When very hot, lay the tenderloins in the pan, not crowding them, so perhaps two at a time. Press down immediately with a spatula, allow to cook for no more than a minute, and then turn them over, press again, and cook for about 30 seconds more.

Remove from the pan and allow to rest for 3 or 4 minutes. Serve scattered with garlic and parsley and pour over the juices from the pan. This is so good with crusty fresh bread to mop up the juices and a glass of robust, naturally produced, red wine.

How to select beef for flavour, nourishment and to sustain nature

Most popular cuts of beef come from breeds bred for meat, such as Aberdeen Angus, Charolais, Hereford and Limousin, or crosses of these breeds from the dairy industry, where there is a constant supply of calves to maintain the production of milk. That's all well and good, but given the misguided fear and avoidance of fat, many popular beef breeds have been further bred so as to reduce the fat and to increase muscle. The answer? Select beef from a traditional less well known, often rare, breed; one that's not been intensively bred and muscle bound, such as Sussex, British White, Longhorn or Devon, for instance. Or, from small-scale, less intensive beef farmers, or from mixed farms, where there's less emphasis on fast-growing methods. If you really want to expand your horizons, find a Jersey or Guernsey dairy farmer who is fattening some steers, as the meat from such pure-bred dairy cattle is exquisitely succulent and flavoursome, with lots of well-distributed fat marbling the meat.

What cattle eat is crucial to their health and therefore to the nutrient density of their meat. Talk to your butcher about his sources because you want beef from slower maturing cattle that have been pastured, meaning that they are out in pastures grazing on grass for as much of the year as possible (and enjoying as many varieties of grass as possible as well as herbs and wildflowers), and then fed hay (or silage) and some grain in the winter months when they are housed in sheds.

How cattle are treated and the quality of their husbandry, as with all farm animals, may not be in the forefront of your mind, but on reflection, will you really be well fed in body and mind if the meat you are eating has come from an animal that's endured a low welfare existence in a feed lot, or other close confinement, and more often than not led a short life? Cheaply produced is more often than not cheap for the wrong reasons, reasons that impact directly and negatively on the animals, their environment,

and of course, on nature in its entirety. Intensively reared, cheaply produced meat is unsustainable and a deeply selfish folly. Make the effort to find a butcher who knows the farmers and their herds and can verify the welfare of the animals, or buy direct from farm shops where you can take a farm tour and see for yourself. Don't be afraid to ask questions, however daft – enlightened and caring farmers love to share their world with the outside world of (largely urban) consumers. As well as the provenance of the animal, be aware, too, of the tasty and economical cuts of beef for stewing, braising and even quick frying. These include offal, tongue, tail, brisket, shoulder steak, skirt and shin. Our ancestors really did understand how to get the most from their animals, eating nose to tail, not just the prime cuts of largely muscle-bound meat we've become obsessed with.

How meat is stored after slaughter before it's sold is a crucial final factor. A lot of prime meat is wet-aged in vacuum packs; this is good for revenue as the moisture and weight are maintained, but bad for flavour and tenderness. Dry-ageing prime meat is a slow process, taking up to a month in a cold store, when the cuts lose as much as a one-third of their weight. Enzyme and fungal activity breaks down connective tissue, increasing tenderness, and moisture loss enhances flavour.

Meat really is a special treat, so it's worth supporting farmers and butchers who understand this, paying with thanks for their produce and savouring every mouthful with respect.

What cattle eat is crucial to their health and therefore to the nutrient density of their meat.

Rare beef and cornichon open sandwich

Sprouted spelt sourdough
(see pages 278–280)

Olive oil

Cooked rare cold beef

Cornichons, small or medium

Mayonnaise (see pages 70–71)

Dijon mustard (smooth)

THIS RECIPE IS IN TRIBUTE TO A PARISIAN CAFÉ, and its most popular sandwich, served daily, year in year out, with the obligatory glass of red wine.

Whenever you cook your pastured beef, try to leave some for cold cuts. Rare, cold and thinly sliced beef creates a simple open sandwich of singular moreishness combined with honest nourishment. Untoasted and with another slice of bread, this is the perfect sandwich to take on a journey, especially a long-haul flight, when you really do need some homely sustenance.

Preheat a griddle or griddle pan until hot.

Slice the sourdough about 1cm thick and brush with a smear of olive oil.

Sharpen your best carving knife and precision cut your beef as thinly as you can.

Slice some cornichons as thinly as possible, into rounds or lengths.

Slap the bread onto the hot griddle. Press down on each side, just for a few moments, more to superficially mark and flavour the bread than cook it.

Spread some mayonnaise and mustard onto the lightly toasted bread, and press into this a layer of cornichons.

Now arrange a succession of two or three slices of the cold beef onto the bread, covering it completely.

Serve with a glass of red wine that's naturally produced, of course.

Hamburgers

Serves 4

500g freshly minced beef from aged chuck or shin cuts that come from pastured traditional beef breeds, with some (10–20 per cent) beef heart (optional)

2 or 3 garlic cloves, smashed and finely chopped

Sea salt and freshly ground black pepper

Olive oil or tallow (see page 86)

4 burger buns, brioche style, freshly made, by an artisan baker

Butter, preferably raw

OF LATE, HAMBURGERS HAVE BEEN REHABILITATED AS A GOURMET TREAT. This is a good thing. For too long a hamburger has been a popular convenience food for all the wrong reasons. Now there are restaurants, cafés and even specialist fast-food chains selling burgers made with high-quality ingredients, such as aged beef from traditional breeds, wild game meat, freshly made buns with simple ingredients, as well as an ever-changing selection of nutrient-rich toppings and fillings, such as raw milk cheeses and fermented pickles.

Making your own super flavoursome and nutrient-dense burgers is extremely simple. All you need is your friendly butcher with his trusted source of pastured (grass-fed) beef that has been (dry) aged, and a willingness to make some mince for you from the richly marbled cuts of meat such as chuck and shin. You don't want lean beef mince here – in fact, not ever. To pimp up the nutrients, have your butcher add some beef heart to your mince.

Unlike other organ meat, beef heart is, of course, muscle meat. It is packed with rich goodness, including enhanced levels of protein, iron, selenium, phosphorus, zinc, CoQ10, folate, thiamine and other B vitamins. CoQ10? This is a co-enzyme, somewhat similar to a vitamin. It is held to give considerable health benefits but there is no clear consensus or understanding as to its precise efficacy. What is certain is that it plays a key part in our metabolic processes, and that given that our food regimes are so often nutrient, trace element and mineral deficient, it is a boon to boost our wellness with such precious natural supplements. That's a good way to consider organ meats: as natural supplements. The trick is how to sneak them into everyday foods; adding about 10–20 per cent beef heart to all your minced beef is a perfect solution.

How to cook hamburgers? It's all about balancing health with taste. What seems clear is that flame grilling and barbecuing can be a rather brutal way to cook foods. Depending on the fuel you use, there may be toxins in the smoke, and if any flames come in direct contact with the meat, there is evidence that carcinogens are created. Use a barbecue sparingly, as a treat, with natural charcoal as a fuel, and make sure that you don't flame the foods. It's okay, however, to cook your vegetables on the barbecue this way. Better to cook burgers, like your steaks, in a cast-iron frying pan, and if you want to mimic the grill, then use a cast-iron griddle or ridged pan.

–

Mix the garlic into the mince, along with a couple of big pinches of salt and some freshly ground black pepper.

Form into 4 patties, slightly smaller in diameter than the buns. Or, if your buns are small, make the burgers no more than 2.5cm thick or they won't cook through properly.

Smear the burgers with a little olive oil or tallow to help prevent them from sticking in the pan. Slice and butter the buns, and prepare any condiments, such as the onions.

Heat your frying pan over a medium-high heat. When it is about to smoke, lower the heat to medium and cook the burgers, two at a time. Press them down lightly onto the pan, and then leave alone for 3–5 minutes each side, depending on their thickness. You're looking for a medium-rare finish; you can't really tell by pressing the burger, so if in doubt, cook for less time. You can always return the burger to the pan.

Place another frying pan, preferably a griddle pan, over a medium heat, and once you've flipped the burgers put the buns butter-side down onto the frying pan and remove when they are lightly browned.

Once you've flipped the burgers, press them down lightly again and cook for a further 3–5 minutes. If you want a cheeseburger, now is the time to lay a slice of cheese on top.

Serve immediately with an array of nutrient-dense condiments.

All-day beef shin stew

Makes plenty for 4, enough for 6

3 or 4 good-sized cuts of beef shin, 2.5cm thick

500ml red wine

20g ghee, or butter and olive oil, plus extra for sautéing the onions

1 litre chicken, venison or beef stock (see pages 78–81)

Several thyme sprigs

3 garlic cloves, minced

½ teaspoon whole black peppercorns

2–3 small pieces of rind pared from an unwaxed or organic orange

500g carrots

400g onions

Sea salt and freshly ground black pepper

To thicken the gravy (optional)

A little arrowroot powder

To serve

Garlic cloves

Flat-leaf parsley

THE BEST CUTS FOR A SLOW-COOKING STEW ARE WELL ENDOWED WITH FAT, either within the meat (marbling) or around the meat, and also with some chewy connective tissue. Both will give flavour, nourishment and body to the stew, and once cooked will be melty to the bite. The best cuts for stewing are often also the least expensive, such as shin, oxtail and chuck. When you cook a stew with shin, you're not looking for veal shin (for ossobuco) in particular, but for beef shin from a traditional breed that has been pastured, and the carcass or cuts dry aged for at least 2–3 weeks.

Have the butcher cut the shin into pieces 2.5cm thick complete with bones. You will be cooking the shin bones in the stew to take advantage of all the nutrient-rich goodness in the bone marrow.

Prepare and begin cooking this stew in the morning. It will be ready for supper. Very slow. Very convenient. Extremely tasty and nourishing.

–

Cut away the meat from around the shank and chop coarsely into 3–4cm cubes. Marinate the meat and the shin bones in the red wine for 3–4 hours at room temperature or overnight in the fridge. Stir the marinade once or twice or when you remember.

You now have the choice of browning the meat before stewing, or merely assembling all the ingredients in your casserole pot. Either way, make sure your casserole pot is big enough; you want no more than three layers of diced meat, or the stew will cook unevenly.

Drain the meat, but keep the wine marinade. Dry the meat by letting it sit in a colander or sieve lined with clean muslin or cheesecloth or a cotton tea towel.

Heat the ghee in a good-sized cast-iron casserole – big enough for your stew. Sauté the cubed meat in small batches. Remove the seared and browned pieces with a slotted spoon and discard any fat remaining. Add the wine marinade and bring to the boil, scraping the pan with a wooden spoon to incorporate any residues from the browning. Skim off any foam. Reduce the wine marinade by about half.

Preheat the oven to 120°C/gas ½. Pour about half the stock into the casserole, bring to a simmer and throw in the thyme, garlic, peppercorns and orange rind. Return all the browned meat and bones to the casserole. Or, if you did not brown the meat earlier, pour off its marinade into a saucepan and bring to the boil, and then simmer to reduce it by about half. Add the meat and bones to the casserole with the reduced marinade.

Ensure that the meat is nearly covered but not fully immersed in stock, and if need be, add more stock and bring to a simmer, before covering and cooking in the oven for 8–10 hours.

About 45 minutes to 1 hour before serving, peel and dice the carrots into roughly 3.5cm cubes and add to the casserole. Peel and similarly dice the onions and sauté in plenty of butter or ghee until they are soft and golden. Put the cooked onions to one side until the stew is cooked.

Thick enough?

If you need to thicken your gravy, use a paste of arrowroot. Make this with equal measures of powder and water and stir into the stew, a little at a time, just before adding the onions, until the gravy is the desired thickness.

Remove the stew from the oven and add the onions. Taste for seasoning and cook for a few more minutes.

Serve this supremely nourishing and comforting stew with boiled potatoes in shallow bowls, alongside a wedge of sprouted sourdough bread (see pages 278–280) to mop up the marrow-rich gravy.

Garlic and parsley

Smash and coarsely chop some garlic, along with some flat-leaf parsley leaves, and scatter this combination over each serving of stew.

The best cuts for stewing are often also the least expensive, such as shin, oxtail and chuck.

Pan-fried rib-eye steak

Serves 4

4 x 150–175g rib-eye steaks (don't worry if you can't finish your steak, it will be great cold in a sandwich or on a salad)

Olive oil

Sea salt and freshly ground black pepper

Butter, preferably raw

Some red wine, water, or chicken or beef stock (see pages 78–81), or a combination

Other ideas for flavour richness

Shio-koji

Rub some shio-koji over the steaks instead of salt (see page 67).

Garlic

Rub some cut ends of garlic onto the meat before cooking.

Garlic and parsley

Smash and coarsely chop some garlic cloves; coarsely chop some flat-leaf parsley leaves, mix together and scatter over the cooked steaks before serving.

ONE OF THE SIMPLEST, quickest and most flavoursome meals is a pan-fried steak, with a reduction sauce and a green salad. Just how nourishing the meat will be is another matter. There are a number of factors to consider: the breed, its feed, the quality and nurture of its life, and for how long the meat is aged. Make a better choice after reading page.

The rib-eye is not a cheap cut, but it is one of the most flavoursome, being rich in nodes of fat as well as good marbling. Sourced from a pastured, slow-growing traditional breed and dry cured for at least 2 weeks, the meat and the fat seem to merge, and are equally succulent, tasty and tender. Rib-eye is taken from the prime or fore rib. For pan-frying ask the butcher to cut the steaks 2–2.5cm thick, no more. Any thicker and you will tend to overcook the outside before the inside is ready; too thin and they will brown and cook through too quickly. To cook a steak well you need to use a well-seasoned preheated cast-iron frying pan, that diffuses the high heat evenly. A thin pan will transfer the intensity of the heat directly to the meat and burn it. If you are making a sauce in the pan after you've cooked the meat, don't use a ribbed or griddle pan.

Drizzle the steaks with olive oil, a few grindings of black pepper and a sprinkling of salt (turn the steaks over in the oil and seasoning). Now, you can either keep the meat refrigerated until just before you cook it, or leave it out at room temperature for an hour or so. Why? Depends on how you like your steak presented. Cold steaks will tend to brown well and stay more raw inside. Steaks at room temperature tend to cook through more readily.

Heat the pan over a high to medium–high heat until it is just beginning to smoke a little (a hot pan and the oil on the meat will ensure that meat does not stick but sears nicely) and place the steaks into the pan. Don't crowd them; if necessary cook two at a time. Press the steaks down lightly, then leave for 2–3 minutes (for rare to medium–rare) or 3–4 minutes (for medium–rare to medium) before turning.

Once you have turned the steaks, press them down lightly again, and after about a minute, place a thick knob of butter on top of each steak and let it melt and sizzle in the pan. Turn down the heat to medium. Cook this side for no more than 2–3 minutes in total for rare to medium–rare and 3–4 minutes for medium–rare to medium. You can tell when the steak is ready by pushing down into the centre of the meat with your fingertips; the softer it is, the more rare it is. Remove the steaks and set aside to rest in a platter (to collect the juices) for about 5 minutes before serving.

Meanwhile, reduce the heat to medium, add some wine, water or stock, or a mixture of these to the pan. Bring to the boil and reduce by about half. Add the juices from the resting meat and a big wedge of butter, stir to mix well, and then pour over the steaks, or serve in a jug.

FISH

Fishcakes with roe

Makes 8 fishcakes, enough for 4 people

150g fresh bread

500g mashing potatoes, such as King Edward or Maris Piper, peeled and quartered

400g marine white fish fillets from sustainably caught cod, whiting, haddock, hake or pollock – or a mix of white fish

150g cod's roe (or mullet, or herring) in its membrane

1 teaspoon zest from an unwaxed lemon, plus a squeeze of juice

A small bunch of chives, chopped

A small bunch of flat-leaf parsley, chopped

25g butter, preferably raw, melted

50g flour, seasoned with salt and black pepper

2 eggs, from pastured hens

Ghee or clarified butter (see pages 36–39), for frying

Sea salt and freshly ground black pepper

To serve

Lemon wedges

Rocket leaves

Olive oil

IF THERE'S ANY WAY TO ENCOURAGE people to eat more fresh fish, albeit wild and sustainably sourced, then bring it on. Fish and marine creatures, from the wild, offer some of the richest sources of nutrients on the planet. The oceans cover about 70 per cent of our planet's surface, and offer up a constantly changing nutrient and mineral soup that marine life seeks out. As long as the hand of man has not spoilt this marine world, its produce is to be cherished, and much respect shown to the responsible fishermen who search and manage the seas for their harvest as hunter-gatherers, not as farmers.

Wild seafood is an excellent source of iodine, iron, selenium and zinc, as well as vitamins A and D. For an even more nutrient-dense and tasty combination, add cod's or other seasonally available roe to your fish cakes. Cod's roe is super high in protein and contains beneficial fats.

Fishcakes made with a combination of the rich and flavoursome soft fresh roe and the mild white meat of the fish are superior in taste as well as nutritional value.

Making your own fishcakes also provides an excellent excuse to make an introduction to your local fishmonger, an endangered species, and to get to know what fresh sea fish is available, week by week and season to season. Only buy the freshest fish that smells sea sweet, and prepare it without delay. For more information on buying fish, see page 189.

–

Preheat the oven to 180°C/gas 4.

Throw the bread cubes into a blender or food processor and make crumbs – as fine as you like. Make a lot, as, once cooled, the baked breadcrumbs freeze well.

Toss with a pinch of salt and about 1 tablespoon olive oil for every cup of breadcrumbs. Spread thinly onto a baking tray and bake until golden brown, moving the crumbs around every few minutes to bake evenly.

Boil the potatoes in salted water for about 20 minutes or until they are soft but still just holding their shape. Drain very thoroughly, place the colander over the warm pan to drip and cover with a tea towel for a few minutes. Empty out any water in the pan, throw in the cooked potatoes, and mash well.

Boil some water in a large deep frying pan and slide in the fish fillets to cook in a single layer. Reduce the heat to a gentle simmer – they will be tender and ready in about 6–8 minutes. Lift the fillets from the pan and break into large flakes, removing any bones.

Loosely wrap the roe in greaseproof paper, adding a squeeze of lemon to the parcel – the paper will hold the roe together if the membrane splits. Steam for about 10 minutes.

Set aside to cool, then remove the roe from the membrane and mix well into the mashed potatoes.

In a medium sized bowl combine the fish, mashed potatoes, melted butter, 2 tablespoons of each of the chopped herbs, the lemon zest, and some salt and black pepper. Mix well together.

Shape into 8 round, slightly flattened, cakes with your hands – ensure they are no more than about 2.5cm thick, with curved edges, or they won't cook through.

Line up two plates and a small bowl in a row. Dredge the first plate with the flour, beat the eggs in a bowl and finish off with a plate of evenly scattered seasoned breadcrumbs.

Prepare each fishcake as follows: first, roll and lay it in the flour, lightly shake off the excess, then thoroughly drench in beaten egg, and finally press it into the breadcrumbs so that the fishcake is evenly coated on all sides.

Heat a very generous amount of ghee or clarified butter in a frying pan until it is almost smoking, turn down the heat a little to medium, and then fry a few fishcakes at a time. Turn over once, when golden brown on the first side. They will take about 3–4 minutes to cook on each side.

Serve with lemon wedges and a handful of rocket leaves drizzled with olive oil.

Potato free

For a fishier cake, leave out the potatoes and use chervil instead of chives. It's a simpler version of the recipe – follow the recipe, then make up your mix with the fish, breadcrumbs, melted butter, herbs, lemon zest and some seasoning. Add ½ teaspoon of cayenne pepper for some spicy heat if you like. Beat the eggs, and then mix in well. Form into cakes and sauté.

Roe for life

Roe is so wonderfully nutritious and full of rich maritime flavours it should be eaten as often as possible when available. Cooked and sliced into rounds, roe is delicious spread on spelt sourdough with lots of raw butter, a squeeze of lemon juice and a sprinkle of fresh coarsely ground black pepper.

Alternatively, dredge slices of the steamed roe in flour and sauté in some ghee. Or, as above, dunk in flour, into egg, then into breadcrumbs and sauté. Serve with wedges of lemon and some coarsely ground black pepper.

Roe is so wonderfully nutritious and full of rich maritime flavours it should be eaten as often as possible when available.

Fish farming

Keeping fish for food is not new; the Chinese, some 4,000 years ago, kept their beloved carp in artificial ponds, easily created after the seasonal floods. Throughout history, moats, lakes and ponds stocked with fish have been a low-impact method of keeping and harvesting fish. But, in principle, until the late twentieth century, most fish caught were from the wild. Now it is estimated to be about 50 per cent.

As wild fish stocks have been depleted by the short-term profiteering madness of overfishing – from inshore waters to an oceanic scale – so the farming of fish and crustaceans in pens has grown, and with equal folly.

There are strong parallels, historically and commercially, between fish farming and beef cattle feed lots, or the sheds and cages of chickens, or the confinement of pigs in crates; can any of this industrial-scale slavery be called farming? Are these creatures given any real welfare in their short, cramped lives? Is it sustainable practice? Is it natural or respectful? Does it create food that is rich in nutrients? Does it damage ocean life and pollute waterways?

In so many ways intensively rearing aquatic life fails on all these counts. Take salmon farming, which, along with Asian shrimp (prawn) aquaculture, is a global industry. Fundamentally, the farming of salmon on such a scale has direct and damaging consequences for the nearby wild salmon and the marine ecosystem in general.

Confining fish in pens in the open sea is like having a beef feed lot dumping its ordure directly into its own water supply. It is impossible to control the level of contaminants and pathogens in the water, which will pollute all marine life in the vicinity. The artificially high density of fish creates the perfect breeding environment for parasites and disease, which are easily shared with the wild fish in the area, whether by contact with escaped fish, or from water-borne pathogens. Since most salmon farms are located along the migratory routes of wild salmon

this unnatural concentration directly threatens the health and viability of the wild stocks of salmon. Migratory routes? Yes, salmon are migratory fish. So how can one justify keeping such magnificent fish in pens, confined and unable to fulfil their natural destiny? Conventional or organic, salmon farms are nothing more than gulags for wild fish. Finally, and most tellingly, consider what farmed fish are fed. Some grain, but predominantly wild caught fish and, absurdly, for every gram of salmon farmed, you'll need to catch, process and feed three grams of wild fish.

So, if the farming practice is so dubious, what of the nutrient density of this food? First, farmed fish are so prone to disease they are likely to be treated with antibiotics, polluting the local marine life and yet again exposing the natural world to the dangers of antibiotic resistance. Secondly, although omega-3 fatty acid levels in farmed salmon are similar to that of their wild relatives, the levels of omega-6 are much higher, which is not good as they need to be in balance.

It's a real conundrum. Wild fish stocks are threatened by factory-sized commercial fleets chasing a dwindling supply, but most fish farming is unsustainable too. There are two good options: consider rejecting all farmed fish unless it can be proven to be sustainable and environmentally responsible for the welfare of ocean life, and select all your wild fish according to the recommendations of the Marine Stewardship Council.

Spicy potted wild prawns

Serves 4 as a starter

100g clarified butter (see pages 36–39)

200g cooked wild brown shrimps or wild prawns, peeled

¼ teaspoon fermented shrimp paste or a splash of Vietnamese or Thai fish sauce

¼ teaspoon fermented Korean chilli paste (Gochujang)

1 unwaxed lemon

PRAWNS, OR SHRIMPS, are nutrient-rich crustaceans that, in the form of fermented shrimp paste, are widely used in southern Chinese and Southeast Asian cuisine; their protein is particularly easy to digest. As a tasty finger food, as easy-going marine protein and as a popular sandwich ingredient, prawns have become a victim of their own popularity, and their good name sullied by an association with intensive, unsustainable fish farming. This recipe calls for wild shrimps, either the smaller inshore brown shrimp or the pink shrimp, also known as the common prawn, which, when harvested far out to sea, are boiled and frozen whole on the boat. Always ask for cooked wild shrimps, frozen or fresh cooked.

Preserving and flavouring shrimps with herbs such as thyme and also some garlic in clarified butter makes for a very simple and delicately flavoured snack with toast or crusty bread. However, to up the sensory impact, add some fermented brute force, such as shrimp paste or Korean chili paste, or both.

–

Melt most of the clarified butter in a pan over a low heat. Keep a couple of tablespoons back to pour over the top of your pots or ramekins. Add the peeled cooked prawns to the pan and stir well.

Now add the fermented pastes or sauce, to taste, then squeeze some lemon juice into the mixture, about 2–3 teaspoons. Spoon the potted prawns into little pots or ramekins.

Melt the remaining clarified butter and pour over the top of the potted shrimps. Let the butter cool, then leave to set in the fridge. The pots will keep in the fridge for 2–5 days.

Serve with toast or freshly made crusty bread.

More caramel?

Use ghee (see pages 36–39) instead of clarified butter. Ghee is better in combination with simple herbs and garlic than the pungent fermented pastes or fish sauce.

Wild halibut

braised in stock on a bed of vegetables

500g filleted wild halibut (with the skin)

Lots of butter, preferably raw

80g each of carrots, small leeks and celery, trimmed, halved lengthways and sliced thinly

75ml dry white wine

500ml chicken stock
(see pages 78–81)

½ unwaxed lemon

A bunch of flat-leaf parsley, stalks removed, leaves chopped medium–fine

Sea salt and freshly ground black pepper

Push the boat out

Substitute wild turbot in place of halibut. Turbot are a smaller flatfish, growing up to 25 kilos, and are found wild in the Atlantic, Mediterranean and Baltic seas. The fish has an exquisite delicate taste and a naturally moist texture to match.

HALIBUT ARE MAGNIFICENT CREATURES, the largest of all flatfish, with meaty white flesh and boneless fillets, making them an ideal candidate for those new to handling and preparing seafood. Despite spending most of their time on the sea bed, halibut can grow to quite enormous sizes, up to 200 kilos. Like all fish stocks, there is less halibut to be found in the wild, and quotas and fishing practices are now tightly controlled, especially in the North Pacific. Given their size in the wild, it's no surprise that halibut sport fishing is extremely popular on the shores of Alaska and British Columbia. Halibut are also farmed, and when nurtured in a slow-growing, low-density environment, they can be a sustainable success, delivering super-fresh fish consistently to a convenience- and homogeneity-obsessed clientele. See more about fish farming on page 189.

Halibut are a naturally lean fish, and a good source of protein, potassium and magnesium. Their thick and dense flesh needs to be cooked with care so that it does not dry out. Braising on a bed of vegetables in stock is an easy cooking method and helps to ensure as soft and melting a texture as possible.

—

Use a very sharp knife to cut the halibut into generous chunks and sprinkle with sea salt.

Select a shallow pan big enough to accommodate all the fish in one layer. Melt a generous slab of butter, about 60–65g, over a low-medium heat. Add the carrots, leeks and celery. Cover the pan and sweat the vegetables for about 5 minutes.

Turn up the heat to medium-high and pour in the wine, let it sizzle; follow with the stock, bring to the boil, then reduce the heat and simmer until the liquid has very much reduced.

Lay the halibut on top of the vegetables, skin-side up, and grind over some black pepper. Reduce the heat to low, cover the pan and let it simmer very gently for 4–5 minutes, or until just before the fish turns opaquely white.

Warm a serving dish and when the fish is nearly done, transfer all the chunks of fish to the serving dish. If there is too much liquid in the pan, turn up the heat and reduce.

Once the sauce is more concentrated, reduce the heat if necessary, add about 30–35g butter and a big squeeze of lemon juice. Stir to melt and combine. Taste and adjust for salt.

Serve the fish on or under a bed of the vegetables and the sauce, with a scattering of parsley.

Poached wild salmon
with traditional Norwegian butter sauce and cucumber salad

Serves 4

4 wild salmon fillets

*For the butter sauce
(Sandefjordbutter)*

200ml raw thick cream

150g raw butter, chopped into small pieces

2 tablespoons finely chopped flat-leaf parsley

Sea salt and freshly ground black pepper

For the cucumber salad

A bunch of spring onions, peeled, trimmed and thickly sliced

1 cucumber, trimmed, peeled in stripes and chopped into medium cubes

2 tablespoons fresh lemon juice

6 tablespoons olive oil

A handful of broccoli sprouts

SALMON, LIKE CHICKEN, WAS ONCE A SPECIAL TREAT. There are so many salmon farms that this fish has largely become the chicken of the sea; a mass-produced industrial food, not a noble wild fish caught with patience and skill by a hunter-gatherer. So now it's time to give wild salmon the highest regard and value, to savour this very wonderful fish, its extraordinary taste and its value as a nutrient-dense food.

Salmon – like tuna, mackerel, swordfish, herrings and sardines – is an oily fish. All fish are valuable sources of protein, minerals, and vitamin D (oily fish are particularly excellent sources of this precious vitamin, more typically than butter or liver). However, oily fish are particularly valuable as sources of long-chain omega-3 fatty acids, known as EPA and DHA. It is now widely acknowledged that these fatty acids support heart and brain health, as well as brain and eye development in babies and children. No wonder fish and seafood were so prized by our ancestors.

–

Put the prepared spring onions and cucumber in a salad bowl ready for serving. Combine the lemon juice and olive oil, add a pinch of salt and a grinding of black pepper, and pour the dressing over the spring onion and cucumber.

Put enough salted water into a large pan (one with a tight-fitting lid) to cover all four fish fillets. Bring to the boil, then lay the fillets in the water, skin-side down. Put the lid on the pan and remove from the heat.

Leave the pan on the side for about 10 minutes or until lightly opaque. If in doubt, undercook fish. It is much more nourishing and better tasting when more raw than when overcooked.

Bring the cream to a gentle simmer over a medium–low heat and leave it to cook for about 5 minutes.

Reduce the heat to very low and stir in the butter. Do not let the cream boil or the sauce will separate. Then add a pinch of salt, a grinding of black pepper and the parsley.

Drain the cooked fillets, place on a warmed platter and pour over the sauce; serve straight away, with the cucumber salad sprinkled with the broccoli sprouts.

White fish goujons

Serves 4

450g skinned fillets of firm-fleshed white fish

3 eggs, from pastured hens

75g plain or sprouted flour – spelt is good

125g baked breadcrumbs (see page 186)

5–7 tablespoons ghee (see pages 36–39) or coconut oil, for shallow frying

Sea salt and freshly ground black pepper

1 unwaxed lemon, cut into wedges

For some heat, mix ½ teaspoon of cayenne pepper with the breadcrumbs

Add a handful of grated Parmesan cheese to the breadcrumbs for a salty moreishness

Try mixing ½ teaspoon of grated lemon zest into the breadcrumbs

Ideal with tartar sauce or mayonnaise (see pages 70–71)

A robust green salad, such as rocket, escarole or frisée, dressed only with extra virgin olive oil and some salt and black pepper goes well with fried fish.

THE SELECTION, PREPARATION AND COOKING OF FISH is not a popular pastime or culinary skill. This is not a new trend. Good fishmongers have been a endangered species for many decades. And yet the era of obsessing over low-fat foods has favoured fish, particularly mild-tasting white fish, as a popular low-fat ingredient for an array of healthy convenience foods, whether fish fingers or a low-calorie ready-meal. Sadly, we've lost our appreciation for one of the healthiest foods known to man.

Anthropologists and nutritional historians agree that traditional peoples living on a diet that included a variety of locally caught seafoods were supremely healthy. This is because ocean fish roam over two-thirds of the world's surface in a marine world that is extremely rich in nutrients – particularly minerals such as zinc and iodine. Much of the world's soils have become selectively depleted of minerals, whereas the oceans remain, on the whole, relatively unspoilt and rich in nourishment for marine life. Many fish are excellent sources of minerals such as selenium and iodine, as well as omega-3 and other long-chain fatty acids. All are terrific sources of vitamin D (particularly oily fish) and a good source of vitamin A, especially in cod liver oil.

A meal of fresh, sustainable, wild seafood once a week is ideal. No wonder this habit has been endorsed by religious belief. Fish on a Friday really is a profound idea. This recipe is a good introduction to buying, preparing and cooking fresh fish from a fishmonger, or even better, from a harbourside fish stall. It's also quick, easy and convenient – and will appeal to the fish finger lover in all of us. Select very fresh wild white fish, not farmed. The firm meaty flesh of whiting, halibut, monkfish, brill or lemon sole works well. You need about 110g of fish fillets per person, so buy one or two whole fish, and ask the fishmonger to fillet and skin it. Keep the skin, head and bones for fish stock.

–

Cut each fillet into little finger strips.

Beat the eggs into a small bowl and sieve some of the flour onto a plate. Season the breadcrumbs with salt and black pepper on a second plate. Warm a serving dish in the oven.

Line up your fish, your plates of flour and breadcrumbs, and the bowl of beaten eggs in a row. Roll each strip of fish in the flour, dip into the egg, and then tumble it across the breadcrumbs.

Melt the ghee or coconut oil in an iron frying pan over a medium heat, and sauté 3, 4 or more fish strips at a time for a few minutes, turning once or twice to crisp and slightly brown the breadcrumbs.

Keep warm in the oven as you sauté the remaining fish – you may need to add more oil or ghee after each batch. Serve with the lemon wedges.

Saba no misoni
Fresh mackerel with miso and ginger

Serves 4 as a starter, or as a main with rice, vegetables and pickles

2 mackerel fillets (1 mackerel)

A bunch of fat spring onions or small leeks, trimmed, washed and cut into little finger lengths

2–3 thumbs of fresh ginger (depends on how much you like ginger), peeled and sliced into very fine matchsticks

Sake

1½ tablespoons rapadura sugar or coconut palm sugar

4–6 tablespoons miso (½ red, ½ white)

Mirin (optional – but only 3-year fermented mirin, please)

WE ALL NEED TO EAT MORE OILY FISH, and mackerel is an ideal species: it's wild and found in abundance in both tropical and temperate waters. Why more oily fish? Largely because they are rich in omega-3 fatty acids. In principle, we function best when the balance of fatty acids in our foods is roughly equal amounts of omega-3 and omega-6. In recent generations the appetite for processed, industrial foods has swung this balance in favour of omega-6 fatty acids.

Mackerel is strongly flavoured and not to everyone's taste. This Japanese recipe transforms the fish, making it soft and delicious, as well as sweet and savoury. It is the way to bring umami to an oily fish – what a perfect combination of nourishment and flavour.

When you buy your mackerel, make sure it's absolutely fresh, smells of the ocean, and has bright and clear eyes. Ask for fillets, with all bones removed. This is quite a finicky task, so be relentless and make sure they are, or do it yourself.

Use a very very sharp knife to slice away the cavity bones. Now run your fingers along the flesh of the fillet, down the middle and at the cut end. When you feel the end of a bone, remove it with a pair of needle-nose pliers, tweezers or pin-bone pliers. Remove every pin bone this way.

Turn the mackerel over and slice each fillet into 3 pieces, then make a slash once or twice into the skin of each piece.

Half fill a big deep-sided frying pan with water and bring to the boil. Add the mackerel pieces, 3 or 4 at a time, and blanch for 10–15 seconds. Remove with a slotted spoon to a bowl of iced water to stop further cooking. This will reduce the fishy aromas in the kitchen.

Fresh, sustainable, wild seafood once a week is ideal.

It's not traditional, but a little heat works well with mackerel. Add, to taste, some gochujang (Korean fermented hot pepper paste) or harissa, to the miso and fish stock mixture.

Empty the frying pan, drain and return the mackerel pieces to the pan. Lay most of the spring onions and ginger on top of the fish. Half cover with water and top up with sake, enough to just cover the fish. Add the sugar. Bring to a simmer over a medium–high heat, then reduce the heat to medium and cover the fish with an undersize lid so that the liquid can evaporate at the sides. Simmer for 15 minutes; the liquid will be very much reduced.

Remove from heat and pour off the liquid into a small bowl. Add the miso, whisking it in to make a smooth paste. If you like, to thin the sauce, add a splash of mirin.

Pour the miso over the fish in the pan and cover again with the small lid and heat over a low–medium heat until it begins to simmer. Let the sauce thicken and caramelise. Remove the lid and spoon the sauce over the fish as it cooks.

Allow the fish and sauce to warm through, which takes 1–2 minutes, and serve with a scattering of the remaining ginger threads.

This dish is also excellent cold.

Raw, fresh, salted sardines and other fish

Serves 4

12 whole sardines 10–13cm long, really super fresh, or 24 fillets, again super fresh (don't buy fillets unless you can watch the fishmonger fillet whole fresh fish right in front of you)

A lot of large-grain sea salt

Super-fresh raw fish is, happily, a taste sensation.

WITHOUT DOUBT, if you can find impeccably fresh, well-raised and clean fish, meat, dairy and eggs, eating them raw will often give you the greatest nutritional benefit. Whether you relish the textures, aromas and tastes is another matter.

Super-fresh raw fish is, happily, a taste sensation. Rather than invoke the Japanese sushi tradition, this Greek recipe is simple and crude, but all the more achievable and evocative for it – as long as you can find very fresh fish. In the Greek islands raw salted sardines, *sardeles pastes*, are especially prized in the summer months, when the fish are the perfect size, 10–13 cm long. Any larger and they take too long to cure; any smaller and there's not much to eat.

You can also use this recipe for super-fresh thinly sliced fish, such as tuna, fillets of small mackerel, herring and, of course, anchovies. All are wild oily fish, and excellent sources of protein and minerals, as well as the health-giving long-chain omega-3 fatty acids, EPA and DHA.

–

Cut off the heads and slice open the fish along the gut with a very sharp knife. Clean the fish inside and out under running water. Rub off the scales and rinse away. To open up the fish, spatchcock it by parting the two sides of the fish, and pressing it down on a flat surface. Pat dry.

Select a glass or ceramic dish that will contain the sardines in a single layer. Cover the bottom of the dish with a layer of large-grain sea salt.

Make a layer with the cleaned sardines skin-side down and cover completely with another layer of large-grain salt. If you have to make more than one layer, put another layer of fish on top of the salt, skin-side down and cover completely with more large-grain salt.

Place the dish in the fridge for no more than 1 hour for a single layer, and no more than 2 hours for two or more layers. Do not chill the fish for too long or its wonderful fresh taste is destroyed. Remove the fish from the dish and rinse off all the salt. Pat dry.

A platter of cured fish, covered, will keep for a day or two in the fridge, but it's really best eaten freshly prepared.

To remove the backbone, take one fin of the tail in each hand and pull the fins apart – the bone should just unzip.

Serve absolutely plain with a squeeze of lemon, some sourdough bread – with tooth butter – and a glass of very chilled ouzo.

Keep it simple as you really want to taste the fish, not the dressing. The best partners are some unfiltered Greek Islands extra virgin olive oil and a sprinkling of finely chopped fresh oregano.

VEGETABLES & SIDES

Roasted winter vegetables with a simple garlic sauce

Makes lots for 4 as a side

1kg mixed winter vegetables, such as carrots, parsnips, fennel, pumpkin, squash, rutabaga, celeriac, turnips, swedes, small onions and small beetroots

400g small Maris Piper potatoes

4 tablespoons olive oil

A bunch of woody herbs, such as thyme and rosemary

Sea salt and freshly ground black pepper

For the dipping sauce

50g mayonnaise (see pages 70–71)

150g crème fraîche

3 garlic cloves, smashed and minced

THE LIFE-GIVING ENERGY OF THE SUN IN SUMMER is captured within the root vegetables of winter. Eat as many of these vegetables as you can throughout winter and into the lean months of early spring. Vary your repertoire, and serve winter vegetables raw, cooked or fermented. The truly seasonal weekly winter veg box may not look exotic, but it will be full of goodness, energy and nutrients to see you through the cold short days.

For variety and a little moreish pungency, make a garlic dipping sauce.

Preheat the oven to 220°C/gas 7.

Trim, peel and cut up the vegetables coarsely but keep the smaller vegetables, including the potatoes, whole and the beetroots unpeeled.

Mix all the vegetables in a bowl, pour over the oil and about 1½ teaspoons of salt, and mix thoroughly until all are lightly glistening with oil and salt.

Tip the vegetables into a baking tray and lay the herbs on top. Roast for about 30 minutes.

To make the dipping sauce, mix the mayonnaise and crème fraîche well together and stir in the garlic. Season to taste.

Remove the herbs before serving, with the sauce on the side.

Vary your repertoire, and serve winter vegetables raw, cooked or fermented.

Tabbouleh with sprouted bulgur

Serves 4

115g bulgur, sprouted (see pages 98–101) and dried, or shop bought

3 or 4 big bunches very fresh flat-leaf parsley, about 300–350g at the start. Note: curly parsley will not do

A bunch of very fresh mint (you need about 1 part mint to 4–5 parts parsley)

A bunch of spring onions, small diameter variety, trimmed, peeled and finely sliced (include the green parts)

2–3 ripe but firm medium tomatoes, cored and chopped (peeled and seeded is optional)

Juice of 1 lemon, or more to taste

60–75ml olive oil

Sea salt

Authentic ideas

Replace the tomatoes with pomegranate arils, or as an extra.

Serve with romaine lettuce leaves, to scoop up the tabbouleh.

WELL-MADE TABBOULEH is a spectacularly fresh and exciting herb salad from the Middle East. The single most important and predominant ingredient is superfresh flat-leaf parsley, and the leaves have to be finely sliced, not torn or mangled, otherwise the salad will be mushy. The same goes for the mint – sliced accurately, not torn. There is a small amount of bulgur in the recipe. Bulgur, or cracked wheat berries, is a popular, or staple grain of eastern Europe, the Middle East and the northern regions of the Indian subcontinent. Authentic shop-bought bulgur is made up of parboiled wheat berries, dried, and then ground, or cracked, to a medium or fine texture according to the recipe. Parboiling the wheat berries helps to reduce the levels of anti-nutrients in the grain, and make it more digestible. Most bulgur is finely ground, about the same as couscous, and indeed you could use couscous instead.

However, for a truly authentic, ancestral, fresh and far more digestible bulgur, you can sprout and dry some soft (red or white) wheat berries. They're easy to sprout (see pages 98–101), just until you can see the sprout, and ready within 2–3 days. Spread them out on an oven tray and put in the oven on its lowest setting overnight (or use a dehydrator at no more than 65°C), until completely dry. Grind them to a fine to medium consistency, ideally in a grain mill, but pulsing in a food processor, or a spice mill will do. Use immediately or store in the fridge. Sprouted and dried bulgur requires no soaking before use.

If you are using bought bulgur, you need to soak it for about 30 minutes, immersed in cold water. Drain thoroughly and squeeze out any water with your hands. You could wrap it in a clean tea towel or muslin and squeeze out the water this way. Fluff up the bulgur with a fork.

Wash the parsley and mint, then shake or spin to dry. Remove all but the very smallest stalks. Use a very very sharp knife to slice a small handful of the herbs at a time, no more, into thin strips; do not chop into a pile of herbs. This precise slicing will take time. It is worth it. Pile up the finely sliced herbs in the serving bowl.

Add the spring onions along with the tomatoes and any juice to the bulgur and mix together. (If you like your tabbouleh less moist, don't use the juice of the tomatoes.)

Combine the bulgur and tomatoes with the herbs in the bowl. Pour the lemon juice over the salad, along with the oil and a big pinch of salt. Mix well. Taste and add more lemon juice and salt if needed, and more oil too. Serve immediately.

Quinoa and aubergine salad

Serves 4 generously

250g white, red or tricolor quinoa

Freshly filtered water

1 lemon, for squeezing

200g haloumi cheese

2 large aubergines, trimmed

Extra virgin coconut oil

Ghee (see pages 36–39)

2 red peppers, halved, cores, seeds and stems removed

Spring/summer: a bunch of spring onions, finely sliced

Summer: 1 or 2 courgettes

Winter: 1 medium or 2 small red onions, unpeeled but halved

1 fresh red chili, diced very finely

1 heaped teaspoon activated and dried sesame seeds (see pages 102–105)

1 dessertspoon activated and dried pumpkin seeds (see pages 102–105)

Tamari sauce

A bunch of flat-leaf parsley, coarsely chopped

Sea salt and freshly ground black pepper

For the dressing

1 garlic clove

Flaked sea salt

1 heaped teaspoon brown rice or barley miso paste

Juice of 1 lemon

Extra virgin olive oil

THIS IS A SPECTACULARLY NOURISHING SALAD, and very much worth all the preparation. Quinoa deserves all of the accolade it has acquired in recent years. Gluten-free and full of nutrients, quinoa has become a valuable export for Bolivia and Peru. It is a false grain (it is not from a grass-like plant) from a bushy flowering annual, closely related to the other wonderfood false grain, amaranth. Ironically, quinoa has been sold in the western world for decades, but as a bird seed… happy birds.

Domesticated for over 4,000 years by the peoples of the Andes where it is a staple, quinoa provides levels of protein similar to oats and wild rice – the most nutritious of grains. Called the mother of all grains by the Incas, quinoa is also a source of calcium – unusual in plant foods – making it a very valuable food for vegans. Quinoa is rich in iron and phosphorus, as well as vitamins B and E. Like all seeds, it comes with its own anti-digestive protective mechanisms. Freshly harvested, it has a coating of saponins, which provide an extremely bitter-tasting defence against bird attack, and which are usually removed. Within the seed itself are the usual anti-nutrients, including phytic acid, which is why it is important to soak quinoa before cooking.

Quinoa is now a fashionable health food, commanding high prices and in ever-spiralling demand – good news for the farmers, when it's fairly traded, until of course the quinoa becomes too costly or too valuable to eat in the Andean farming communities. Replacing locally grown quinoa with imported highly refined white rice or wheat flour is not good at all for the health of the quinoa growers. Quinoa thrives in poor and dry sandy soils. It is a very undemanding and vigorous crop, and in principle could be grown more widely, without irrigation or artificial fertilisers. Quinoa is now grown commercially in the USA and the UK.

Rinse well and soak the quinoa overnight; this will both activate it, allowing more nutrients to be available, and also speed up the cooking time. If you add a squeeze of lemon, it will help to neutralise the phytic acid.

When cooking the soaked quinoa, rinse well first and use a ratio of 1 measure of quinoa to 1.5 measures of freshly filtered water. For unsoaked quinoa, use the ratio of 1 measure of quinoa to 2 measures of freshly filtered water.

Put the quinoa and water in a large pan and cook uncovered at a gentle simmer until it is just done, no more: it should be light and nutty. Quinoa becomes translucent when cooked and it's best to taste often, as the cooking time will depend on just how long you soaked the quinoa for. Presoaked quinoa will cook in about 5–7 minutes. Unsoaked, it will take about 15 minutes.

Quinoa deserves all the accolade it has acquired in recent years.

Soak the block of haloumi in filtered water for about 30 minutes to release its salt. The longer you soak, the sweeter it will be. Pat dry and keep ready for grilling or sautéing at the last minute.

Dice the aubergines coarsely. Salt the cubes generously and leave for about 30 minutes to let the aubergine weep. Rinse and pat dry. Rub the aubergines with a generous coating of coconut oil, sprinkle with flaked sea salt and some freshly and coarsely ground black pepper, then sauté in some ghee in a heavy frying pan over a medium heat. Turn frequently and let the cubes colour nicely. Remove and set aside.

Roughly cut the red peppers into lengths, brush with coconut oil, and grill skin-side up until the skin blisters and starts to blacken. Allow to cool, then peel off the skin and tear apart or dice the flesh coarsely. Set aside.

Trim the courgettes, slice lengthways in half, rub with coconut oil and grill until just cooked, then chop coarsely. Set aside.

Roast the red onion halves with their skin on at 180°C/gas 4 for about 15 minutes until nicely caramelised. Allow to cool, peel off the outer skin and chop coarsely. Set aside.

Heat a small heavy frying pan over a medium heat and gently dry-roast the seeds until they colour. Remove from the pan immediately and when nearly cool sprinkle with tamari sauce and a generous pinch of flaked sea salt. Stir to mix.

For the dressing, peel and crush the garlic, then mince with a generous pinch of flaked sea salt. Use the flat of a sharp knife to press the garlic and salt into a paste. Mix a heaped teaspoon or so of miso with lemon juice to make a creamy paste, then combine with the salt and garlic paste in a small bowl. Drizzle and stir some olive oil into the paste – make lots of dressing as it keeps well in a jar in the fridge. Keep tasting as you add the oil until you have the consistency and intensity you like.

When it's time to serve the salad, fry the haloumi in some ghee, or griddle, or grill, until it is golden on all sides, then pull the block apart into smallish pieces and squeeze some lemon over it while still hot.

Mix the quinoa and all the vegetables in a large serving bowl, pour over as much dressing as you like and toss. Scatter the haloumi, parsley and seeds onto the salad, and serve.

Some latecomers to this salad festival, especially whatever is seasonal and freshly picked...

A little fresh turmeric root grated into the dressing adds another dimension of colour and flavour.

Some small fresh mint leaves scattered with the parsley.

No parsley? Use coarsely chopped rocket leaves or watercress.

Soil is not dirt

In an October 2014 edition of Farmers Weekly (the UK magazine for all farmers) this small entry appeared (in fact was buried) within a side column:

'The UK has only 100 harvests left in its soil due to intensive overfarming, a study has claimed. Scientists are warning that the UK is facing an "agricultural crisis" unless dramatic action is taken to reverse the depletion in soil nutrients. Researchers from the University of Sheffield found that soils under Britain's allotments were significantly healthier than soils that have been intensively farmed.'

There are three striking aspects to this report. First, this is a warning from mainstream scientists, not from a fringe natural living fraternity. Secondly, the study is about the soils of the UK, the legendary green and pleasant land, not a marginal scrubland. Finally, this news is very old news and it could equally apply to millions of once-fertile soils across the Americas, Europe, Africa and Australia.

Humans have been treating soil as a substance to mine and exploit for thousands upon thousands of years, as if it will last forever. Throughout history most civilisations fail because of the collapse in fertility within their local or regional soils. In pursuit of maximising yields, traditionally largely for annual grain crops, ancient forests and grasslands have been, and continue to be, cleared and put to the plough. These ancient ecosystems have developed living soils over hundreds of thousands of years. Stripping these soils of their robust and perennial, rich varieties of vegetation is like peeling the skin from an animal; it exposes the soil to the elements, and when farmed selfishly and relentlessly, there is no chance for either the nutrients or the soil itself to regenerate. This is especially true in a marginal ecosystem, whether subarctic like Greenland, or seasonally hot and cold like the American Midwest, arid like Greece and the Levant, or tropical like the Amazon basin. All share the same story of agricultural abuse and environmental collapse, whether in a few decades or over countless generations.

Living soil? Yes, it's not dirt. A healthy soil is teeming with life and with nutrients. There is way more macro- and microbiotic life in a tablespoon of good healthy soil than humans on the planet, by a factor of about 10 to 1. As ever, belatedly, we are beginning to realise, like our own microbiome, that we need to nurture these microbes (bacteria and fungi) in the soil, not tear them apart physically and chemically. Think of the soil as a digestive system of nature; this now has a name – the soil food web. There is a complex and symbiotic relationship between soils releasing nutrients to plants and those plants feeding the soil microbes with sugars derived from photosynthesis. This relationship is called the liquid carbon pathway, trapping the sun's energy and making it available to the teeming microorganisms in the soil. Feeding the soil food web takes place most dynamically when plants are growing strongly and before they divert energy to their seeds. The diverse, remarkably rich life in the soil is sustained and regenerated when it supports and is supported by a diverse selection of young, powerful plants, and also by traditional mixed farming practices, those that integrate arable crops and animals. By contrast, leaving fields fallow or repeatedly growing the same crops (monoculture), starves the soil food web and selectively depletes it of minerals, as well as destroying its physical structure.

In other ways, there is a parallel between how we have come to feed ourselves and how we think we are feeding the soil and therefore plant life. We really are inextricably intertwined. We crave and thrive on variety in our diets. Yet we have taken a wrong turn in both repects. Repeatedly spreading the plants and soil on which we depend with narrow-spectrum chemical fertilisers, predominantly ammonium nitrate, is like having a diet based only on highly processed junk foods. Both are addictive, both weaken their consumers, and both are unsustainable for healthy life. Plants need at least 16 mineral elements to exist. This is the warning of the scientists, and of many of our farmers too. We must therefore learn how to return nutrients sustainably to the soil, how to make available the nutrients within the soil, and as a result encourage its biodiversity and health. This is the essence of biodynamic farming.

The soil on this planet is in percentage terms and on average much thinner than human skin. And, like our own skin, it is living, protective and precious. Healthy soil sustains healthy farming, it supports healthy people and of course, environmental health in the round. It's time we recognised this fundamental truth: we should respect, feed and sustain our living soil and, most importantly, regenerate the vital resource we have taken for granted for so long.

Quick ratatouille

Serves 4 either as a side or with some crusty bread and butter

1 large aubergine, purple or freckled, trimmed and chopped medium-coarse

5 large, firm and ripe tomatoes (gnarly heirloom ones are a good choice), cored and chopped medium-coarse

3 medium courgettes, trimmed and chopped medium-coarse

2 red or orange peppers, trimmed, deseeded and chopped (more coarsely than the other vegetables)

4 garlic cloves, smashed and finely diced

2 bay leaves

Thyme sprigs

100–150ml olive oil

A small bunch of fresh flat-leaf parsley, leaves coarsely chopped, to serve

Sea salt and freshly ground black pepper

BY MID- TO LATE SUMMER, once you've had your fill of the wealth of fresh tomatoes, courgettes, peppers and aubergines spilling over the stalls in farm shops and farmers' markets, and from your garden or allotment, it's time to make lots of ratatouille to enjoy freshly made or to freeze. The summer and early autumn glut of fresh vegetables is a boon, but they don't keep, and so our recent ancestors spent much time preserving this wealth by fermenting, cooking and sealing in a jar, or if very frontier, by cooking and canning themselves. We have the luxury of freezing to add to these preservation techniques. Cut the vegetables to a similar size, not too small, as you don't want your ratatouille to be at all mushy.

–

Preheat the oven to 200°C/gas 6.

1. One-dish method

Put the prepared aubergine, tomatoes, courgettes and red or orange peppers into a roasting tin or baking dish.

Throw in the garlic and herbs, pour over about 100ml of olive oil, and sprinkle with lots of salt and some grindings of black pepper. Jumble it up to coat everything thoroughly with the oil, adding more oil if need be to keep it moist. Roast for 35–45 minutes, turning over the vegetables from time to time.

Remove the thyme sprigs and the bay leaves and serve sprinkled with the freshly chopped parsley.

2. With a tomato and onion sauce

If you like onions in your ratatouille, in addition to the above, peel and dice 2 medium onions medium-coarse. Smash, peel and finely dice 3 of the 4 garlic cloves. Peel the tomatoes if you wish or just core and chop them coarsely without peeling.

Warm 3 tablespoons of olive oil in a pan over a low-medium heat and add the onions. Allow them to sweat a little and soften but not colour, then add the chopped garlic and continue to cook for a minute, no more. Add the tomatoes and simmer, uncovered, for about 10 minutes.

Assemble the rest of the vegetables in the baking dish as above, and tuck in the remaining clove of garlic. Pour over the tomato sauce and stir, adding as much olive oil as necessary to moisten everything generously.

Roast.

Potatoes: boiled, fried, baked and roasted

Buy your potatoes to suit your cooking needs, and to celebrate the seasons.

POTATOES MUST RANK AS ONE OF THE ALL-TIME COMFORT FOODS, and also one of the most versatile of vegetables. They are especially good when cooked or served with nutrient-dense and tasty fats such as goose fat, lard, tallow, ghee and butter. Sadly, so many commercial fried potatoes are not only no longer cooked in tallow or lard, they're also likely to be pimped up with a cocktail of flavour enhancers, including sugar and lots of salt; all designed to enhance moreishness synthetically. Which is why such fries so often make you very thirsty, and also unsatisfied. Fresh, well-grown potatoes are not only starch rich – starch is filling – but are also sources of vitamins B and C as well as iron, manganese, potassium and phosphorus. Buy your potatoes to suit your cooking needs, and to celebrate the seasons. There's nothing quite like the taste of the very first new potatoes, glistening with melted butter. If you can, keep the skin on the potatoes when cooking; the skin is a good source of fibre, and also a lot of the nutrients are found just under the skin, so baked potatoes come into their own during winter months when we really need our vitamins. The only potato that is best stored in the fridge is a new potato. Keep main crop potatoes in a cool and dark place. Don't eat any that turn green. However, if your potatoes sprout, just break off the sprouts when small, they are still good. Many potatoes are now sprayed with a sprout inhibitor; organic potatoes are not.

–

Boiling potatoes

Served whole: any new potatoes; *otherwise:* Desirée, King Edward, Maris Piper, Wilja

Submerge the potatoes completely in cold water and bring to the boil. Cook until you can push the point of a sharp knife into them quite easily. Salt whenever you like – at the start or when boiling. If you have time, bring the potatoes to the boil, cover with a lid, turn off the heat and within 25–30 minutes they will be cooked.

Mashed potatoes

Desirée, King Edward, Maris Piper, Wilja

There's no end of opinions as to exactly what makes the best mash. Ultimately, mash should not be lumpy, watery, stale tasting or bland. And there's universal agreement that it's crucially important to use the right potatoes. All the varieties listed above are suitable.

Cut the potatoes into even, medium-sized pieces before boiling. Make sure they are cooked through – they are ready to mash when you can cut them easily with a blunt knife. Drain thoroughly and leave in the colander covered with a clean tea towel in the hot pan over a very low heat for a minute or two before mashing – this will help to dry them out. Drain any water from the pan, tip the cooked potatoes back into it, and add a splash of milk and a tablespoon of cream. Keep the pan over a very low heat. Mash. Add a little more milk and cream so that the mash begins to become smooth.

Now add as much butter, cut into small pieces, as you like. Keep mashing and stirring. Taste for butter and for salt. Serve immediately. Mash made in advance and kept warm is horrible.

Some umami? Add a teaspoon or two of sweet miso paste when you mash, and use shio-koji (see page 67) instead of salt.

Sautéed potatoes
Golden Wonder, King Edward, Maris Piper

When you prepare boiled potatoes, cook too many and save the surplus for sautéing. Sautéed potatoes are best made with cooled boiled potatoes. How well cooked? Well, if you like slightly furry-edged sautéed potatoes, boil them until completely cooked. If you like crispy sautéed potatoes, undercook when boiling.

Cube your boiled potatoes small to medium, and shallow-fry in plenty of hot fat – lard, tallow, goose fat or ghee. The fat should be very hot but not smoking. Flip the potatoes over so that they are evenly coloured. Remove from the pan with a slotted spoon to a warm platter and scatter with flaked sea salt.

Baked potatoes
Estima, King Edward, Maris Piper, Wilja

Baked potatoes are a good excuse for more butter, both mashed into the scraped-out potato, and then more butter again, spread cold and thick onto the inside of the crispy skin.

For a crispy skin, prick all over with a fork or cut an end off (all of which will prevent a potato blow out), smear or brush with lard or olive oil, scatter over some sea salt, and bake at 200°C/gas 6 for 1–1½ hours. Once cooked, cut open immediately and serve, or the skins will soften.

Roast potatoes
Cara, Desirée, Golden Wonder, King Edward, Maris Piper

There are two distinct styles of roast potatoes: those that are crispy and crunchy on the outside, and those that are also crispy and crunchy but with a laminated, rough exterior that oozes the fat they are cooked in. The former comes from roasting boiled potatoes cooked for a short time, about 5 minutes, and the latter from roasting boiled potatoes that are almost completely cooked, but still hold their shape well. Whichever style, boil the potatoes and drain well. Shake the fully cooked potatoes in the colander to roughen their edges. If you have time let the boiled potatoes cool before roasting.

Roast at 200°C/gas 6 for the crispiest results. Place your roasting tray in the oven as it preheats, together with some big wedges or many tablespoons of lard, tallow, goose or duck fat. Once the fat is hot but not smoking, place the potatoes in the pan and either spoon the fat over them or roll them around in the fat. Roast for 45 minutes–1 hour, turning once or twice.

Potatoes dauphinoise

Serves 4

Some butter, preferably raw, in its paper, plus extra, cubed, for topping

750g potatoes (see pages 212–213 for your preferred variety), peeled and cut into 1.5mm slices

500ml thick cream, ideally Jersey or Guernsey, or a mix of cream and creamy milk

Sea salt and freshly ground black pepper

WHEN YOU BAKE SLICED POTATOES IN CREAM AND MILK, don't spare the quality or butterfat richness of the dairy; find some super-creamy Jersey or bright golden Guernsey cream and milk, and you will take this comfort food to a new level of satisfaction.

If you want your potatoes to remain intact, you need waxy potatoes for this recipe, such as Yukon Gold, Maris Piper or Charlotte varieties, or Jersey Royal new potatoes. Or, if you like your potatoes beginning to disintegrate in the creamy sauce, use floury ones, such as Russets, Maris Piper or King Edward.

–

Preheat the oven to 180°C/gas 4.

Rub a medium-size baking dish thickly with butter. Not a smear, more like a render of butter.

Wash the potato slices until the water runs clear; drain. Lay the slices of potato into the dish, forming overlapping layers, seasoning each layer as you go with salt and black pepper. Gently pour thick cream, or milk and cream mixture over the potatoes, so that the top layer is just visible. Add more liquid if need be.

Dot the top of the potatoes with lots of cubes of butter. Transfer the dish to the middle shelf of the oven and bake for about 45 minutes, then press the potatoes into the liquid so that the top layer does not dry out too much.

After about 1–1¼ hours when the potatoes are soft and the top is golden, it's ready.

Ways to add even more goodness and flavours:

Peel and flatten 2 whole garlic cloves and rub them hard around the inside of the dish before buttering it.

Sprinkle chopped fresh herbs between the layers, such as flat-leaf parsley or thyme.

Sauté in butter some sliced wild garlic, small leeks or sorrel and lay them between the layers of potatoes.

Roughly grate some Parmesan or Gruyère cheese over each layer, and, 20 minutes before it's ready, even more on the top.

Replace half the potatoes with sliced parsnips.

Porcini and potato sprouted wheat tartlets

Makes 8 x 12.5cm tartlets, 4cm deep

For the pastry

500g sprouted wholewheat flour

250g unsalted butter, preferably raw, cubed

70ml ice-cold water

For the filling

900g small new potatoes

600g fresh, small and young porcini mushrooms (ceps), wiped clean if necessary with a damp cloth

20g unsalted butter, preferably raw

1 teaspoon fresh thyme leaves

360ml double cream, preferably raw, otherwise Guernsey or Jersey

6 eggs, from pastured hens, lightly beaten

100g Parmesan cheese, freshly grated

Generous pinch of sea salt and freshly ground black pepper

THESE SIMPLE-TO-MAKE tartlets reveal the naturally sweet and richly flavourful nature of sprouted flour when used for pastry. In addition, the highly prized wild mushrooms provide a rich and creamy meaty umami as well as some important nutrients, especially protein, B vitamins, zinc and other minerals, as well as fibre.

Supremely creamy and cheesy, these tartlets are perfect as a light meal with a summer's garden salad and a glass of fresh, lightly chilled natural white wine.

—

Preheat the oven to 170°c/gas mark 3.

Pulse the flour and butter in a food processor to make breadcrumbs. Gradually add the cold water and pulse to combine – you want a slightly wet texture as this will give some stretch and a crispness to the pastry.

Knead the pastry into a flat puck and place in the fridge for about 30 minutes.

Remove the pastry from the fridge and roll it thinly so that it hangs a little over the sides of the lightly greased tartlets. Press lightly into place and trim the edges to fit. Bake blind for about 25 minutes, or until crisp and golden brown. Set aside.

Boil the new potatoes in salted water until just cooked and crush them crudely with a fork.

Slice the porcini in half lengthways and sweat in a pan with the butter and the thyme. Remove and leave to cool.

Combine the cooled crushed potatoes with some of the porcini (reserve 8 slices for the top), cream, eggs and three-quarters of the Parmesan. Fill the cases with the mixture, finishing with a slice of the reserved porcini.

Sprinkle the remaining Parmesan on top of the tarts and bake for 15–20 minutes, or until the cheese has melted and crisped lightly on top.

Wild mushrooms provide a rich and creamy meaty umami.

Cavolo nero and bacon or pancetta

Serves 4 as a side dish

2 big bunches of cavolo nero, stalks removed, leaves washed and coarsely chopped

Lard (see pages 82–85) or ghee (see pages 36–39)

135g slab of smoked streaky bacon, cut into cubes, or use pancetta

3 garlic cloves, smashed, peeled and chopped medium-fine

Sea salt and freshly ground black pepper

CAVOLO NERO, OR TUSCAN KALE, long appreciated in Italy, is now an increasingly popular leafy green vegetable that can survive being sautéed, and is robustly flavoured too, holding its own alongside the likes of garlic, chilli and cured pork.

Cavolo nero, with other members of the brassica family including broccoli, cabbage, Brussels sprouts and kale, has been rightly elevated to near-superfood status in the refined realm of plant-based afficionados. Rich in lutein (a carotenoid), fibre, as well as vitamins A, C and K, this hardy vegetable is also a good source of calcium, iron, manganese and copper. So whether you are green juicing or sautéing with bacon, cavolo nero will nourish you.

All brassicas, especially green ones, benefit greatly from being blanched before sautéing. Blanching ensures that the bright green colouring is maintained, enhances succulence and speeds up the finishing of the dish in the pan.

—

Bring a large pot of salted water to the boil. Have a big bowl of ice-cold water, with ice cubes, ready by the hob.

Blanch the cavolo nero for about 30 seconds, then remove, drain and immediately immerse in the ice-cold water. Drain the cavolo nero once more, then spread out on a clean tea towel. These part-cooked leaves can be kept for future use, in the fridge, for a few days.

Melt 2 very big slabs of lard or ghee in a large heavy frying pan over a medium heat. When hot, add the bacon or pancetta, and sauté, turning and stirring from time to time, until the fat begins to colour and render.

Tip the chopped blanched cavolo nero into the pan, and stir and toss to coat in the fat. Sauté until heated through, about 3–4 minutes, then add the garlic. Stir and toss again, and leave to cook for a further minute or two.

Check for seasoning and serve.

All brassicas, especially green ones, benefit greatly from being blanched before sautéing.

Beetroot and goat's cheese salad

Serves 4 as a starter

4 medium beetroots, preferably 2 red and 2 yellow, scrubbed, trimmed, roots intact

1 red onion, halved and roughly diced

1 Tarocco blood orange (or 1 orange will do), peel and pith removed and segments chopped coarsely

180g goat's cheese with a light, fresh texture and only a hint of goat – Dorstone is ideal – or goat curd, cut into 1cm cubes

A handful of winter purslane or purslane

For the vinaigrette

3 tablespoons olive oil

1 tablespoon nut oil (walnut or hazelnut)

2 tablespoons red wine vinegar

1 unwaxed lemon

Sea salt and freshly ground black pepper

Beetroot salad, going solo

Freshly made beetroot salad is delicious on its own – cook and cube as above, sprinkle with red wine vinegar and salt, taste for tartness, then pour over some olive oil.

This is a fresh and nourishing winter salad. The health-giving properties of beetroot are legion. Its earthy taste and colour belies the long-held belief of its potency as a tonic for the blood. Here, the beetroot is cooked but if you like your beetroot raw, use fermented beetroot (see page 58). Goat's milk is remarkable in many ways. It is naturally homogenised, its composition is far more similar to breast milk than cow's milk, it has less lactose, as well as more easily digestible forms of casein, or milk protein. That's all well and good, as long as you like the taste. Goat's milk does, however, make wonderful cheese, and very willingly. All you need to do is let raw goat's milk curdle, and then drain and press the curds. France is justifiably well known for the range, variety and excellence of its goat's cheese, but many new artisan cheese makers are making fabulous goat's cheese from around the world. Support them.

Blood oranges come but once a year; it's worth seeking out the best, such as the Tarocco from Sicily – an exquisitely sweet and juicy variety. These blood oranges have the highest vitamin C content of any orange, due primarily to the fertile soil around Mount Etna, and their beautiful red colouring is derived from anthocyanin, another powerful antioxidant. For a leafy vegetable, purslane has a uniquely high concentration of omega-3 fatty acids, which are normally associated with wild fish and other marine life. It is also rich in vitamins A, C and E, as well as magnesium, iron and potassium (and calcium). Children who are averse to green food will eat winter purslane – making that vitamin C content very welcome in the winter months. You can also use common purslane for even more nutrients and a lemony flavour contrast.

Preheat the oven to 180°C/gas 4.

Drop the beetroots into a heavy casserole and pour in enough water to come about 1.5cm up the sides. Sprinkle the beets liberally with salt. Cover and roast in the oven for about 1–1½ hours – check after 1 hour. If a knife or skewer can be pushed into the beets without too much effort, they are done. Remove from the casserole, drain and leave to cool, then cut off the roots and neaten the tops. Peel and cut into 1cm cubes.

For the vinaigrette, combine the oils in a small jug. Pour the vinegar into a small bowl, with a squeeze of lemon juice, and add salt and black pepper. Stir to dissolve the salt and taste, adding more salt as you like. Start to add the oil mix a little at a time, beating with a small whisk or fork. Pause from time to time and taste – and stop when it's just right.

Mix the beetroots and onion gently in a serving bowl or on individual plates, then scatter the orange pieces and goat's cheese over the top. Place some of the purslane on the salad and pour over as much of the vinaigrette as you like.

Masdoor dal

Serves 4

250g masoor dal (red split lentils) or toovar dal (also known as toor dal or yellow lentils) – you want the washed, not the oily, variety

¾ teaspoon ground turmeric

1–2 teaspoons sea salt

5 tablespoons ghee (see pages 36–39)

6–8 garlic cloves, smashed and sliced

A bunch of fresh coriander (flat-leaf parsley will do), leaves separated from stalks and chopped coarsely

Optional

Pinch of asafoetida

1 teaspoon whole cumin seeds

½ teaspoon cayenne pepper

LEGUMES, the generic term for a wide variety of lentils, beans and peas, are a truly ancestral food, appreciated in almost all traditional food cultures, very often as a filling supplement to the historically scarce or scant availability of meat. Rich in vegetable protein, minerals and B vitamins, legumes are in theory a good source of nutrients, but only once they have been carefully prepared to make the nourishment bio-available. This involves many or all of the following processes: soaking – often for an extended period – rinsing, cooking and also fermenting. Raw legumes can also be sprouted very successfully (see pages 98-101). All of these time-honoured practices ensure that the anti-nutrients in the legumes, such as phytic acid and enzyme inhibitors, are deactivated and the complex sugars are broken down to simpler sugars. If all this sounds a familiar scenario, then you're right. Similar or identical methods are required for the preparation of grains and other seeds and nuts. After all, they are all merely dormant life forms that are understandably reluctant to give up their nutrients to a destructive predator.

Dried legumes, known very generically as dal, are a cornerstone of the culinary traditions of the Indian subcontinent. They are used in a multitude of dishes, either as a main course with meat, vegetables or both as a truly hearty stew, or simply puréed with ghee and served as a side dish, poured over boiled rice or eaten with flatbread. A simple supper of dal, rice (see below), fresh spinach cooked in butter or ghee (see page 236) and fermented vegetables should be the fallback meal in every household. Many dal recipes are simple to prepare and they chill and freeze well. This one is made with masoor dal (a salmon-coloured hulled split pea that is also known as red split lentils) or toovar dal (hulled split pigeon peas, also known as toor dal or yellow lentils). They are readily available and extremely cheap to buy. You need to check them carefully to make sure there are no tiny stones or other tooth-cracking objects in with the lentils.

—

Weigh out your lentils and examine them to check there are no small stones. Immerse and rinse the lentils in many changes of water, and leave to drain. Fill a heavy pan with 1 litre of cold water, add the lentils, stir and bring to the boil. Have a little sieve or strainer handy as you will need to skim off the foam or scum that will rise to the surface as the lentils come to the boil. Simmer, stir and skim until the water is clear.

Add the turmeric and stir to combine. Reduce the heat to low, cover partially and simmer, stirring from time to time, until the lentils are soft – 30 minutes–1 hour, depending on the type of lentils. Add 1 teaspoon of salt, stir well and taste. Add more salt if need be. The dal should be pourable but not too runny. Adjust with more water if necessary.

Dried legumes, known very generically as dal, are a cornerstone of the culinary traditions of the Indian sub-continent

Keep the dal warm while you make the flavoured ghee to pour over the dal in a serving bowl or, traditionally, in individual bowls.

Melt the ghee in a small frying pan over a medium heat. Once the ghee is nicely hot throw in the garlic, stir and let it sizzle until it colours lightly, no more. Pour the scented ghee with the garlic over the dal, sprinkle with the chopped coriander leaves and serve.

To the hot ghee you can also add a pinch of asafoetida (an aid to digestion and a natural flavour enhancer), followed by the cumin seeds. Stir once as they sizzle for a few seconds, then add the sliced garlic. Let the garlic sizzle and colour lightly. Remove from the heat, sprinkle over the cayenne pepper and stir. Pour over the dal and serve with some chopped fresh coriander leaves.

Once cooked, the lentils can be refrigerated for 3 or 4 days or frozen until needed. Chilled or frozen dal tends to thicken, so when you reheat it, you may well have to add some water to achieve a pourable, but not too runny consistency.

Sprouting all year round

The vital energy of a sprouting, fast-growing seed is extraordinary. Just as an egg is a complete container of nutrients for a chick, so a seed contains valuable proteins, fat and starches that, until sprouted, remain in an inert and dormant form. Through the action of plant enzymes, sprouting converts these nutrients into amino acids, essential fatty acids and simple sugars – and most of all this simple and miraculous nourishment is available to us raw.

What is even more exciting is that it's possible to sprout grains, nuts, seeds and pulses regardless of the seasons. A jar, some water, and a selection of organic seeds sold for sprouting and you are ready to grow your own superfoods.

(Packaged everyday seeds, nuts and legumes have usually been stabilised – by cooking or with chemicals – in effect to kill them, and so will not sprout.)

Sprouted peas really do taste of freshly picked garden peas – they're sensational. You can eat them raw, as a salad or part of a salad, but they also stand up to being sautéed. The Chinese, who have been thriving on sprouted foods for millennia, recommend lightly cooking sprouts before giving them to anyone with a weak constitution, or to calm the vigour and impact of certain larger bean and nut sprouts when you first introduce them to your diet. For more about sprouting see pages 98–101.

Warm salad of sprouted peas and sprouting broccoli

Serves 4

As much extra virgin olive oil, lard, ghee or coconut oil as you like

3–4 large handfuls of short-stemmed, very young and fresh sprouting broccoli

150g sprouted organic peas (see pages 98–101)

A bunch of flat-leaf parsley, coarsely chopped

Flaked sea salt and freshly ground black pepper

WE ALL YEARN FOR FRESH FOOD. And there's nothing quite so vigorous, appealing and tasty as freshly harvested spring vegetables and salads. What is so wonderful about sprouting your own vegetable seeds and pulses for salads is that you can enjoy this spring-like energy all year round. Sprouted peas provide amino acids, fibre, minerals and carbohydrates, as well as vitamins A and C. Purple and white sprouting broccoli is also wonderfully nutritious, and being hardy, will survive frosts and snow. It is particularly welcome in the late winter/early spring, between Brussels sprouts and first spring cabbage. Choose very fresh, short and tender-stemmed sprouting broccoli, or discard ruthlessly the fatter, woody stems.

–

Melt/heat your favourite fat in a wok or frying pan over a medium heat. I prefer a slightly caramelised ghee (see page 38) as this adds a subtle nutty flavour.

Throw in your sprouting broccoli and sauté quickly, tossing and turning; after a few minutes add the peas. Continue to toss and turn lightly for a minute or two. Pour over any remaining fat and mix the parsley into the salad.

Season as you see fit. Serve warm or at room temperature.

Variations

Sauté some bacon and lightly cook your sprouted peas in its fat (see page 85).

Stir-fry some coarsely chopped mushrooms – especially chanterelles – add some crushed, roughly chopped garlic, before adding your sprouted peas. Garnish with coarsely chopped parsley.

Fry the sprouted peas on their own in butter, just for a few moments, add a sprinkle of flaked sea salt and coarsely ground black pepper, and enjoy wiping out the bowl with a slice of sourdough bread.

Jumbled sprout salad

Makes 4–6

½ tablespoon fenugreek seeds

½ tablespoon shelled sunflower seeds

1½ tablespoons mung and adzuki beans

1½ tablespoons mix of lentils – brown, red and green

IN PRINCIPLE there are two types of sprouts anyone can grow easily and harvest year round. For the first, micro-greens, the seeds are germinated and the leaves and stems of the young plant are harvested, and the growing time is between 6 and 14 days; and for the second, sprouts, the objective is to eat just the germinated seed, which is a much shorter process, taking about 2–4 days.

The best-known commercially grown micro-green is probably wheatgrass, predominantly used for fresh juicing. Micro-greens are grown either in trays of soil, and only the stems and/or leaves are harvested, or without soil in a purpose-made tower of mesh trays that will need regular irrigating. Without soil, it's possible to eat the whole plant, as long as you can prise it from the plastic mesh or from its seed case.

Tray-grown micro-greens for salads and juicing include wheatgrass and barley grass, sunflower, buckwheat, garlic, onion and leeks, as well as the more lettuce-like salad greens, such as broccoli, red clover, radish, alfalfa and fenugreek. You will need to buy the equipment to grow these effectively, and to be most convenient and effective, with an automatic watering system.

To grow sprouts for salads, all you need is a sprouting jar or two (see page 101). Legumes are most popular as they are easy, quick and delicious, both raw, or if one of the larger legumes like green peas or soya beans, lightly sautéed. You can grow green peas, soy, mung and adzuki beans, shelled sunflower seeds, different kinds of lentils, as well as fenugreek in a jar. They all take about 2–4 days to sprout and be ready to eat.

It's worth the initial investment and time to do this, as you will be able to grow micro-greens and sprouts all year round; just consider, you will know exactly where and how your salad has been grown, and you will be able to enjoy the freshest, most nutrient-dense form of edible plants, harvested in your own home, and straight to the plate within seconds.

Always buy your seeds from specialist sprouting seed suppliers, soak and wash seeds thoroughly, and make sure you eat your sprouts when fresh. If in doubt, throw them out and start again.

–

Soak the seeds and pulses overnight in a 1-litre sprouting jar three-quarters filled with freshly filtered cold water.

Drain then rinse with plenty of cold water. Let the jars sit and sprout draining on the rest. Do not leave in the full sun.

Rinse twice a day, morning and evening, and return the jar to the draining rest each time. After about 18–24 hours you should see the sprouts emerging.

The sprouts should be ready to eat after about 4–5 days. Taste them after 3 or 4 days. Once you are happy, rinse in a bowl and let any seed coats float to the surface, and discard.

Delicious as a snack to munch on, or as a small salad with some good olive oil and a sprinkle of sea salt, or a light vinaigrette.

Drained and stored in the fridge in an airtight container most sprouts will keep for about 7–14 days.

You will be able to enjoy the freshest, most nutrient-dense form of edible plants.

Fresh pesto with activated pine nuts

Makes about 250–300ml

35g activated pine nuts
(see pages 102–105)

3 garlic cloves, smashed

Sea salt

25g Parmesan cheese,
freshly grated

A very large bunch of very fresh
basil, leaves only

125ml olive oil

IF THERE'S ONE DISH THAT MOST CHILDREN WILL EAT, it has to be pasta, and the most convenient sauce to serve is shop-bought pesto. There are two easy ways to improve this dish, and for really good reasons: for the pleasure of eating, and also for nutritional benefits. First, serve fresh pasta – handmade shop-bought pasta is of course fine (and cooks in moments) – and secondly, make your own superfresh pesto. The scented reward you savour as you pound basil leaves in a mortar is unforgettable, and always improves one's humour. So, slow down and make your own pesto. And don't just serve it on pasta. Pesto makes a wonderful dipping sauce, goes well with fresh tomatoes, is terrific on pizzas, and also alongside fish.

Pine nuts are packed with goodness, including lots of protein, minerals and fibre, but are vulnerable to rancidity if not refrigerated or even better, frozen. So buy your pine nuts very fresh, then freeze, and thaw them out a small batch at a time, then keep them in the fridge. You can soak pine nuts overnight to activate them (see pages 102-105). Pine nuts generally taste better for being lightly toasted.

Lightly toast the pine nuts in a medium–hot dry pan. Set aside to cool.

In your molcajete (see page 230) or mortar, grind the garlic and about ½ teaspoon of salt to a paste.

Now add the toasted cooled pine nuts, pound a little, then add the Parmesan and pound some more. Scrape the mixture into a bowl. Start to mash the basil leaves in the mortar. Be prepared for the most heavenly scents as you do this.

Return the garlic, salt, pine nuts and Parmesan mixture to the mortar and pound into the basil roughly to combine, drizzling in the olive oil as you do so.

Taste for salt. Use immediately.

Other herbs and salad leaves?

Add some rocket leaves to the basil.

Use flat-leaf parsley or coriander leaves instead of basil.

Combine all three herbs with some rocket.

Only fresh, honest olive oil, please

Good olive oil is such a simple food. It is, after all, just a fruit juice, no more than the liquid squeezed from olives. Long before Roman times and continuing to this day the small-scale methods of production for best-quality olive oil are unchanged. To make the finest extra virgin olive oil, only top-quality olives must be picked, and only when they taste their best. They must be pressed within 24 hours of picking and the oil, unfiltered, stored in airtight containers in a cool, dark place. Simple, natural and delicious. So, don't hoard your best oil: light, heat and oxygen will quickly turn it rancid. Once the bottle is open, use it liberally.

Such top-quality freshly made oil is packed with all kinds of nutrient-dense goodness, such as phytonutrients, polyphenols, antioxidants and anti-inflammatories. Consuming 2–3 tablespoons a day is not only a health-giving routine, but also a sensory pleasure. But like all foods, you only benefit from such nutrient bounty when the oil is fresh and produced sympathetically and sustainably. Given that good olive oil is a high-value food, and has been a significant trade good since ancient times, it is no wonder that olive oil is one of the most adulterated of foods. Olive oil fraud is at least 5,000 years old; cuneiform tablets dating from 2400BC warn against the fraudulent practices of olive oil dealers.

It's not straightforward to understand what constitutes good honest olive oil, especially in countries where olives do not grow and the purchase of olive oil relies on imports from dealers. In the regions of the northern hemisphere where olives do not grow, historically, there is a better appreciation for, and understanding of, tallow, lard and butter, as the most readily sourced fats. In the absence of a direct handshake contact with the producer, the best way to select the freshest, natural and most delicious olive oil, is to take time to read and understand the label.

Extra virgin is supposedly the best. The quantity of oleic acid in the oil gives a simple grade for the quality; extra virgin should have between 0 and 0.8 per cent – the lower the acidity the better. Supposedly an extra virgin? As always, production and trading (in particular of the most premium and valuable grades) is open to abuse; lab tests focusing on extra virgin olive oils have uncovered the use of inferior oils blended to lower acidity, deodorized to disguise rancidity, and the inclusion of seed oils coloured with industrial chlorophyll and flavoured with beta-carotene.

Virgin is oil from freshly picked olives, but of lower quality (0.8–2 per cent acidity); the olives may be bruised and damaged and may not have been taken to the mill for pressing quickly enough after harvesting.

Olive oil above 2 per cent acidity is classified as unfit for human consumption (often called lampante or lamp oil) – that is, until it is pasteurised and becomes pure olive oil; yes, it is now clean, but stripped of most of its nutrients in the process.

Don't just follow the acid test: the taste and smell are critical, as is the freshness of the oil. Look for producers who openly indicate the month and the year of harvest. Buy the freshest. Beware of trusting Best Before dates, which describes the two-year span from the date of bottling the oil; prior to bottling it could have been hanging around in tanks for months, even years.

Open a bottle and sniff: if you are pleasured with clean and lively aromas such as grassy, fruity and citrus, it's likely to be good oil. Too many oils smell neutral or unpleasant, being rancid, musty and unclean. If the oil smells good, take a swig, rolling the oil and sucking in air from the corners of your mouth as you do so, just like wine tasting, to develop and appreciate complexities in taste. A kick of pepperiness is also a good indication that the oil is fresh. Colour is less important – taste is what matters. And what sort of flavours do you like? There are over 700 cultivars of olives producing different kinds, densities and flavours of oil that all vary according to climate, soil and methods of farming. So, think of olive oils in the plural and how you might use different oils for different foods, and different oils for cooking, or simply raw for dipping.

Top-quality, fresh olive oil is neither cheap nor consistent. Thank goodness. Like natural wines, its taste will vary each year according to nature's seasonal variety.

Guacamole

Serves 4

1 medium onion, diced
medium–fine

A bunch of fresh coriander,
main stalks discarded, chopped
medium–coarse

3–4 hot little chillies, stalks
removed, finely diced with
the seeds

3 ripe medium avocados,
or 4 small ones – I like Hass

2 handfuls of ripe but firm
cherry tomatoes (any colour),
quartered, or 4–5 medium ripe
but firm tomatoes, peeled, cored
and chopped

Sea salt

THE AVOCADO, as one of the most fashionable foods of now, have earned the almost universal blessing of not only our ancestors, but also our food scientists, as well as the nutritionists, and, most importantly of all, obviously, our beloved celebrities. We should celebrate this extraordinary meeting of minds by eating more avocados, and in guacamole, you have the perfect simple recipe that will make a welcome change from squished avocados on toast.

Let's not forget, however, that the late twentieth century fat phobia did not help the popularity of this wonderful fruit. Avocados typically have a fat content of between 5–22 per cent; however, like homemade lard or butter from pastured animals, or coconut oil and manna, this fat is, especially when fresh, a combination of good fats, so don't be anxious. Avocado fat is predominantly (75 per cent or so) monounsaturated oleic acid, which is of course fresh and natural, and endowed with vitamins C, E, K, some B vitamins, and a good selection of minerals, namely potassium, magnesium, phosphorus and zinc. Added to this, when ripe, avocados are easy to stone, peel and mash – another of nature's naturally convenient superfoods for the modern world – and happily, they are also delicious.

Guacamole (meaning avocado sauce in Aztec) was the fast food of Mesoamerica, and was, typically, made in a very solid and seemingly crude mortar and pestle made of rough basalt. A molcajete and its pestle, the tejolote, are perfect for grinding spices, herbs, and for crushing salsas and guacamole. The rough surfaces season over time and impart a distinctive texture to the foods, and sometimes lingering flavours from previous ingredients too. A molcajete makes a perfect serving bowl, and an ideal conversation opener on the subject of ancestral foods and tools.

Crush about two-thirds of the onion, along with 4 tablespoons of coriander, salt to taste and the chillies in your new molcajete using its tejolote, or your less exotic pestle and mortar, to make a paste.

Cut the avocados in half and pop the flesh out of the skin, or scrape it out into the crushing vessel. Mix and pound roughly with the paste, then stir in about three-quarters of the tomatoes. The overall texture should be lumpy and coarse.

Serve with a sprinkling of chopped tomato, coriander leaves and the remaining onion.

Avocados are another of nature's naturally convenient superfoods for the modern world.

Late summer garden salad

Green salad leaves

Edible flowers

Rocket

Mint

Chives

Sorrel

Summer savory

For the dressing

1 garlic clove

1 tablespoon apple cider vinegar
(see pages 62–66)

A handful of capers

1 teaspoon smooth Dijon mustard

3–4 tablespoons walnut oil

Sea salt and freshly ground
black pepper

Extras

2 ripe figs, torn apart roughly

100–150g feta cheese, torn apart
into small–medium pieces

Or

1 perfectly ripe pear, cored
and sliced

A handful of activated broken
walnuts (see pages 102–105)

75g blue cheese, crumbled

FRESHLY PICKED OR PLUCKED SALAD LEAVES, edible flowers and herbs are some of the greatest treats of the summer. You don't need a walled garden or greenhouse to grow your own; plant seeds or seedlings in window boxes or pots on your windowsill, patio or deck. You may not have a sizeable harvest, but it will be all the more special, tasty and memorable when grown by you. What is more, the plants will be nurtured and grown without pesticides and in good humus-rich soil; when you harvest your crop, you will be able to rinse and dry it in fresh water, not the heavily chlorinated water used by commercial growers. And your ingredients will be more nutrient dense too, because, from the moment the leaves, stems or flowers are cut, the vital energy of the plant is dissipating.

If you can't grow your own, make friends with a gardener or allotment holder, or buy direct from a local trusted market gardener who cuts and rinses fresh salads morning and evening during the season. Even better, ask if you can walk along the rows, plucking from and tasting the varieties. Take the children. If they are resistant to green food, they will delight in the variety of taste and texture sensations, especially those that are sweet and soft, or subtly earthy or savoury, and – even more exciting – in the experience of eating an edible flower.

–

Wash the capers and soak them in water for 30 minutes .

For the dressing, smash and mince the garlic with salt to form a paste.

Pour the vinegar into a small bowl and stir in the capers, and the garlic and salt paste. Taste. Salt and vinegar have a wonderful affinity. Adjust or not, then add some black pepper. Taste again.

Now stir in the Dijon mustard to combine. Whisk in a little of the walnut oil, then some more. Keep tasting as you add more oil, and stop when it is thick and you are happy with the flavour.

Put all the salad ingredients in an oversize bowl, pour in the dressing and gently toss.

Buying vegetables and fruits wisely

In principle, everything we eat or drink should be grown or reared sustainably, and we should strive to nurture the soil to maintain its natural fertility. Both of these practices are entirely logical and prudent, because first, soil is not a commodity to be mined until it's all used up but a living, vital, life-giving, fragile and very thin skin on our planet, and secondly, if we don't care for the soil, how can we ensure food supplies for future generations?

With these thoughts in mind we should, as consumers, unite to end the use of pesticides and artificial fertilisers and campaign against farming practices that are environmentally disastrous, such as unsustainable irrigation and arable farming in marginal ecosystems. Organic, particularly biodynamic, farming embraces such standards. If a farm claims such practices and has no certification, you will have to visit the farm and see for yourself.

So, for selfless shopping, both for nature and for our health and well-being, whenever possible we should buy certified organic or biodynamic produce (a holistic agricultural approach that works with, not against, nature and treats the entire farm, whether the soil, plants, animals or workers, as a part of an entire organism – the farm organism). In circumstances where it isn't possible to stick to organic, it is worth knowing which fruits and vegetables are most contaminated by pesticides, and which are least reliant on chemicals, as well as whether they are grown with a sustainable source of water.

Fruits and vegetables that are most likely to be contaminated with pesticides
The list is largely logical; thin-skinned or very watery fruits and vegetables are likely to be most contaminated.

- Soft fruits: strawberries, blueberries, raspberries, grapes
- Tree fruits: peaches, nectarines, apples
- Vegetables and salads: celery, lettuce, cucumber, tomatoes, chillies and peppers, spinach, kale, collard and other loose-leaved greens and potatoes

Of these, research from the USA showed that the average potato contained more pesticides by weight than any other produce, while some soft fruits tested contained between 13 and 15 different types of pesticide.

Fruits and vegetables that are least likely to be contaminated with pesticides
Again, it's a more or less logical selection, as thick-skinned produce prevails, including ones that are naturally disease and pest resistant.

- Fruits: honeydew melon, kiwis, pineapple, mangoes, papayas, grapefruit
- Vegetables and salads: avocados, asparagus, sweet potatoes, onions, cauliflower, aubergines, sweetcorn and cabbage

Of these, avocados were least likely to show pesticide contamination.

For you, your children and for the planet
What makes sense for ourselves and for the planet? Buy organic whenever you can, even better, buy biodynamic produce and wash all produce thoroughly with filtered water.

Whenever possible, we should buy certified organic or biodynamic produce.

Vegetables cooked with lots of butter

Butter not only adds considerable nourishment, its very presence ensures that the nutrients in the vegetables themselves are more accessible to our digestive system.

THERE ARE TWO VERY GOOD REASONS for cooking many vegetables with a lot of butter; first, they taste better, and secondly, the butter not only adds considerable nourishment, its very presence ensures that the nutrients in the vegetables themselves are more accessible to our digestive system. Take carrots, for instance; about 3 per cent or less of the beta-carotene is available when raw. Cooked in butter, the bio-availability increases tenfold.

The two prime and everyday contenders for the butter treatment are carrots and spinach. Carrots can be truly dreary when boiled in water, especially when overcooked. You will just about save the day if you cook them until they're nicely firm to the bite, drain well, then toss them in the pan with lots of butter and a handful of chopped fresh flat-leaf parsley. Much better to coat them in some butter and honey, followed by chicken stock and water, then simmer to reduce, glazing the carrots nicely. Carrots are a well-known source of beta-carotenes (eat too many raw carrots and your skin really will take on a orange hue), vitamin A (only when the beta-carotenes are fully accessible), vitamin K, manganese and potassium. Look out for purple, red and yellow carrots, or combinations thereof; they are all equally nutritious.

Spinach is a health-food legend in its own right, being, potentially, a rich source of iron, magnesium, manganese and vitamins A, C and K. It is also a pretty good source of calcium, potassium, fibre and vitamins B and E. Potentially? Not only will the level of nutrients depend on where and how the spinach was grown and how fresh it is, but also whether it is eaten raw or cooked. The iron and calcium in raw spinach are not fully accessible because of the presence of substances that inhibit the absorption of iron, including oxalates, which also reduce the bio-availability of calcium. High levels of oxalates will encourage the removal of iron from the body. Cooking neutralises the oxalates. So eat spinach cooked in butter regularly, but raw, as a salad, much less often.

Serves 4 as a side

Lots and lots of spinach
– about 1kg

About 100g butter, preferably raw

1 medium onion, peeled, halved
and finely diced or sliced

Spinach with onions and butter

If necessary, destalk the spinach, then wash and spin lightly in a salad spinner so that the leaves remain moist but not dripping wet. If the leaves are big, gather them in bunches and chop coarsely.

Melt 60g of the butter in a large frying pan and sauté the onion over a medium heat until is has softened and coloured just a bit.

Start to add the spinach leaves, filling the pan, and stirring into the butter and onions. The spinach will collapse as it heats, so keep adding more, stirring to combine. If there is a lot of water in the pan, increase the heat and leave the pan uncovered to reduce. If there is little water, cover the pan and simmer. Cook for as long or as little as you like. When ready, add another 40–50g of butter and let it melt into the spinach. Serve, pouring over any sauce, and season individually.

Ghee?

If you'd like to add the rich caramel taste of ghee, substitute for the butter, or use half and half.

Serves 4 as a side

60g butter, preferably raw, plus extra for the sauce

2 garlic cloves, smashed and crushed

500g carrots, trimmed, peeled and sliced into rounds or batons

1 tablespoon raw honey

100ml chicken stock (see pages 78–81)

A small bunch of flat-leaf parsley, leaves separated from the stalks and chopped coarsely

Sea salt and freshly ground black pepper

Carrots in a butter glaze

Melt the butter in a heavy medium-sized saucepan over a low heat. Add the garlic, stir and leave to cook for a minute or two. Add the carrots to the butter, along with the honey, a grinding of black pepper and a small pinch of salt. Stir to coat the carrots. Pour over the chicken stock and add a little water if need be so that the carrots are just immersed. Bring to a simmer, then reduce the heat, cover and cook for 4–5 minutes, until the carrots are just beginning to soften.

Take off the lid and increase the heat so that the liquid is boiling merrily. Reduce the liquid to almost nothing. Add two more good-sized pieces of butter and stir in to melt. Taste and adjust for salt.

Serve, pouring over the wonderful sauce with a sprinkling of parsley.

Hatsuga genmai
Sprouted wholegrain rice

Serves 4

300g wholegrain brown rice

Place the rice into one or more sprouting jars. Fill with water, rinse and fill again, so that the rice is fully submerged. Leave to soak overnight.

The next day; drain off all the water and rinse again. Invert the jar in its drainer so that any water can drain away.

After 12 hours of draining, rinse and drain again. Repeat, rinsing and draining, 2–3 times daily for 1–2 days.

WHITE RICE is one of the most widely eaten foods in the world, especially in Asia. And yet it is well known that white rice is deficient in certain nutrients, so much so that in some countries it is obligatory to fortify white rice artificially. This is not a wise solution, especially when you realise most of the nutrients are removed during the processing of brown rice to create white rice. They are both dehulled rice grains. White rice is then further milled and often polished. These processes remove the bran and the germ, leaving only the starchy endosperm. The bran and the germ contain the important nutrients, including B vitamins, fibre, rice bran oil, magnesium and iron. So why is white rice milled and polished? Well, white rice cooks more quickly, is more fragrant, many might say it looks more appealing and more sophisticated, it takes up any flavouring more readily, and finally, it keeps better.

It is thought that our ancestors did eat mostly wholegrain brown rice and that the milling and refining of rice is a relatively recent practice, perhaps over the last 750 to 1,000 years. (Let's not forget that rice has been cultivated for over 10,000 years.) Rice is a gluten-free grain and is therefore easier for some of us to digest than grains with gluten, such as wheat (and spelt), barley and rye. But rice, as a seed, does contain anti-nutrients to protect itself. Our ancestors knew this and therefore soaked grains to help neutralise the toxins, and also to speed up the cooking time.

'Hatsuga genmai', meaning germinated whole rice, is the new (introduced in Japan in 2004) throwback technique, where wholegrain brown rice is soaked and allowed to germinate, but only just. In this way all the beneficial nutrients are realised, the anti-nutrients are reduced, the flavour is enhanced, and – best of all in this day and age – it's convenient to cook, taking the same time to prepare as white rice. Once dried, it will also keep much better. It's also known as GABA rice, as it contains enhanced levels of gamma-aminobutyric acid, much needed by our nervous systems. You can buy sprouted and dried brown rice, and flour, or you can sprout the rice easily.

–

Once you see little tails beginning to form on the rice, it is ready to cook or dry. If you allow the rice to continue to sprout it will become very sweet as more and more of the starch is converted to simple sugars. Drain the sprouts well and cook as per white rice.

The sprouted rice will keep in the fridge for several days in a sealed container.

To store the rice and to make flour too, dry in a dehydrator or in the oven at a low temperature (50°C for 5 hours), then store in a sealed container or grind into flour.

SWEET THINGS

Chocolate, raisin, seed and nut cookies

Makes about 24

120g unsalted butter, preferably raw, softened, plus extra for greasing

150g rapadura sugar, jaggery or coconut palm sugar

1 egg, from pastured hens

1 teaspoon finest-quality vanilla extract

130g sprouted wholewheat or spelt flour

½ teaspoon flaked sea salt

Pinch of bicarbonate of soda

½ teaspoon baking powder

100g raisins

75g mix of activated pecans and slow-dried hazelnuts (see pages 102–105), coarsely chopped

60g mix of activated or sprouted and dried sunflower (30g), chia (15g) and linseed (golden or brown flax seeds) (15g) or any combination of activated seeds (see pages 102–105)

75g dark chocolate (70 per cent cocoa solids), coarsely chopped (keep the pieces a generous size)

ONCE YOU HAVE GOT INTO THE HABIT of activating your nuts and seeds, you will realise just how flavoursome they are in baking too. Cookies may be an occasional indulgence, but these are doubly moreish, as they are packed with nutrient-dense, readily digestible ingredients, and also taste wonderful. Yin and yang in a cookie.

Of the nuts and seeds recommended, chia seeds are the new wonder ingredient, lauded for their high-quality protein, antioxidants and mineral content, including calcium, phosphorus and magnesium and as an excellent source of plant-based omega-3 fats. Chia seeds are not new to mankind, for they were an everyday food of the Mayan and Aztec civilisations, who appreciated this energy-packed seed for its sustaining qualities.

These cookies should be gooey, crunchy and deeply satisfying to the bite. To achieve this cookie nirvana you need to be careful with their cooking time. This is because cookies bake in a short time, and are very sensitive to small changes in temperature and timing. A cookie, being small, takes but moments to dry out from moist perfection to a burnt frazzle. They are also deceivers. At first sight they can look underdone, when in fact they are ready. Watch the edges, if they start to brown, whip them out. It's much better to have underdone than overcooked cookies.

–

Preheat the oven to 170ºC/gas 3 and butter some baking sheets, or better, cover baking trays with non-stick baking parchment.

Cream the butter and sugar together in a medium-sized mixing bowl. Beat in the egg until the mixture is very smooth and holds together. Stir in the vanilla extract.

In a separate bowl, mix the flour, salt, bicarbonate of soda and baking powder together, and add to the wet mixture, a little at a time, beating as you go, until you have a very thick batter. Note: If you are using unsprouted flour do not add all the flour at once, but add sufficient to make a very thick batter, and no more.

Stir in the raisins, nuts, seeds and chocolate. The dough should now be so thick you could almost roll it into a ball with your hands. Use two serving spoons to scoop out and drop small, firm, walnut-sized dollops of cookie mix onto the baking sheets. Space them about 6–7cm apart to allow for spreading. Bake for 10 minutes, then check for consistency – if you like your cookies more firm, cook for up to 15 minutes.

Remove the sheets from the oven and allow to cool, so you can handle

Chia seeds are not new to mankind, for they were an everyday food of the Mayan and Aztec civilisations.

them without oven gloves, before transferring the cookies to a wire rack to cool. This will take about 2–3 minutes. Do not leave the cookies on the sheets for longer than this or they will become more or less welded to the metal if you're not using baking parchment.

Eat warm... try to eat only a few at a time.

Store in an airtight container.

Grinding or cracking dormant seeds

If you decide to use organic raw seeds that have not been activated or sprouted, it is best to crack the smaller seeds before using them. Linseed and chia seeds are very small and very robust, which makes them structurally highly resistant to digestion. Many, if not most, will not be ground or cracked when you bite into the cookie, so the best solution is to crack/grind the small seeds using a mortar and pestle just before you add them to the dough. Do not store cracked or ground seeds – they will quickly go rancid.

Seeds: you could use any mixture of dried seeds, such as activated pumpkin seeds, sprouted alfalfa and broccoli.

Nuts: try activated chopped almonds and peanuts.

Apple cobbler

Serves 6

8 tart, fresh organic apples

Juice of 1–2 unwaxed lemons

2 tablespoons rapadura sugar, jaggery or coconut palm sugar

Grated rind of 1 unwaxed lemon

1 tablespoon arrowroot

½ teaspoon cinnamon

Topping

160g crispy almonds (see page 103)

120g unsalted butter, preferably raw, softened

175g sprouted organic spelt or wheat flour (bulgur)

60g rapadura sugar, jaggery or coconut palm sugar

¼ teaspoon flaked sea salt

1 teaspoon vanilla extract

FOR CHILD AND ADULT ALIKE, an apple has an innocent and sentimental allure. Imagine the smell, the feel, the colour, the bite and the fresh satisfaction of the first of the season's Cox's Orange Pippins. Over generations of simple plant breeding we have developed more than 7,500 varieties of apples suitable for picking and enjoying fresh from the early autumn to the early summer, and locally. Sadly much of this astonishing variety has been shunned for the sake of standardisation and convenience. Over the past 50 years we've partially commoditized apple farming on an international scale in order to enjoy the same boutique style apples the year round – by chasing the autumn harvest in both hemispheres, and developing ever more unnatural ways to keep apples perfect in shape and size, unblemished, as well as shiny and fresh looking.

Apples are indeed healthy. They're rich in boron, which helps to reduce osteoporosis, and they also have a low glycemic index, so that despite often possessing an exquisite sweetness, they do not create a surge in blood sugar levels. This is because apples also contain pectin, a soluble fibre, which helps slow blood sugar absorption, making apples a suitable fruit for diabetics.

Cobblers were first cooked by the American settlers, who, without suet, used simple dumplings or crushed biscuits to make a filling and sweet topping to a dish of stewed fruit. It's worth exploring the world of cobblers. Varieties include the Grunt, the Slump, the Sonker and a Pandowdy. In the UK, a cobbler is often made with a scone topping.

Warm the oven to 175ºC/gas 4. Liberally butter a baking or soufflé dish.

Peel, core and slice the apples and toss with the lemon juice. Mix the 2 tablespoons of sugar with the lemon rind, arrowroot and cinnamon and mix thoroughly into the apples. Place the apple mixture into the baking dish.

For the topping, grind the almonds to a powder in a food processor. Add the butter and flour, 60g sugar, vanilla and salt and process until smooth. Layer this mixture on top of the apples, and bake for 1 hour. Serve with raw cream, or homemade vanilla ice cream (see page 321).

Peach cobbler

Use 8 ripe peaches in place of the apples and leave out the cinnamon.

Blueberry cobbler

Substitute the apples with about 1kg blueberries, and again, don't add any cinnamon.

What is real chocolate?

Real chocolate is a heavenly food. Break off a piece. Close your eyes and slowly let it melt on your tongue to taste its many nuanced flavours. Please don't just chew it. Real chocolate is made from a hyper-nutritious seed, roasted to bring out its flavours, ground to a fine paste, and finally sweetened with sugars, preferably unrefined ones from the juice of sugar cane, or the nectar of the coconut flower. The cacao seed is said to contain the secret to longevity, happiness and good sex. It is a veritable superseed.

In fact, when the father of modern plant taxonomy, Carl Linnaeus, searched for a botanical name to describe the fruit tree from which chocolate is derived, he found that only a superlative would suffice: Theobroma cacao means food of the gods. The ancient Mayas had called the shade-loving rainforest tree 'kakaw' and arguably developed the first-ever recipe to make chocolate. They discovered how to soften the bitterness of the cacao seed (or bean, by its shape) through fermentation and drying. However, they preferred to drink chocolate rather than eat it, since water filtered the heavier particles in the stone-ground paste and diluted any remaining astringent flavours that are present in the seed to defend it from being eaten.

It was not until the mid-nineteenth century that machines could be built powerful enough to crush cacao seeds mechanically. With such presses, cacao and cacao butter, contained in the seed in equal measures, could be refined and emulsified to a degree that was palatable and chewy. In this way, the finest and purest of chocolates could be made – and this nearly 200-year-old process is now exciting a new generation of real chocolate-makers and consumers.

However, this is not how most chocolate is made. The fast-growing chocolate industry of the twentieth century settled for a more profitable, predictable and homogenous technique in which the fat is extracted from the seed to separate the cacao butter and cacao powder. Once broken down into its components, chocolate can be reconstituted by mixing the bitter cacao powder with refined beet sugar to create a cheap, replicable taste profile sold as 'drinking chocolate'. To reduce costs, the precious cacao butter is often part or wholly replaced with milk fat, other plant fats, and fillers like caramel.

This process lies behind a global industry for chocolate products that have assumed a powerful position in our imagination, largely associated with happiness, generosity and luxury.

Despite the myths and marketing, chocolate's magic as delicious, nutritious and potent food got lost along the way. Our mothers were right to keep those super-sweet snacks containing chocolate as rare treats rather than considering them as food. And we now know that the story does not end with the dubious nature of the chocolate in its garish packaging; behind the scenes lies an unsavoury and unsustainable mix of social exploitation of the cacao farmers and mindless degradation of tropical forests and soils, let alone apart from the nutrient-poor cheap calories of processed chocolate bars.

Happily, over the course of only a few years, a new culture of real chocolate has retraced its roots back to the heavenly rainforest tree and the simple, pure traditions of the ancient cacao cultures. The best of these chocolate-makers know the terroir of their cacao plantations as intimately as a top winemaker would, and are able to create a food that is pure and yet sparkles in texture and flavours more complex than wine. Since land and farming practices are once again the main criteria for the quality and taste of chocolate, respect for origins and direct purchase have become currencies in the new real chocolate trade. For the planet, palate and body, the new real chocolate culture promotes a more meaningful and pleasurable way of enjoying chocolate: less really is more.

Sprouted spelt muffins

Makes about 12

450g sprouted spelt flour

¾ teaspoon finely ground sea salt

1¼ teaspoons bicarbonate of soda

1 tablespoon baking powder

250g rapadura sugar, jaggery or
coconut palm sugar

170g unsalted butter, preferably
raw, melted

475ml raw buttermilk, or yogurt,
or soured raw milk (you need
about 10 per cent less soured raw
milk) – all from pastured cows

2 teaspoons finest-quality
vanilla extract

3 eggs, from pastured hens

SPROUTED FLOUR IS JUST RIGHT, in so many ways, for our day and age. First, it is so flavourful; secondly, it is extremely digestible; and thirdly, it is so convenient to use, as it is ready for mixing and baking straightaway without any soaking or fermentation.

This makes sprouted flour particularly relevant for simple instant batter recipes, such as for muffins and pancakes, where there is no fermentation process, and the raising agents are baking powder and baking soda. This chemical leavening will not release the nutrients or neutralise the enzyme inhibitors found in dormant seeds, or in grains that have not been fermented.

These muffins, therefore, are an exciting example of how one really can combine great flavours, and health; all you need to do is to take a moment to find just the right ingredients, and you will create muffins that are indulgent, nourishing, and also easily digestible.

–

Preheat the oven to 180°C/gas 4. Line a 12-hole muffin tray with paper cases.

Mix together the flour, salt, bicarbonate of soda, baking powder and sugar in a medium-sized bowl.

In a separate bowl, whisk together the melted butter with the buttermilk (or yogurt or soured milk), vanilla extract and eggs.

Little by little add the wet mix to the dry ingredients, stirring and mixing carefully. Make sure all the ingredients are blended well together and add just the right amount of wet ingredients to make a thick batter.

Fill each muffin case with batter, to just below the top of the case. Bake for about 10 minutes, then turn the tray around and bake for a further 10–15 minutes, until the tops are golden and a skewer inserted into the centre of a muffin comes out clean.

Leave to cool in the tray for 15–20 minutes, then remove and allow to cool completely on a wire rack.

Chocolate and banana

Chop 2 ripe bananas and mash 1 ripe banana and add to the batter, along with 350g coarsely chopped dark chocolate, 70 per cent minimum cocoa solids. For more crunch, sprinkle a few broken activated walnuts (see page 102–105) on each muffin before baking.

Blueberry and poppy seeds

Add about 400g fresh blueberries to the batter. Don't use dried blueberries, ever, unless they are completely sugar free. Check the ingredients carefully, most are stuffed with sugar to preserve them, bulk up the weight and to provide flavour. Dust the muffin tops with poppy seeds before baking them.

Super seeds and nuts

Add 75g coarsely chopped activated pecans, 50g each of organic activated or sprouted chia seeds, sunflower seeds and pumpkin seeds (see pages 98–101). Sprinkle some chia seeds over the muffin tops before baking.

Brown rice pudding with cardamom

Serves 8

Butter, for greasing

3 eggs, from pastured hens

325ml cream, preferably raw, otherwise Guernsey or Jersey

125ml maple syrup, or 125g coconut palm sugar

½–1 teaspoon freshly ground cardamom seeds, to taste

⅛ teaspoon sea salt

450g short-grain brown rice, sprouted (see pages 98–101) or unsprouted

175g crispy pecans (see pages 102–105)

300g or more raisins or sultanas, or a mixture of the two

RICE PUDDING IS ONE OF THE GREAT COMFORT FOODS. Rather than making it with refined white pudding rice, use whole (brown) short-grain rice and you will benefit from extra fibre, B vitamins, magnesium, iron and vitamin E. Brown rice has more flavour too – it's rather nutty and more satisfyingly chewy. It will need longer to cook as brown rice is the whole grain, and contains the bran and the germ, which are removed when the grain is milled and polished to create white rice. Brown rice has, however, a shorter shelf life than white rice. This is because the bran and the germ contain fats, which will go rancid, so it's important to buy brown rice that has been stored carefully, and, once opened, store in an airtight container in the fridge.

For the ultimate brown rice pudding, sprout your brown rice. It will taste even better and cook more quickly. See pages 98–101 for how to do this. Once sprouted, the rice will keep for a few days in the refrigerator, or you can dry it in a dehydrator or warm oven for longer-term storage.

–

Preheat the oven to 170°C/gas 3 and generously butter a casserole, soufflé or pie dish.

Beat together the eggs, cream, maple syrup, cardamom and salt. Stir in the rice, pecans and dried fruits, and pour into your dish. Bake on the middle shelf of the oven for about 50 minutes.

Increase the heat to 200°C/gas 6 for the last 5 minutes if you like a browned and caramelised skin.

Cinnamon and vanilla

Replace the cardamom with ½ teaspoon of ground cinnamon and 1 teaspoon of vanilla extract.

No nuts?

No problem. Leave them out.

Brown rice has more flavour too – it's rather nutty and more satisfyingly chewy.

Not all sugars are equal

Unwrapping a chocolate bar with greed in your eyes? Licking the cream spoon and smiling pleasurably? You're not alone, or unusual. Humans are genetically coded to seek out, gorge on and hoard three fundamental building blocks for life – salt, sugar and fat. This is because historically all three have been difficult to find, or costly to acquire, grow and nurture, or only very seasonally available. So we are highly sensitive to their taste, smell and after-effects – in short we are salt, sugar and fat junkies. However, in the natural world, salt and fat are usually far easier to obtain than sugar, which is why the craving for sweetness is so overwhelmingly powerful. Until very, very recently the only sources of concentrated sugar were wild, primarily honey and tree syrups, along with the naturally occurring sweetness from sugars in sun-ripened fruits and vegetables. Concentrated sugar was therefore scarce, highly seasonal and/or unknown to most humans until about 500 years ago, when sugar cane production and processing rapidly evolved into a global trading phenomenon.

Sugar cane is indigenous to Southeast Asia, and it is thought that the peoples of present-day India discovered that cooking sugar cane juice produced a stable (sugar is a preservative), solid block of intense sweetness that is easy to handle and ship; this is jaggery. Jaggery was perhaps the first easily transported, stored and traded international commodity, but it was the start of the rot in more ways than one. The insatiable desire for this sweet opiate swept through the Islamic world into Europe and when the conquistadors took sugar cane to the New World, production switched to the Caribbean and the Americas, creating immensely rich sugar empires and also the slave trade.

If jaggery is the rough diamond of the sugar world, refined white sugar is a far distant cousin, now the most widely traded and consumed form of sugar. Refined white sugar was created with typical ingenuity and complete disregard for the wellbeing of the consumer. Easy and cheap to produce from sugar cane or sugar beet, it looks pure and perfect, dissolves fast, acts as a great preservative and has a long shelf life. Significantly, sugar beet is a simple root vegetable that, unlike sugar cane, can be widely grown outside the tropics, and sugar is extracted from beet in a single process, rather than the two-step process required to extract cane sugar. The same European nations that made their fortunes from cane plantations overseas now grow their own crop, threatening the fragile economies of Caribbean countries.

Sugar is a highly addictive substance, so for the big food companies, the production of cheap refined sugar is a licence to print money – legally. Humans love it, so give them more. And more. And in sneakier ways. Sugar has been a glorious ally to the proliferation and popularity of convenience foods. One of the earliest partnerships was sugar and tomatoes. Before refrigeration, it was discovered that fresh tomato purée lasted longer and was made seductively moreish with the addition of refined sugar. Tomato ketchup was the first of the many sweetened refined foods that we adore. You will be very surprised (or not) to find that refined sugar is used in many rather unlikely foods, including savoury ready meals, and even dried fruits. With our love of sweet things and a decades-long preoccupation with demonising fat, we have ignored the fact that despite a low-fat dietary obsession, people are on average getting fatter...

Thankfully, it would seem that the refined sugar honeymoon is losing its lustre. Lifestyle advisers now preach not only low-fat mantras, but support the new, sensational, evangelical anti-sugar lobby. Sadly, the demonising process is often a catch-all, crowd-pleasing set of sweeping statements: just as all fat is bad, makes you fat and hastens your death, so all sugar is now the really bad stuff that will make you spotty, blotchy, moody, bad tempered, fat, ill and, of course, die early. This is absurd but inevitable. Be ready for the sugar damnation brigade, and for the low-sugar or sugar-free sweeteners (such as stevia or sucralose) to take the moral high ground. But we will all suffer, as usual, from this simplistic evangelism. Think of raw honey (from a small producer), organic maple syrup, rapadura (unrefined cane sugar), coconut palm sugar and, of course, jaggery. Do you add them to your Bolognese sauce? No. To stewed rhubarb? Of course. These are all wild or unrefined sugars to be appreciated and savoured, and used sparingly. They come complete with a complex, ever-changing selection of nutrients, vitamins and minerals. Used in moderation, following our ancestral wisdom and patterns, they not only give pleasure, but also support rude health.

Berry ice cream

Makes about 1 litre

500g fresh or 450g frozen
organic berries – a mixture of
tart and sweet berries

2 egg yolks, from pastured hens

500ml cream, preferably raw,
otherwise Guernsey or Jersey

Maple syrup

ICE CREAM AND ICED JUICES ARE NOT MODERN LUXURIES.
Before refrigeration and temperature-controlled transport, ice and
snow were precious commodities, gathered in the mountains or hard
winters and stored in underground icehouses. Over 2,500 years ago,
Persians made the simplest of sorbets with snow and fruit juice. And this
is how iced treats should be made – with very few, simple, preferably
seasonal, and very high-quality ingredients – and then eaten freshly
made. You will also be inspired to make homemade ice cream and sorbet
once you've taken the time, and a magnifying glass, to read the list of
ingredients on most ice creams. There's a simple mantra to follow for
all foods and drinks: if you can't pronounce it, spell it or it's not in your
larder, don't eat it.

–

If using frozen berries, let them thaw a little. Whip up the berries, egg
yolks and cream in a blender until smooth. Taste. Now begin to add
maple syrup, a little at a time, and continue to taste, until you've reached
your sweet spot.

Churn and freeze in an ice-cream maker. Enjoy as much as you can
when freshly made, when it has a light and whipped texture. Any
leftovers are best crammed into as small a container as possible, covered
with waxed paper, sealed tightly and frozen. Don't store for too long.
Remember to give your ice cream plenty of time to thaw before eating it.

Strawberries only – make with
about 750g of fresh organic
strawberries and add ¼ teaspoon
of almond extract to enhance the
already sublime fresh fruitiness.

Most fresh berries are not only
fragile but lose a lot of flavour
when washed. Use organic berries
only so you can be sure they have
not been sprayed, and take the
time to pick over the berries
to remove spoiled fruit and
anything alive.

Make a chocolate glaze with
coconut oil for your ice cream
– melt about 1 tablespoonful of
chocolate in a bowl over a pan
of boiling water, and stir in about
1 tablespoonful of coconut oil.
Pour over the ice cream. It will set
into a shiny shell.

Compotes and fools

THE SUMMER AND AUTUMN abundance of fruits is a celebration of the sweetening, flavour-enriching energy of the sun. For our ancestors this was heavenly, perhaps all the more so because it was so very local, and therefore so short lived. Yes, of course, some fruits, such as apples could be stored dry and cool into the winter months, and others fermented or salted for preservation. Fragile and short-lived soft fruits, however, were another matter, and as manufactured sugar was scarce and expensive, using it as a preservative to make jams was not widely practised until relatively recently.

Many of us can now pick and choose from all manner of fruits, local and exotic, all year round. The wisdom and sustainability of this remains to be seen. A few fruits, like bananas, are purpose-made for travel, as they are picked green and ripen on the boats. Others, like plums, are picked unripe and they never fully ripen in flavour or texture. What is clear is that rock-hard, dull-hued strawberries on sale in winter, sealed in a protective atmosphere, chilled and flown or trucked from a long way away do not give the same pleasure, in taste, texture, fragrance or sentiment, as a freshly picked ripe strawberry from a local farm or garden. It's also clear too that certain varieties of fruits travel and store better than others, and so the majority of stores display these, and very little other variety or choice. All fresh produce also loses its vitality and nutrient density from the moment it is picked or harvested, so grow your own varieties, or shop carefully from local producers who appreciate soft fruits for flavour and choice, and accept their naturally short harvesting period.

To extend the soft fruit season, without resorting to jam making, it's better to transform a wide variety of soft fruits into lightly sweetened compotes, uncooked or simmered gently for a short time; they keep for a week or so when chilled, and once lightly cooked, throughout the winter in the freezer as a reminder of the seasonal abundance. Compotes are perfect at breakfast time on top of porridge, or for puddings with ice cream, or stirred into whipped cream to make a fruit fool.

All fresh produce loses its vitality and nutrient density from the moment it is picked or harvested, so grow your own varieties, or shop carefully from local producers.

Serves 4

4 big handfuls of strawberries

2 or 3 handfuls of raspberries, or replace part of with 1 handful of tayberries and 1 handful of loganberries, when available

1 handful of blueberries or local wild berries, such as wimberries or cloudberries

Rapadura, jaggery or coconut palm sugar

Juice of 1 lemon

Serves 4

500g strawberries

Rapadura sugar, jaggery or coconut palm sugar

1 unwaxed lemon or orange

Orange juice?

Replace the lemon juice with freshly squeezed tart orange juice and use less sugar.

Fresh berry compote

If you have to buy soft fruit from a conventional farm, wash it gently and leave to dry. Otherwise, simply hull and chop the strawberries coarsely. Tayberries or loganberries may need halving if they are large or very firm.

–

Mix the berries together in a serving bowl and sprinkle over 1 tablespoon of sugar and about half the lemon juice. Stir gently so that the sugar dissolves. Taste and add a little more lemon juice or sugar, or both. Cover and set aside to develop the flavours for about 30 minutes.

Lightly cooked strawberry compote

Wash, hull and drop the strawberries, without letting them dry, straight into a pan over a low-medium heat. Use a potato masher to crush the strawberries lightly, but don't mince or pulverise them.

–

Stir in 2 or 3 tablespoons of sugar, and a big squeeze of lemon or orange juice. Let the sugar dissolve, then taste the compote, adding more sugar or juice as you like. Let it simmer gently, stirring from time to time, for no more than 7–10 minutes.

This will freeze well. For a porridge sensation, freeze the compote in an ice-cube tray, then drop a cube into your steaming bowl of sprouted oat porridge (see page 120), along with a spiral of raw cream.

Fruit fool

This is a very simple pudding indeed. Make a lightly cooked but not too sweet compote with whatever fruit is in season, such as rhubarb (strictly a vegetable), strawberries, raspberries or loganberries. Let the fruit cool, then chill. Whip some raw Guernsey cream a little and chill. Make up some bowls of compote and stir in some of the whipped cream, or layer fruit and whipped cream in a sundae glass.

Dutch-style gingerbread loaf with spelt and honey

Makes 2 x 450g/1lb loaves

Butter, for greasing

2 eggs, from pastured hens, beaten

400ml raw milk

500g sprouted organic spelt flour

2 teaspoons bicarbonate of soda

2 tablespoons gingerbread spice mix (see below)

Finely ground sea salt

150g raw honey, warmed if it isn't runny

Gingerbread spice mix

2 tablespoons freshly ground ginger

2 tablespoons freshly ground cinnamon

1 tablespoon freshly ground cloves

½ teaspoon freshly ground nutmeg

¼ teaspoon freshly ground white pepper

¼ teaspoon freshly ground cardamom seeds

THIS RECIPE WILL BE FAMILIAR TO ALL DUTCH PEOPLE, as a gingerbread loaf is a traditional snack, or served for breakfast. Indeed, this cake is known in the Netherlands as *ontbijtkoek*, which means breakfast cake, or *kruidkoek*, a spiced cake. As with many traditional sweet treats, such a cake was once reserved for a special occasion and as an expensive indulgence. The exotic spices from the Orient and Asia were especially valuable and costly in the Middle Ages, and it is likely that the original sweetener was indeed honey. Sugar was as rare and often more expensive than spices until the seventeenth century.

The original flour would have been a coarse rye. Sprouted spelt flour makes for a lighter cake, yet rich with tempting honey-sweet spiciness that's full of readily available nutrients, and so much easier to digest. The spices not only provide moreish flavours, but also offer real benefits to well-being, as they are a concentrated source of antioxidants and minerals. Indeed, most spices have specific medicinal qualities and benefits.

The perfect companion for this treat is good butter. A lot of butter. All bread is but a vehicle for butter, and this gingerbread is no exception. Best eaten Danish-style, so that when you can see the teeth marks it's known as *tandsmør*, meaning tooth butter. You should barely be able see the gingerbread for the thick layer of nourishing unsalted, preferably raw, butter from pastured cows. For more about butter and its life-enhancing nourishment, see pages 31–33.

Preheat the oven to 180°C/gas 4. Butter two 24cm loaf tins.

Stir the eggs and milk in a medium-sized bowl.

In a separate bowl, mix together the spelt flour, bicarbonate of soda, gingerbread spices and a big pinch of salt. Little by little, add to the eggs and milk, and stir carefully.

Stir in the honey to mix well. Divide the mixture between the two tins and level the surface.

Transfer to the middle shelf of the oven and bake for 35 minutes, but check after 30 minutes – especially if you like the centre of your gingerbread to be softish.

Allow the gingerbread to cool slightly in the tin, then turn out onto a wire rack. Best enjoyed while still warm, spread with a thick layer of tooth butter.

SNACKS

Sprouted oats and activated seed flapjacks

Makes 12 bars

250g butter, preferably raw

1 tablespoon blackstrap molasses

90g rapadura sugar, or use less and make up the weight with date syrup

300g sprouted rolled oats, or jumbo oats, or a mix of jumbo and porridge oats

A mixed handful of activated and dehydrated pumpkin, sesame and sunflower seeds (see pages 102–105)

10g quinoa pops

MOST SHOP-BOUGHT OAT BARS ARE CRUDELY SWEET, and are either too hard and brittle, or too soft with a pappy mouthfeel. And to sustain a maximum shelf life, they will be made with vegetable oils rather than butter. The best flapjacks are made at home with lots of butter and the finest-quality, nutrient-dense and richly sweet unrefined sugars.

The combination of good butter and sugar is a real treat. For the best oaty flavours and greater digestibility, use sprouted rolled oats and add some nourishing crunchiness with activated seeds.

Please don't overcook these flapjacks, they should be soft and moist with a pleasing, ever so slightly crunchy oat and seedy bite.

‒

Preheat the oven to 200°C/gas mark 6. Grease and line a medium-sized baking tray or dish.

Melt the butter, then add the molasses and sugar, and stir to mix thoroughly. Now tip in the oats, the seeds and the quinoa pops, and stir so that they combine completely. Turn out onto the prepared baking tray or dish and level the surface. Transfer the tray to the bottom shelf of the oven and cook for about 10, and definitely no longer than, 12 minutes.

Remove and allow to cool a little before cutting into 12 bars. Leave in the tin to cool completely before turning out.

Store in an airtight container. Simply brilliant alongside a glass of fresh, raw milk.

More seedy?

Add some chia seeds, golden linseeds or poppy seeds; make your own unique combination.

Some nuts?

Activate, dehydrate and break up some hazelnuts and almonds, and add these to the mixture.

The best flapjacks are made at home with lots of butter and the finest-quality, nutrient-dense unrefined sugars.

Activated seed and nut energy balls

Makes 8–12

100g mix of activated and dried brazil nuts, hazelnuts and almonds (see pages 102–105), very roughly chopped in a processor

50g mix of activated and dried seeds, such as pumpkin, sesame, sunflower and chia (see pages 102–105)

50g mix of dried fruits, such as dates, apricots and figs, roughly chopped

Raw white tahini

Gomashio (see pages 72), or hulled sesame seeds, or coconut flakes

STICKING A COLLECTION OF NUTS, seeds and dried fruits together with tahini makes a naturally gluten-free snack. Use activated nuts and seeds for full flavour and increased nourishment. Double check that any dried fruits you buy are sugar free. Refined sugar, or sugar in the form of juice concentrate, is often added to increase weight, to act as a preservative, and to add sweetness and flavour, especially to rather bland dried fruits like blueberries.

Tahini is, in essence, sesame seed butter, and offers a less sweet alternative to a nut butter. Tahini is sold hulled (white tahini) or whole (brown or whole tahini), and both types are available roasted or raw; brown tahini is, however, more bitter than white. Sesame seeds are a valuable source of protein for vegetarians as they contain amino acids not normally found in vegetables, as well as calcium.

–

Mix the nuts, seeds and fruits together in a bowl.

Drop the tahini, a spoonful at a time, into the mixture, until it starts to come together into a rough dough. Sprinkle the gomashio, sesame seeds or coconut flakes (or a mixture of the three) on a tray.

Break off a lump of dough, about the size of a golf ball, roll it into a ball, and then roll over the seeds or coconut flakes in the tray to coat all over.

Refrigerate if you don't eat them straight away.

More flavour?
Mix in some cardamom or ground cinnamon, or a little star anise.

Tahini is, in essence, sesame seed butter, and offers a less sweet alternative to a nut butter.

Sprouted oat and chocolate chunk biscuits

Makes about 18

175g unsalted butter, preferably raw, plus extra for greasing

100g coconut palm sugar or maple sugar

160g sprouted rolled oats or jumbo oats

75g sprouted oat, spelt or wheat (bulgur) flour

¼ teaspoon bicarbonate of soda

85g dark (70 per cent cocoa solids) chocolate, chopped coarsely or broken into chunks

Pinch of sea salt

THESE BISCUITS ARE VERY RICH AND SATISFYING. Oats have a natural affinity for dairy, not only as a flavour combination, but to encourage the release of nutrients from the oats, and of course, to increase the sense of fullness and satisfaction. For a more pleasing texture, body and bite, use big and thick oat flakes, sold as jumbo oats, or coarsely milled sprouted oats.

—

Preheat the oven to 170°C/gas 3 and butter 2 or 3 baking trays, or line them with nonstick baking parchment.

Cream the butter and sugar until smooth, and then stir in the oats, flour, bicarbonate of soda, chocolate pieces and salt until mixed well.

Form about 18 balls of dough and place on the trays, spaced well apart. It's best to bake no more than 6 per tray. Bake for 15 minutes, or less if you like your biscuits chewier.

Some other ingredients to try

Add some raisins or unsweetened cranberries to the dough.

Throw into the dough a big handful of broken activated crispy pecans (see pages 102–105).

Seeds go well with oats, particularly activated sunflower seeds, and also pumpkin seeds.

Oatcakes

**Makes about
8 x 6cm and 8 x 4cm oat cakes**

225g medium-grade oatmeal
or dehydrated sprouted oats,
milled medium–coarse, plus
extra for dusting

1 teaspoon sea salt

¼ teaspoon bicarbonate of soda

75g leaf lard (see page 82), ghee
(see pages 36–39) or raw butter,
melted, or olive oil, plus extra
for greasing

AN OATCAKE, like good bread, should be made with very few
ingredients: oatmeal, fat, some baking powder, a hint of salt and some
water. Don't use oatmeal flour, but seek out stone-ground, medium-
grade oatmeal – it gives a wonderfully crumbly texture and an intensely
oaty aroma and flavour. In principle, traditional Scottish oatmeal is
available in four grades: pinhead (steel-cut berries or groats), coarse
(the pinhead milled a bit), medium (milled a bit more) and fine or flour
(milled a lot). For more about oats, see page 117.

Sprouted oatmeal? The natural sweetness of the germinated oats makes a
particularly delicious oatcake. Sprout some hulless oat berries until they
have only just germinated, dehydrate them and then use a home flour
mill to grind medium-coarse. Easy? Yes, but only with hulless oat berries,
which when soaked for an hour, will sprout in a jar within 2–3 days.

–

Preheat the oven to 170°C/gas 3 and lightly grease a baking tray.

Mix the oatmeal, salt and bicarbonate of soda in a bowl. Add the melted
fat or oil and sufficient cold water to form a firm but pliable dough.
Scatter some oatmeal onto a board and roll out the dough so that it's
about 8-10mm thick.

Cut out rounds using a 6cm cutter and also smaller rounds for children
and transfer them to the prepared baking tray. Bake for no more than
25 minutes.

Leave to cool completely on the tray before storing in an airtight tin.

Spelt and rye

Substitute some of the oats with
spelt or rye flour, sprouted if
possible. Use about half oatmeal
and half spelt, but no more than
one-third rye as its flavour is
overpowering and its bite too firm.

Seeds

Add some seeds, activated if you
like, to the dry mixture, such as
poppy, chia, black sesame and
golden linseed.

A sweeter biscuit

Mix 1 teaspoon of rapadura or
coconut palm sugar into the
dry mixture.

Porridge fritters

DON'T THROW AWAY LEFTOVER PORRIDGE. Our ancestors never did. In the old Scottish crofting world it was poured onto a platter, allowed to set and then eaten as a snack or an evening dish, more like a wet floppy flapjack. Cooked porridge can also be cooked again for breakfast the next day; just add a little water or milk and warm gently.

Simple porridge fritters

Break an egg or two into a bowl, whisk, spoon in some cold porridge and stir to combine; it will be a wet paste. Heat some ghee, butter, coconut oil or lard in a heavy frying pan over a medium heat and, when hot, drop big spoonfuls of the eggy porridge mixture into the pan. Flip over when lightly browned and press down lightly. Serve when set. Extremely popular as an after-school snack with some maple syrup or honey and a glass of raw milk. As for how good they are: the egg increases the protein content of the porridge, and adds vitamin D (important for children's bone growth) and vitamin B12 (which is only found in animal products – important for vegetarians).

Savoury porridge fritters

You can develop a porridge fritter into a main meal if you like. All you need is more leftovers. Mix together until it makes a good paste that is neither too dry nor too loose. If it's too wet, add a little sprouted flour or sprouted rolled oats. If it's too dry, some raw milk. Whisk 3 or 4 eggs in a bowl, add and stir in the leftover porridge, then combine with whatever is to hand, such as: some chopped onion, a crushed garlic clove, a big handful of grated strong cheese, leftover cooked rice and vegetables chopped small, some seasoning: sea salt, freshly ground black pepper, paprika or cayenne pepper, and chopped fresh parsley or chives.

Cook as for the Simple Porridge Fritters until crispy and light brown, and serve immediately.

Coconut oil and butter – how many ways do I appreciate you?

Coconuts may have less protein than other nuts, but they more than make up for this with their superb balance of rich nutrients, and in particular fatty acids. The creamy rich texture, taste and satiety of coconut flesh and milk is mostly derived from its high fat content. Coconut is 60 per cent fat, of which 92 per cent is saturated fat. Of these fatty acids, perhaps the most important is lauric acid, an extremely powerful medium-chain fatty acid that not only helps to strengthen the immune system, but also offers potent antiviral, antifungal and antimicrobial benefits, as well as providing a quick source of energy. Coconut (especially the meat) is also rich in calcium, iron, magnesium, phosphorus, potassium and iodine. Coconut deserves to be respected as an authentic superfood. Once you've developed a taste for the finest-quality, cold-pressed raw coconut oil – and also coconut butter, the puréed raw coconut meat, which contains fibre as well as the fat – you will want to explore the many ways in which you can use and thrive on this wonderful food.

Coconut oil and butter in the kitchen

- Coconut oil has a medium–high smoke point of around 180°C – about the same as extra virgin olive oil or butter. Use it for medium-temperature frying, roasting vegetables, and for baking, as well as for brushing on vegetables and other foods before grilling.

- As an ingredient, use coconut oil to make mayonnaise (see pages 70–71)

- Mix coconut oil with a pinch of ground cinnamon and some honey, and spread on toast; think instant cinnamon bun.

- With your black coffee – add a big teaspoon of coconut butter and stir it in thoroughly. Any bits left in the bottom of the cup are a bonus. Others like coconut oil in their espresso.

- Activate the turmeric in turmeric and ginger tea (see page 316) with a teaspoon of coconut oil.

- Add some big spoonfuls of gently softened coconut oil or butter to a juice or smoothie in the blender, or to save on washing up, stir into the drink itself.

- Make popcorn with coconut oil (see pages 264–265).

- A spoon of coconut butter on porridge, please.

- Oil your cast-iron frying pans and saucepans with coconut oil, and your wooden chopping boards.

Coconut oil as a tonic

- Take at least a teaspoon a day; just like good-quality extra virgin olive oil, taking raw coconut oil is said to keep the doctor away by aiding digestion and by supporting and boosting the immune system.

- How about coconut oil pulling? Take 1–3 teaspoons of oil and keep it in your mouth, moving it around for 20 minutes or so. Swish it and squidge it between the teeth; just imagine it's a mouthwash. When you're done, spit out the milky residue then rinse out your mouth with warm water. It is said to cleanse and to improve teeth and gum health.

Coconut oil for beauty

- The moisturising properties of coconut oil are self-evident, so use it as a body oil and as a wonderfully natural baby lotion. Its gentle healing properties also make it ideal as a nappy cream.

- Coconut oil works well as a make-up remover, and can be plastered on as a night-time moisturiser. Wipe off with a warm cloth.

- Coconut oil possesses natural sun protection qualities. Use it to give some protection from the sun, applying every 2 hours or so, as well as to moisturise the skin after being in the sun.

- Coconut oil is a great moisturiser for the lips and should help clear up cold sores.

- Use coconut oil as a wonderfully aromatic massage oil. In the tropics, where coconut palms grow, the oil is an everyday moisturiser and hair conditioner. Massage coconut oil into the scalp and hair and comb it through, tie up in a towel and leave it in overnight or for at least 40 minutes. Shampoo.

- Coconut oil works well as a shaving oil and aftershave moisturiser.

- Mix coconut oil with some sea salt and lemongrass oil, or with some bicarbonate of soda, and rub into the skin as an exfoliator. Rinse with warm water.

Popcorn with coconut oil

Makes 1 large bowl

1 tablespoon coconut oil

85g popping corn

MAKING POPCORN is an entertaining process for children and adults alike; neither grows tired of the explosions and the magical heaving of the lid as the popping corn expands. If you're going to make popcorn, then make it with the best-quality, freshest corn kernels and some coconut oil. The brightly coloured popcorn kernels, like red or blue corn kernels will have an even greater antioxidant profile than the typical yellow/white corn.

If you would like a real treat, seek out some sprouted popping corn. The sprouting process transforms some of the starches to simple sugars, so sprouted popcorn is naturally sweeter and more aromatic.

–

Heat the oil in a large pan with a lid over a medium–high heat. Make sure that there is enough oil to cover the bottom of the pan.

Once the oil is hot, pour in the corn and give the pan a shake to coat all the kernels. As soon as the first of the kernels explodes, it's time to put the lid on. Shake the pan once or twice as the popping continues, and again as the popping dies away to make sure no kernels are burning or others remain unpopped.

While the corn is popping, you can make the flavours up.

Cinnamon and coconut sugar

Melt 1 tablespoon of coconut oil in a pan. Once melted, add 1 tablespoon coconut sugar and 1 teaspoon ground cinnamon, and stir. Once the corn has been popped, pour the mixture over the popcorn, stir and indulge!

Pemmican

Makes 300g

150g dehydrated strips of lean wild game meat, such as from a haunch of venison

150g rendered fat from venison, or from pastured beef suet

IN THIS FOOD-OBSESSIVE ERA, there are very few ready-to-eat and sustaining foods that meet fashionable and supposedly healthy criteria, such as gluten free, grain free, paleo, plant based and raw. Pemmican meets and exceeds most of those criteria, and indeed some would say it is the only complete food that one needs to survive. In essence, pemmican is a dried meat snack bar, held together with rendered fat (tallow), so this is not a food for advocates of a raw or plant-based diet.

Pemmican is a derivative of the Native American Cree word for grease or fat. It was the convenient and complete ancestral food of the semi-nomadic Plains Indians who roamed widely in the scorching summer months. Wrapped in rawhide purses and bags, their edges sealed with fat, pemmican lasts almost indefinitely, regardless of the season. It's highly portable, nutrient-dense and preserving qualities were perfect for, and appreciated by, Arctic fur traders and explorers and the military during the eighteenth, nineteenth and early twentieth centuries.

The meat must be lean and, historically, from small and big game, and the fat the most nutrient-dense, which is that found in the cavity and around the vital organs. Bison, moose, elk or deer hunted in the autumn months would have been perfect for making pemmican, as the animals would be at their healthiest, having grazed widely under the life-giving summer sun, laying down fat reserves for the harsh Plains winter ahead.

It's time for a pemmican revival. You can make pemmican with equal amounts of low-temperature dried lean meat from wild game, and the rendered suet (tallow) from game or pastured beef cattle. Meat from wild game that is slow dried at or below 48°C retains the maximum level of nutrients possible. You can add some well-dried wild berries, such as blueberries, but only up to 5 per cent of the total weight. Just 15 grams of pemmican provide about 1,500 nutrient-dense calories. So pack light and enjoy your adventures, powered by pemmican.

Slice the haunch into thin strips and place in a single layer on a mesh tray in the oven at its lowest temperature or a dehydrator at no more than 48°C, for as long as it takes for the meat to be completely dry so that a strip will crack and break when bent double, not just bend.

Smash the meat to a coarse powder in batches in a processor.

It's time for a pemmican revival.

Render your fat and make tallow (see page 86), and warm it gently so that it remains a liquid.

Combine equal amounts of powdered meat and tallow in a bowl. Mix well so that all the meat is coated in the fat and none remains in the bottom of the bowl.

Form the pemmican into 15g balls, the size of small golf balls, or press into small cupcake trays lined with paper cases, or place on a shallow baking tray lined with baking parchment, which once cooled, can be cut into bars and wrapped in greaseproof paper.

Once cold, the pemmican sets pretty hard. Sealed in an airtight and moisture-proof container and stored in a cool, dry place, well-made pemmican will last for a very long time. You can freeze pemmican too.

BREAD

Creating a sourdough mother in 5 days

Ingredients for each day, for 5 days

50g wholewheat, or whole spelt, or whole rye flour – depending on what sorts of bread you want to make (you can of course nourish more than one mother at a time)

50ml freshly filtered water (you will need more if you use sprouted flour). The developing mother should have the consistency of pourable porridge

Equipment

A small bowl or container to start with, and then a larger container with a lid that will hold about 300–400g of the mother, one that will fit in the fridge

MAKING BREAD WITH THE SIMPLEST OF INGREDIENTS IS A THRILLING EXPERIENCE. Flour, water, yeast and salt. That's all you need. Of these, the yeast is your catalyst of fermentation, as it devours the sugars in the grain and creates carbon dioxide, which leavens, or expands, the dough. Yeast is a fungus, and wild strains have been utilised for thousands of years by bakers throughout the world. Over the past two hundred years or so commercial yeasts have been cultivated for both the baking and brewing industries.

Wild yeasts, unlike commercial strains, are made up of a happy union of fungi and bacteria (*lactobacillus*), where the fungi digests all the sugars, except the maltose, and produces carbon dioxide (the rise), and the lactobacillus digests the maltose and other sugars, and produces glucose, which the fungi can digest. The lactobacilli act anaerobically, meaning in the absence of oxygen, and, in digesting the sugars, they produce lactic acid, lowering the pH, and so create the sour taste in the dough. The very best sourdough has just the right combination of sweet yeastiness with a hint of sour. Some sourdoughs are famous: San Francisco sourdough is renowned for its tangy flavour. The species of lactobacillus first found there is named after the city, *Lactobacillus sanfranciscensis*, and is cultivated commercially and sold to bakeries worldwide to replicate this distinctive sourdough flavour profile.

Rather than buying commercially produced fresh or dried cultivated yeast, you can create and nurture your own happy union of wild fungi and bacteria, using only flour and water. All the fungi and bacteria you need are floating in the air around you. Once it comes alive, your wild yeast is known as a mother. Fed and kept well, it will last indefinitely, and its offspring, the starters, will provide you with an endless succession of wild yeasts for baking, as often as you like.

You will also be creating your very own and unique wild yeast. Your sourdough mother is energised by the combination of microorganisms present in the air in your kitchen and home, which means that she'll be helping you to make bread with your own individual and special flavours. (Naming your mother is highly acceptable. My rye mother is Peggy, after an inspirational sprouted-grains pioneer, and my spelt mother, Arthur, is more paternal, in tribute to my father, who loved baking bread.)

Your sourdough mother is energised by the combination of microorganisms present in the air in your kitchen and home.

Your mother will be happily left alone in the fridge until the next time you need to bake, up to a maximum of 2 weeks. If your mother starts to sweat some greyish water when chilled, don't worry, just pour off the liquid.

Sprouted sourdough mother

Yes, you can create and nurture your mother with sprouted flour and make the most wonderfully flavoursome and digestible wild-yeasted breads; when you refresh your mother you will notice a more rapid and lively reaction. Sprouted flour, being naturally sweeter, will ferment more quickly.

Day 1

In a small to medium-sized bowl mix 50g of flour and 50ml of freshly filtered water together thoroughly with your finger, then cover the bowl with a cloth or muslin and leave out at room temperature.

Day 2

Stir in the same weight of flour and volume of water to your day 1 mixture.

Day 3

Repeat as for day 2. By now or by day 4 you may well need to move your mother to the larger container, which will become her permanent home.

Day 4

Repeat as for day 3. By now you should see your mother coming alive, and forming a light crust, under which will be a sponge of gently bubbling activity.

Day 5 and storing the mother

Repeat as for day 4, but from this day forward cover the container and keep your mother in the fridge, unless you are refreshing (feeding) her. The wild yeasts will stabilise at between 2–4°C, and as they slow down their activity they will live quite happily for about 2 weeks, undisturbed, before they run out of nourishment.

Feeding the mother and creating a starter for baking

To ensure that your mother thrives you need to feed her at least once every 2 weeks – and in doing so you can remove a portion of the mother, known as a starter, for your bread-making. At any time within the 2-week period, remove the mother from the fridge, and refresh with the same quantity of flour that you will be removing as a wild yeast (sourdough) starter. So, if your bread-making requires 150g of sourdough starter, feed the mother with 150g of flour and 150ml of water; stir to incorporate fully and then leave out at room temperature for 8 hours before returning her to the fridge.

If you are unable to feed your mother beyond 2 weeks, then freeze her. She'll be up for coming back to life once thawed and fed again.

Sprouted lavash

Makes 4 sheets

1 teaspoon active dried yeast or
8g fresh yeast

350ml freshly filtered water

680g sprouted wholewheat flour,
plus extra for dusting

50g extra virgin olive oil, plus
extra for brushing

28g fine sea salt

¼ teaspoon cayenne powder

*For coating and sprinkling,
in combinations as you wish:*

1 large egg, from pastured hens,
beaten, or some more olive oil

Raw or toasted poppy or sesame
seeds – or try cumin, caraway or
fennel seeds

Sea salt flakes and coarsely
ground black pepper

LAVASH IS AN UNLEAVENED THIN FLATBREAD, or when dried out, very much a crispbread or cracker, typically made from only flour, water and salt. Originally of Armenian origin, it is a popular flatbread of the Caucasus, Iran and Turkey. Baked in a wood-fired tandoor, or clay oven, lavash is rolled out very thinly and then slapped against the sides of the oven, where it cooks in moments. Soft and doughy at first, it quickly dries out and has terrific keeping qualities – up to 12 months (stored in an airtight container). You can revitalise and soften it by sprinkling with water and reheating it, albeit gently. Warm lavash, freshly made, makes a perfect wrap for kebabs, and for simple goat's cheese and herbs. When dried and broken up, it's a flavoursome cracker or a scoop for hummus, baba ghanoush or cream cheese. Before baking, the dough really benefits from a sprinkling of flaked sea salt, and either raw or toasted sesame or poppy seeds. This lavash is particularly light, tasty and easily digestible – it combines all the benefits of sprouted flour with a little yeast, and the cayenne powder gives it a very gentle heat too.

–

Dissolve the yeast in a jug of all the water and let it sit in a warm place for 10–15 minutes.

Put all the ingredients into the bowl of a mixer and use a dough hook to combine all the ingredients, or mix thoroughly by hand, until the dough pulls away from the side of the bowl.

Divide the dough into 4 equal portions, lightly brush each one with olive oil, wrap in greaseproof paper and then place them in the fridge for 45 minutes to 1 hour.

Preheat the oven to 170°C/gas 3. Line two baking sheets with some lightly olive oiled baking parchment, or brush olive oil directly onto the baking sheets.

Flour the work surface and roll out each portion of lavash as thinly as possible. Lay two sheets of lavash onto each prepared baking sheet, one sheet at a time. Stretch out the lavash to fill the sheet using your fingers – it doesn't have to be a regular shape, but it does need to be very thin.

Prick the dough randomly all over with a fork; this will prevent it from blistering and bubbling. Brush the dough with either a smear of beaten egg or some olive oil, and then sprinkle over the seeds of your choice, some sea salt flakes and black pepper. If you use an egg wash the seeds and seasoning will stick more firmly to the lavash.

Slide the baking sheet into the oven and bake for 8–10 minutes, turning once. Be careful not to burn the lavash, especially if you are worried that they are too soft at first. (Even if you're after a crispbread texture, once they cool, they soon become very brittle indeed.) Leave to cool a little on the tray, then lay out on a wire rack.

Sprouted sourdough pizza

Makes 4 smallish pizzas

For the pre-ferment or poolish

30g starter from your mother (see pages 270–272), refreshed 7–8 hours before

50ml freshly filtered lukewarm water

50g sprouted spelt or whole-wheat flour

For the pizza base

250g sprouted spelt or wholewheat flour, plus extra for dusting

4g fine sea salt

4g fresh yeast

120–130ml freshly filtered lukewarm water

Toppings

4 garlic cloves, crushed and finely chopped

Extra virgin unfiltered olive oil

400g tin chopped tomatoes

2–3 balls (125g each) mozzarella

Kalamata olives, stoned

Flaked sea salt and coarsely ground black pepper

And then, any combinations of

Anchovies (in olive oil)

Chorizo, sliced or small cubes

Salami, thinly sliced

Prosciutto, very thinly sliced

For when you serve

Handfuls of fresh rocket

Equipment (nice to have)

Wood-fired pizza/bread oven (there's no substitute, really)

Baking stone (or a clean oven tray)

Baker's peel (or a light chopping board)

THE SECRET OF A GREAT PIZZA is the combination of a thin, light base, crisped to perfection in a seriously hot oven, and then topped with a selection of savoury treats, arranged with a light touch.

A sensationally flavoursome pizza can also provide a truly nourishing and fully digestible meal – as long as you make it using a combination of sprouted flours and a pre-ferment – in this case a sourdough pre-ferment, called a poolish. The sourdough pre-ferment will give your pizza base terrific structure that is light but elastic and strong. The sprouted flours guarantee better nourishment and convenience too; they are ready to use, and as the grain has germinated, it's now a plant not a seed, so that its nutrients are generously available for easy digestion.

A seriously hot oven? That's not so easy to solve. Domestic ovens top out at 240°C/gas 9. Pizza ovens reach temperatures in excess of 400°C, so that a pizza is cooked within a minute or two at the most. If you have a garden, you could build or purchase a wood-fired pizza and bread oven... but in the meantime, buy a pizza or baking stone, preheat the stone in the oven set to its maximum temperature, and you can bake a crispy pizzeria-style pizza within 5 minutes.

Day 1: Make your poolish
In a measuring jug, stir together the refreshed starter with the water until it blends into a muddy-looking soup.

Select a bowl big enough to take all your ingredients, and weigh out 50g of flour. Add the starter mixture and stir well to mix completely. Cover with a cloth and leave out at room temperature for 8–12 hours.

Day 2 (or evening of day 1): Make your dough
By now your poolish will be lovely and bubbly and smell sweetly fermented. Tip the flour and salt onto the poolish.

Dissolve the yeast in the water, then pour this onto the mixture and stir to combine, using a spoon or your hands. Make sure the mixture has come together completely.

Flour your work surface and then scrape out the dough onto it.

Stretch your dough
Stretching out the dough develops its gluten, which will provide the elasticity you are looking for when you shape your pizza base into a light and thin round.

Use the heel of your hand to push down and forward simultaneously, so that the dough is stretched out away from you. Be vigorous. Keep rolling the dough back, turning and stretching in one continuous movement. It's a pretty good workout if you really focus on working the dough

thoroughly. Fairly quickly the dough will feel more alive, more supple, and also less wet. Continue for a good 8–10 minutes.

Cut the dough into 4 or 5 equal-sized pieces and form each into a round, and then cover them all with a cloth and leave to rest and prove for 1 hour at room temperature. The dough should double in size.

Prepare your toppings
Tomato sauce: Crush, peel and finely chop the garlic.

In a small to medium-sized saucepan heat a very big glug – about 4 tablespoons – of olive oil over a medium heat until it begins to simmer a little.

Throw in the garlic, let it simmer for an instant, and then pour in the chopped tomatoes and two big pinches of salt. Stir to combine. Simmer, stirring occasionally, until the sauce begins to reduce a little, about 15–20 minutes.

Press the sauce with a potato masher so that it is not lumpy. Remove from the heat and leave to one side.

Mozzarella: Pour away the water and let the mozzarella sit in a sieve or colander to drain completely; you don't want any water from the mozzarella appearing on the pizza.

Once it is much drier, don't slice the mozzarella but peel, then tear it into strips ready for use.

Olives et al: Leave whole or halve the olives lengthways, and prepare your other toppings as you wish.

Baking stone in, oven set to max
Always let your baking stone heat up and cool down with the oven. So, place the baking stone in the middle of the oven, and turn it up to its maximum. If you don't have a baking stone, use a clean oven tray.

Shape the dough
Either flour or scatter polenta onto a lightweight chopping board or your baker's peel – this will allow the pizza to slide off the wood onto the baking stone.

Flour your work surface and shape a piece of dough into a flat round with both hands. Now lift up and start to rotate the flattened dough, stretching the centre of the disc while keeping a thicker rim around the edge. Keep juggling and rotating so that as the disc grows in circumference it becomes thinner in the middle, while remaining intact.

If a hole develops, lay the base onto your peel and patch it by bunching up some adjacent dough and pressing it over the hole. Once your base has reached the size and thinness you like, lay it on the peel.

Toppings please
Use a serving spoon to smear some tomato sauce evenly and thinly over the base.

Add some torn mozzarella, olives and other delights.

Bake and serve

Slide the pizza off the peel and onto the baking stone. Bake for 5 minutes, turning once.

Scatter some rocket over the pizza and drizzle with extra virgin olive oil (olive oil infused with chillies is very good too) and a generous scattering of flaked sea salt and coarsely ground black pepper.

It's pretty well much obligatory to enjoy pizza as good as this with a glass of red wine; a robust one from one of the many Italian natural wine producers, of course.

Sprouted spelt sourdough, the no-knead method

Makes 1 large or 2 small loaves

150g refreshed (8 hours before) sourdough starter from your mother (see pages 270–272)

375ml freshly filtered water (or 350ml if not using sprouted flour)

500g sprouted spelt flour, or 500g freshly milled spelt flour, plus extra for dusting

10g fine sea salt

Equipment

Proving basket (banneton) 22cm in diameter, suitable for a 500g loaf, or 2 smaller, 13cm-diameter bannetons

Misting sprayer – a simple spray bottle will do

Baker's peel or lightweight chopping board

Baking stone if possible, but an oven tray will do

Polenta, semolina or coarse flour, for dusting the peel

THIS SOURDOUGH RECIPE IS EXTREMELY EASY TO MAKE and in principle requires only some simple time management to incorporate into a wonderfully rewarding weekly routine. It's easy to see why artisan bread-making can become such an addictive process. There's a deep-rooted innate appeal in making loaves of crunchy crusted sweet-savoury smelling bread, time after time, using methods unchanged for thousands of years, and as ever with only flour, water and salt.

Making bread as good as this is a fundamental part of the process in regaining one's relationship with nourishing, flavoursome foods, made at home, by hand. Since mankind began farming, the making of bread or the preparation of rice has been the centrepiece of our daily sustenance, and therefore acquired deep religious and cultural significance, reverence and respect. Once you make your own sourdough bread, you will be connecting with the best of our ancestral wisdom, and in so doing you will be nourished, not just in body, but in mind and spirit too.

Timings: this is a simple 3-day method.

–

8 hours before Day 1

Take your mother from the fridge, and refresh by stirring in and mixing well 150g organic spelt flour and 150ml freshly filtered water. Leave out at room temperature, covered by a cloth, for 8 hours.

Day 1

Time to complete: about 1 hour 15 minutes. Time to rest: 12–24 hours.

Make a liquid of the starter

Measure 375ml freshly filtered water into a bowl, and then drop 150g of the starter from the refreshed mother into the water. It should float, showing that your starter is full of life and ready for further fermentation and baking. If it sinks, your mother is not refreshed enough. Stir the starter into the water, thoroughly. Seal and return your mother to the fridge.

Make a dough without salt

Weigh out 500g of sprouted spelt flour into a bowl that will subsequently fit into the fridge and make a well in the centre of the flour.

Pour the starter liquid into the well and gently mix for about 1 minute by hand, using your fingers like forks, just enough to combine the liquid and the flour. Cover with a cloth and leave out at room temperature for 1 hour, no longer.

This resting time for a dough without salt is known as the delayed salt method, or autolysing. Without salt present the wild yeasts in the starter are not held back, so that not only is the gluten being swiftly broken down into strands, but the flour absorbs more water. By the end of the hour your dough will be more developed and also be slightly stringy.

It's easy to see why artistan bread-making can become such an addictive process.

Add the salt then stretch and fold the dough

Sprinkle the salt onto the dough along with a splash of water. Mix the salt and the splash of water into the dough by hand, gently but thoroughly, for about 30 seconds, no longer. All you want is for all the salt to be incorporated into the dough. Immediately the dough will tighten as it literally sucks in the salt. The salt slows down the energy of the starter, the gluten now forms into sheets and the dough becomes shiny too.

Leaving the dough in the bowl, make the first of the simple stretches and folds to add structure and air to the dough. Grasp one side of the dough and stretch it away from you, about 8–12cm, then fold it over onto itself. Rotate the bowl or the dough 90 degrees, and do the same again. Do this a total of four times. Cover the bowl with cling film or a cloth and refrigerate for 12–24 hours. This resting period will allow flavours to mature and a firm structure to be created.

Day 2
Time to complete: about 2 hours 10 minutes. Time to rest: 8–24 hours.

Stretch and fold some more

Remove the bowl from the fridge; the dough will look more together and will be much firmer to the touch.

Ease the dough onto a suitable work surface – no need to flour the dough or the surface. Hold the dough in both hands on the surface and stretch it away from you – by about 8–12cm – and then fold it back and over onto itself. Turn the dough by 90 degrees and repeat, until you have stretched and folded back the dough four times.

Cover with your upended bowl and leave to rest for 30 minutes.

Repeat the stretching and folding and rest for a further 30 minutes. This stretching and folding will gather air into the dough to give it a more open structure, revitalise the starter and further develop the gluten.

Shape into a round

Flour your work surface and your hands too. Lay the dough onto the floured surface and then, gently but positively, stretch a small portion of the dough away from you by about 5 cm, before folding it back to the centre of the dough. Continue to stretch out and fold back small portions to the centre, while rotating the dough, until you've completed one complete circle. That's about 8 or 9 small folds.

Now turn the dough over, and dust your hands and the boule with flour again. Use a rotating and cupping action to shape the dough, so that you squeeze tension into the dome of the boule. Your hands should rotate, cup and lift the dough all at once, and you should feel the edge of your palms meeting each other under the boule. What you want is a boule that feels and looks tight and round.

Into the basket and the fridge again

Dredge the banneton and the surface of the boule with flour, and place your boule into the banneton, seam-side up. Cover with a cloth and leave to rise for 1 hour at room temperature.

Transfer to the fridge, covered with the cloth, for between 8–24 hours.

Day 3

Time to complete: about 3 hours 30 minutes.

Remove your banneton from the fridge and leave out, still covered with the cloth, at room temperature for about 3 hours. This is the final rise.

Prepare the oven

Place either a baking stone or a flat baking tray on the middle shelf of the oven. Turn the oven to its maximum, about 240°C/gas 9. Make sure your misting bottle is full of fresh, filtered water and place it next to the oven.

Bake your loaf

Scatter polenta, semolina or coarse flour onto a baker's peel or a smooth and light chopping board. The coarse grains will allow the loaf to slide off the board and into the oven.

Now turn over the banneton and turn out the boule onto the centre of the peel or board. Score the loaf with a sharp serrated knife or a baker's lame twice or four times in one direction and then again at right angles, to make a simple criss-cross pattern.

Misting bottle at the ready, open the oven door, slide the loaf onto the scalding hot baking stone or tray and, working quickly, spritz as much mist as possible all round the oven and then close the door.

Bake for about 15 minutes, then turn the loaf round and bake for about a further 15 minutes; you may want to check after 10 minutes. Your loaf is ready when it has a golden brown crust and sounds hollow when you tap the bottom.

Let the boule cool on a wire rack. This will take a surprisingly long time, about 30 minutes.

Dutch oven

Baking a no-knead recipe loaf in a 20cm Dutch oven or any large, heavy pot such as a cast-iron casserole is extremely simple, and replicates the cooking environment of a large commercial baker's oven, ensuring that you bake a perfect loaf every time.

Following the recipe above, and once your boule is ready to bake, ease it into a Dutch oven, cover with the lid and bake for 30 minutes at 240°C/gas 9.

After 30 minutes remove the lid, and bake for a further 10 minutes to finish and to ensure that you have a perfectly crusty crust. Turn out and cool as above.

Sprouted gluten-free buckwheat bread

Makes 1 loaf

350ml freshly filtered lukewarm water

2 teaspoons dried active yeast or 19g fresh yeast

2 teaspoons rapadura sugar, jaggery or coconut palm sugar

2 eggs, from pastured hens

2 tablespoons raw coconut oil, plus extra for greasing

400g sprouted certified gluten-free buckwheat flour

1 teaspoon fine sea salt

1 teaspoon apple cider vinegar with the mother (see pages 62–66)

Equipment

A 900g/2lb loaf tin

CONFUSINGLY, DESPITE ITS NAME, buckwheat is not related to wheat, and unlike wheat, it is gluten-free. Buckwheat is related to rhubarb, sorrel, the common dock and knotweed, and is a vigorous plant, becoming full-grown in about 11 weeks, making it ideal for the short growing seasons of northern latitudes. Its triangular seeds are particularly distinctive, and as with all seeds, the best way to make its nutrients available to us is by fermenting or sprouting.

Roasted and coarsely milled, or cracked buckwheat, known in Russia as kasha, has been a staple food for centuries in Eastern Europe and Western Asia. Cooked as a casserole or gruel, mostly with broth, it is very much a savoury porridge. Fermented buckwheat batters are also popular for making light and foamy pancakes, known as blinis in Russia (see pages 126–128). Further east, buckwheat noodles are a delicious speciality of Japan (soba) and also Korea.

Buckwheat is rich in readily available protein, the minerals zinc, copper and potassium, and it's also high in fibre. You'll not be able to miss a honey derived entirely from the flowering buckwheat nectar, as it is as dark as molasses, with a forthright flavour to match.

Pour the lukewarm water into a measuring jug and add the yeast and sugar. Mix well and leave for 10 minutes for the yeast to become active. Preheat the oven to 190°C/gas 5 and grease the loaf tin with a little coconut oil.

Break the eggs into a bowl and add the coconut oil. You may need to warm the coconut oil very gently to liquefy it if your kitchen is cold. Beat well until the mixture is frothy.

Tip the flour into a large bowl and make a well in the centre. Sprinkle on the salt, then pour in the egg mixture, vinegar and activated yeast mix. Stir well with a spoon until you have a thick batter which drops sluggishly off the spoon. Add a little more water if it is too thick. Pour the batter into the lightly greased loaf tin and spread evenly.

Slide the tin into a large food-safe plastic bag, and leave in a warm place to allow the mixture to rise to about one and a half times its original size. Keep an eye on it; you want it to rise, but not to rest for any longer. If you leave it too long after it has risen, it will tend to collapse once in the oven. It should take about 1 hour to rise fully.

Transfer to the middle shelf of the oven and bake for 25–30 minutes. Leave it in the tin to cool completely before turning out.

Eat fresh as this bread does not keep well – certainly no longer than 2 days. The best way to store and get the most out of this bread is to slice it and then freeze it. It makes very good toast.

Sourdough rye bread

Makes 1 small loaf

For the pre-ferment

140g freshly filtered water

75g sourdough starter from its recently refreshed mother(see pages 270–272)

100g freshly milled or sprouted rye flour

For the loaf

Pre-ferment mixture (see above)

175g freshly milled or sprouted rye flour, plus extra for dusting

7g finely ground sea salt

130ml freshly filtered water

½ tablespoon blackstrap molasses

Seeds or dried fruits (optional) – see suggestions at the end of the recipe

Equipment

Misting bottle filled with freshly filtered water

450g loaf tin, ideally long and thin

RYE IS A ROBUST GRAIN – not only in taste but also in hardiness. It can be grown in poorer soils than wheat and will survive in a colder climate too. This in part explains why rye breads are so various and so popular in north Germany, Eastern Europe and Scandinavia. This recipe is very simple, and is more like a cake mix than a bread mix.

Rye does contain gluten but less than wheat, and it also has enzymes that will break down the dough structure; low gluten and high enzyme levels both ensure that, typically, rye bread will rise less and have a dense crumb structure. There are two ways to achieve a lighter rye bread: either by combining rye with other grains such as wheat, or, the best way, by leavening dough made with 100 per cent rye flour with a sourdough starter. The wild yeast, being more acidic than baker's yeast, will survive well in the rye dough, providing a better rise and a much better, lighter, crumb. Well-made rye bread has good keeping qualities, measured in months rather than days, it is moist and is also extremely filling. Slice very thin, spread with tooth butter (see page 252 if you need an explanation) and enjoy with strong cheese, some soup and a hearty natural red wine.

Sourdough mother and starter – if you like rye bread it's worth creating and nurturing a rye mother just for your rye bread baking.

8 hours before Day 1

Refresh your mother with 75g flour and 75ml water, and leave out of the fridge at room temperature for 8 hours.

Day 1: Make the pre-ferment

In a measuring jug mix the water with the starter to make a slurry.

Select a bowl big enough to take all the ingredients, weigh out the 100g rye flour, make a well in the centre, then add the water and starter mixture.

Mix by hand until the flour and starter have combined. This will take about 1 minute, and will create a loose mixture. Cover with a cloth and leave out at room temperature for 18–24 hours.

Day 2: Mix your dough

Have a look at your pre-ferment; it should be active, and therefore bubbly.

Tip the 175g rye flour into the pre-ferment, along with the 7g salt, and then add the 130ml water.

Mix by hand – use one hand like a big fork – for about 1 minute, and then add the molasses (and any seeds or fruits), and continue to mix coarsely until all is combined, which will take no more than another minute.

Well-made rye bread has good keeping qualities.

Shape, roll and prove your rye loaf

Sprinkle a lot of rye flour onto your work surface and a little into the tin. Scrape your dough out of the bowl and onto the floured surface.

Flour your hands and then shape the dough into a rectangular block, about the length of the tin. Now slightly flatten the block and then roll one long edge of the dough over onto itself, creating a coarsely shaped rectangular loaf with a seam. Roll the dough through the flour so that it is well coated all over and then drop it into the tin, seam-side down.

Cover with a cloth and leave to prove for 2 hours.

Bake

After 2 hours the rye dough should show signs of marbling or cracking on its surface. It's now ready for baking.

Preheat the oven to as high as it will go, preferably 240°C/gas 9, and have your misting bottle ready by the oven.

Once the oven is to temperature open the door, slide the tin onto the middle shelf and then, with haste, spritz filtered water all around the oven, and then close the oven door.

Bake for 15 minutes, then turn the tin around and reduce the temperature to 180°C/gas 4 and bake for a further 15 minutes.

Rest, set and mature

Remove from the oven and tap the loaf out of the tin, but then leave it to sit in the tin, but with one end up, resting on the end of the tin, for 8 hours. The rye loaf is a very wet mixture and it needs to cool and set.

Once cool, wrap in a cotton cloth and leave for as long as you like, or wish, or can, to mature. It will improve with age.

Seeds and fruit?

The robust rye character pairs well with strong-flavoured seeds, such as caraway, coriander and fennel, and with dried fruits like raisins and figs.

Suggested pairings:

Seeds: add 2 teaspoons of caraway seeds and 2 teaspoons of coriander seeds.

Seeds and fruits: try 1½ teaspoons of fennel seeds and 1 tablespoon of raisins.

Sprouted multigrain soda bread

Makes 1 large loaf

250g sprouted spelt flour, plus extra for dusting

250g sprouted wholewheat flour

150g sprouted porridge or flaked oats

1 tablespoon raw honey

1 tablespoon blackstrap molasses

500ml buttermilk or live yogurt (or 450ml soured organic milk), from pastured cows

1½ teaspoons bicarbonate of soda

1 teaspoon fine sea salt

SODA BREAD IS KNOWN AS A QUICK BREAD, and it's not only very quick but also extremely simple to make. There are no complex sequences or steps, or any kneading or any proving, or indeed, much waiting at all. Soda breads are leavened with bicarbonate of soda (also known as baking soda), which was first introduced about 150 years ago, and was adopted with enthusiasm in Ireland and Scotland, already the home of many simple unleavened breads. Bicarbonate of soda breaks down chemically when heated to form the gas carbon dioxide and sodium carbonate, which is washing soda and alkaline, and as might be expected, has a soapy taste. To reduce or neutralise the sodium carbonate all quick breads are made with just the right amount of baking soda and include ingredients that are mildly acidic, such as honey, molasses, soured cream or milk, yogurt and buttermilk. The acidic ingredients speed up the release of carbon dioxide and ensure that any residual salts are mild tasting.

Nutritionally, soda breads made from flour or milled grains that have not been sprouted or fermented are not ideal. All grains, as seeds, contain anti-nutrients and enzyme inhibitors to protect themselves from being digested before they can germinate. Our ancestors knew this very well, and devised simple (but to us, somewhat time-consuming) methods to neutralise the seed's toxins and release its nutrients as fully as possible. Chemically leavened, or quick breads, made with industrially milled unsprouted flours tend to be neither easy to digest nor fully nourishing. Replacing modern highly processed flours with sprouted flours is the perfect solution. Now you can prepare and bake soda bread that is easy and quick, and nourishing too. Old practices meet this so-called modern and convenience-obsessed world, and get on. Result.

–

Preheat the oven to 200°C/gas 6. Cover a baking sheet with a piece of baking parchment.

Mix together all the dry ingredients, then make a well in the centre, and pour or spoon in the honey, treacle and buttermilk. Work everything together with your hands until you have a loose, wet dough.

Dust flour onto the work surface and over your hands too, and then drop the dough onto the floured surface and shape the dough into a round, or boule. Place your round in the centre of the prepared baking sheet and score a deep cross across the top of the dough with a sharp knife or a baker's lame.

Transfer to the middle shelf of the oven and bake for about 45 minutes, turning once, or until the bread sounds hollow when tapped on the base.

Transfer to a wire rack to cool and cover with a lightly dampened cloth.

Sprouted wholewheat quick loaf baked in a Dutch oven

Makes 1 small loaf

250g sprouted spelt or wholewheat flour, plus extra for dusting

200ml freshly filtered water

3g fresh yeast

5g fine sea salt

Polenta, semolina or coarse flour, for dusting the casserole

Equipment

Proving basket (banneton) 22cm in diameter

18cm (Le Creuset) cast-iron casserole

The liberating ingredient is, of course, sprouted flour.

IF YOU WANT TO MAKE YOUR OWN BREAD THAT IS FULL-FLAVOURED, digestible and also convenient, quick and easy to make, then read on. This recipe will create, in a single day, such a loaf, one that has, until now, only been possible to achieve with the 2- or 3-day long techniques that combine to best effect the fermenting power of wild yeasts in the slow proving of dough, and that ultimately creates a sourdough.

The liberating ingredient is, of course, sprouted flour. With its reduced gluten and phytic acid content and largely neutralised enzyme inhibitors, sprouted flour is a nutrient-dense, ready to use ingredient. It is possible, therefore, to bake with either wild yeast and make a sourdough sprouted flour loaf with its keynote sour taste (see pages 270–272) or to make a quick loaf using cultivated yeast.

As promised, this is a supremely simple recipe, so that there's no kneading, and no folding and resting to plan for. The loaf is shaped in a banneton into a boule, and then baked in a Dutch oven (a cast-iron casserole with a lid) to maintain its shape and moisture content.

–

Mix

Weigh out your flour into a mixing bowl.

Measure the water in a jug, and then add the yeast to the water and stir using your finger to dissolve fully.

Make a well in the flour and pour in the yeasted water. Use your hand like a splayed fork and gently bring the mixture together until you have created a slightly sticky dough. If necessary, squeeze into the dough with your fingers to make sure that all the flour and yeasted water have combined. Cover with a cloth and leave out at room temperature for about 40 minutes.

After about 40 minutes, sprinkle the salt and a tiny splash of water (about a teaspoonful) onto the dough and then gently stretch the salt into the dough. The dough is very eager for the salt and will absorb it readily, and begin to glisten.

Prove

Now cover your dough with a cloth or cling film, and refrigerate for about 8 hours.

Shape

After about 8 hours, remove from fridge. Dust your work surface with flour and drop your dough onto it. At the same time dredge a banneton with lots of flour, and your hands too.

Now, gently but positively, stretch a small portion of the dough away

from you by about 5cm, before folding it back to the centre of the dough. Continue to stretch and fold back small portions to the centre, whilst rotating the dough, until you have completed one complete circle. That's about 8 or 9 small folds.

Turn the dough over, and dust your hands and the boule with flour again. Use a rotating and cupping action to shape the dough, so that you squeeze tension into the dome of the boule. Your hands should rotate, cup and lift the dough all at once, and you should feel the edge of your palms meeting each other under the boule. What you want is a boule that feels and looks tight and round.

Dust the top of the boule with flour and then place it into the banneton seam-side up. Cover with a cloth and leave to rise for 2 hours.

Bake

Preheat the oven to 230°C/gas 8 or, ideally, 240°C/gas 9.

Dust a cast-iron pot with polenta, or dredge it with flour.

Place your dough into the pot, seam-side down. Score the top of the dough with a razor blade or a serrated sharp knife, place the lid on and slide it into the oven. Bake for 30 minutes with the lid on, and then a further 10 minutes with the lid off to allow a delicious crust to form.

Remove from the oven, tip the boule out of the pot and let it cool – it needs about 30 minutes.

Sprouted flour cornbread

Serves 6–8

55g organic butter, preferably raw, or ghee (see pages 36–39), melted

240g sprouted organic yellow maize flour or sprouted organic yellow cornmeal

120g sprouted spelt or wholewheat flour

1 teaspoon bicarbonate of soda

3 eggs, from pastured hens, lightly beaten

475ml whole buttermilk or dairy kefir (see pages 22–25), from pastured cows

Note: if using conventional cornmeal flour, use about 300ml buttermilk

1 teaspoon fine sea salt

CORNBREAD, LIKE SODA BREAD, IS A QUICK BREAD and much loved in the southern and southwestern states of America. Corn is indigenous to the Americas, and the Native Americans have developed, over thousands of years, a keen understanding of how to get the best out of corn, both in flavours, variety of recipes and in nourishment. European settlers, accustomed to their diet of wheat, barley and rye, were slow to adapt and viewed corn as a lowly local grain. 'Corn' in North America is known as maize in the UK, so don't confuse maize flour with cornflour. Derived from European quick bread recipes, cornbread is a terrific sweet-savoury accompaniment for barbecues, chilli con carne and beans. America's northern and southern states conduct a lively debate regarding the rightness of the ingredients and nature of cornbread: southern cornbread is more savoury, and contains buttermilk, whereas the northern style, typically, includes sugar and is more of a sweeter cake.

Adding wheat or spelt flour to the cornbread recipe provides a lighter structure, and the use of sprouted flours – as with all quick breads – ensures that nutrients and flavours are richly available, despite the fact that there is no yeast fermentation.

Cornbread is often made in a frying pan, and in frontier lore, over an open fire and served with beans. A baked frying pan of cornbread goes by the name of a 'pone of cornbread' in some states and regions. My recommendation is to bake this bread in a shallow glass dish; the glass radiates the heat very quickly and contributes to the light and moreish texture of this cornbread.

–

Preheat the oven to 170°C/gas 3.

Smear butter or ghee around the inside of a 25 x 35cm glass or ceramic dish, then sprinkle or sieve some sprouted flour onto the fat.

Mix the flours, salt and bicarbonate of soda in a large bowl, and make a shallow well in the centre. Pour in the beaten eggs and the melted butter or ghee, and most of the buttermilk or kefir. Stir together. You're looking to create a pourable batter, so if it's too thick add more buttermilk or kefir to achieve the desired consistency.

Pour the batter into the buttered and floured dish. Transfer to the oven and bake for about 1 hour or until it has a golden crust, and a skewer inserted into the centre comes out clean.

Pone of cornbread

You will need a large, heavy cast-iron frying pan with an ovenproof handle.

Preheat the oven as before, and follow the cornbread recipe opposite.

Heat the pan until it's about to smoke, and then drop onto it a hefty chunk of good lard (see pages 82–85). Now pour in the batter – it will sizzle and smell divine. Slide the pan into the oven and cook as before.

Enjoy with a thick wedge of homemade butter (see pages 31–35), some beans, or a mutton stew – and a tin mug of coffee.

Honey-crust sprouted spelt bagels

Makes 8

380ml freshly filtered water

15g fresh yeast

1½ tablespoons rapadura sugar, jaggery or coconut palm sugar

500g sprouted spelt flour, plus extra for dusting

1½ teaspoons fine sea salt

Olive oil

1 tablespoon raw honey

Raw or toasted poppy or sesame seeds (optional)

Spelt is an ancient hybrid, and until about 150 years ago, it was the bread grain of choice in Europe since antiquity.

BAGELS ARE THE EVER-POPULAR SHINY, CHEWY, ring-shaped bread rolls that have a rather unusual genesis, as they are boiled (poached really) as well as baked. Bagels are of course associated with Jewish communities, especially in New York City, known for their perfect pairing with cream cheese and lox (cured salmon). Their origins can be traced back some 500 years to Poland where they were a staple of the region. The hole in the middle? It's practical – the dough cooks more evenly throughout, and for the baker, it was, traditionally, a novel way to display and sell bagels either in rows on a stick or strung up on a length of string.

Most bagels are made with highly refined wheat flour, which is high in gluten and lacks the coarse bran or germ. At best they are made more nourishing and digestible if the dough is fermented overnight but there's no doubt that their moreish, sweet, tender (when fresh), dense and chewy texture is derived for the most part from the use of refined wheat flour and refined sugars, making them unsuitable for the increasing numbers of gluten-sensitive and gluten-intolerant individuals, let alone those wanting to avoid refined sugar.

This recipe manages to combine the best of both worlds; by using sprouted spelt flour and unrefined, or wild, sugars the amount of gluten is reduced, the digestibility and nourishment are improved, yet you can still have your chewy, crusty mouthfeel and superior flavours. You want convenience too? It's right here. Made with sprouted flours complete with their readily available nutrients, including simple sugars rather than starch, these bagels do not require proving overnight.

Spelt. So what's all the excitement? Spelt is closely related to wheat, and therefore contains gluten, but, crucially, less gluten than wheat. Spelt is an ancient hybrid, and until about 150 years ago, it was the bread grain of choice in Europe since antiquity. Replaced in the last century by more recent wheat hybrids, spelt is making a welcome return in popularity, especially in organic farming, as it's less dependent on the use of artificial fertilisers. Spelt has a far more interesting flavour profile than wheat; it's nuttier, and sweeter too, and for those sensitive to gluten, spelt can often be tolerated.

Activate

Pour 100ml of the water into a small bowl, crumble in the yeast and sprinkle over the sugar. Leave for 5 minutes, then stir to dissolve.

Mix the flour and salt together in a large bowl. Make a well in the centre of the flour and pour in the yeasted water. Pour in the remaining water and then mix to form a firm, moist dough.

Knead and leave to rise

Turn out the dough onto a well-floured work surface. Knead until smooth and elastic, which will take about 10 minutes. As you knead the dough, feel for its texture. You need this dough to be quite stiff and firm. If it's too moist, gradually knead in some more flour.

Wipe the inside of a bowl with some olive oil, then roll your dough around the inside of the bowl. Place the dough in the bowl and cover with a cloth. Leave to rise in a warm place until doubled in size, which will take about 1 hour.

Knock back the dough, then leave to rest again for 10 minutes.

Shape and rest

Scrape the dough out of the bowl and return it to a lightly floured work surface. Cut into 8 equal-sized pieces and shape each piece into a ball. Poke a floured finger into and through the centre of each one to form a ring.

Place the bagels on a lightly (olive) oiled baking sheet, cover with a damp cloth, and leave to rest for 10 minutes.

Meanwhile, preheat your oven to 220°C/gas 7.

Poach

Bring a large, wide pan of water to the boil, reduce the heat to a simmer, and then add the honey.

Use a slotted spoon to lower the bagels carefully into the honeyed water, 2 or 3 at a time.

Boil each batch of bagels on one side until they rise to the surface and puff up, then turn each one over and remove them once they rise to the surface again.

As you remove the bagels, let them drain well. If you are coating them in seeds, this is the time to do it. Put the seeds in a shallow bowl and dip the top of each bagel lightly into seeds.

Bake

Return the drained bagels to the lightly oiled baking sheet. Transfer to the oven and bake for 20 minutes, turning once, or until golden and shiny. Leave to cool on a wire rack.

Bagels are at their best within 2 or 3 days of baking, when fresh. They do freeze well. Slicing into two half rings before freezing is recommended.

Water is life

We are so familiar with water that we take its nature for granted: it's liquid, ice or vapour. Water is water. Scarcely a further thought and, also, precious little enquiry is made about it. This is extraordinary, considering that water is so omnipresent, so essential for life, whether on our planet, or on other planets, that surely we should be devoting much more thought and respect for the truly miraculous nature of water. And indeed, new research is beginning to confirm just how little we know about water, and the more that is discovered, the more we should value water as an energy-rich form central to nature, rather than merely a component of life.

We don't need to know or understand any science to appreciate the living nature of water. We can see it, touch it, feel it, and taste its properties. Think of the vitality in water, which you see, feel and hear in a downpour, let alone a thunderstorm. Consider the taste and texture of different waters. Mountain spring water is hydrating, delicious and refreshing, whereas municipal waters are often stale tasting, thin and unsatisfying.

New understanding and experiments are revealing that these properties arise from the levels of natural energy that water contains. In simple terms, water is storing and releasing, or perhaps sharing, more or less energy depending on the dynamic levels of electrical charge within it. The differences in the electrical charge within water are created and driven by the presence of another form of water that some scientists are calling 'structured water'. Very tentatively, but with full scientific, reductionist thinking and rigour, their exciting and brave research is beginning to reveal that, as well as water, ice and vapour, there is a fourth form of water, which is structured differently – H_3O_2, with three hydrogen molecules and two oxygen molecules, so it's not the familiar H_2O.

From this scientific research, it's becoming apparent that structured water is made up of organised layers of pure H_3O_2 and studies show that plant and animal cells are rich in structured water. Structured water, and plant and animal cells too, are negatively charged, whereas H_2O can carry positive charges.

When they sit alongside each other in a tube (think of a capillary in your body) a flow of water is generated. The strength of this flow is dependent upon the energy levels of the structured water. What's fascinating is that structured water receives its vitality from radiant energy, and expands, and is energised, by such energy. We all know that we feel more alive when the sun shines; might this be because our water-filled cells are being invigorated by the solar energy?

In many ways this makes sense, especially in view of the fact that our bodies are made up of about 70 per cent water by weight, but we're 99 per cent water when measured by numbers of molecules. It seems logical, therefore, that the more structured water, to an extent, that we can source or create, the more our cells and therefore our bodies will thrive. The opposite is also true.

Sourcing structured water? Well, there are indications that water that's been refreshed and purified by nature's natural cycle is most beneficial. This includes glacial and snow melt waters (think of mountain streams) and spring water. Heaven forbid that this is a call to action to buy bottled water from far away. But if you are near a spring, drink deep. And at home, how about installing a filter to remove the chemicals that keep the water safe in municipal storage, but are not needed by your body.

Intrigued? Raising the awareness of the significance of the quality of water we consume in relation to our health and wellbeing is a good thing. It is also clear that there are many more astonishing and revelatory discoveries yet to be made. Increasingly, it's being realised that this is not the stuff of conjecture and fancy; it could well be one of the most important breakthroughs in the fundamental understanding of the pivotal role of water in nature.

DRINKS

Beet rassol or kvass
Fermented beetroot tonic

Makes just less than 1 litre

1 large beetroot, topped and tailed

Freshly filtered water

Large pinch of sea salt

Ideas for more flavours and fermenting energisers:

Some whey (see pages 41–42)

Some white or red cabbage, finely shredded

Some fresh ginger, finely grated

Some fresh horseradish root, finely chopped

Some fresh jalapeño peppers, finely chopped

It makes a wonderfully potent, and with time, rather pungent drink.

WHEN YOU FERMENT BEETROOT to make a kraut (see pages 44–49) you also create small quantities of a brightly coloured, highly flavoured brine – try some. It makes a wonderfully potent, and with time, rather pungent drink. This is of course a fermented and soured juice, sometimes known as beet kvass, and certainly as beet rassol (in Russian, rassol is brine). Beet, cabbage and cucumber rassols are somewhat worthwhile in Russia, as they are renowned tonics for a hangover.

This recipe uses beetroot, but you can make a rassol with lettuce, cucumber, cabbage or combinations of vegetables. All will contain the living cultures and much of the nutrients from the fermenting vegetables. Best enjoyed as a tonic rather than as a refreshment. You could dilute it over ice with some sparkling water and it's also perfect to add to soups or to a vinaigrette.

Chop the beetroot roughly into 1cm dice and drop them into a 1-litre pickling or flip-top jar. Fill the jar with filtered water to within 2.5cm of the top.

Add a big pinch of salt and also your optional assistant ferments, such as a tablespoon of whey. For flavour and also to assist with the fermentation, add some very finely shredded, more like grated, white or red cabbage and, if you like, some finely grated fresh ginger root or finely chopped horseradish or jalapeño peppers. Stir.

Seal the jar, and leave it out at room temperature. How long the rassol will take to ferment and develop will depend on so many factors, such as temperature and the freshness of the vegetables. So, taste daily. The fermentation process may take a few days or it may take a week. It may pressurise a little and be slightly fizzy, or it may not.

Once the juice has reached the flavour you like, pour through a strainer and bottle. Refrigerate.

You can now make at least one more batch of rassol using the same vegetables. Once you've finished making rassol, eat the remaining vegetables – the beet will be crunchy and most satisfying.

For some fizz, once you've bottled the rassol, leave the bottles out at room temperature for a day or so: it will naturally carbonate. For safety, always keep your fermenting and carbonating bottles inside a cardboard box just in case they can't handle the pressure and either leak or burst.

A very important note about carbonation in bottles and jars when making fermented foods and drinks

Fermentation produces carbon dioxide, which makes many fermented foods and drinks naturally and delightfully fizzy. Dependent on the ambient temperatures – warmth makes for faster fermentation – and the mix – some ferments are more gassy than others – the build-up of gas under pressure can cause sealed bottles or jars to burst. So, it is wise to prepare and store your bottles and jars as follows:

Label each bottle or jar with date of making and ingredients.

Keep your more volatile ferments (usually the carbonated drinks that involve ginger...) such as kvass, kombucha, water kefir, ginger ale and beer in a robust cardboard box on the floor in a store room. Don't forget about them...

Wrap bottles of your liveliest ferments in old tea towels before placing in the cardboard box.

When bottling a batch of bubbly drinks, make one of the bottles plastic. Once the plastic bottle begins to firm up with the pressure of carbonation, you will know it is time to refrigerate and drink this batch.

Burp (and taste) your bottles or jars daily during the ambient temperature fermentation; this way you can monitor their progress as well as relieve the pressure in the bottles or jars.

Once fermented to your taste, store your ferments in the fridge. The low temperature will slow and stabilise the fermentation, so that carbonation will not increase.

Chill your ferments before opening. Open with care and over a sink. This will reduce the chance of your refreshing drinks ending up on the ceiling rather than in your glass with a slice of lemon and some ice cubes. Open in stages. Ease open the flip top or screw top, release some pressure, seal again, let the mixture settle, then repeat until it is ready to pour.

Green juicing, as a tonic

Makes 2 small glasses

1 large or 2 small apples (or pears), quartered, cored and chopped

1 or 2 celery sticks, washed (keep any leaves for stock)

½ cucumber (at least 10cm), quartered into sticks

4cm piece of fresh ginger, peeled

Some fresh turmeric – 2 or 3 pieces (no need to peel if fresh)

Some handfuls of washed cavolo nero, spinach, kale, watercress or parsley, or combinations of these. Rocket is good too, and nicely peppery, of course

Optional

A squeeze of lemon juice

Some ground cayenne pepper or a small jalapeño pepper

ONE OF THE GREAT CHALLENGES in understanding how to eat right is to know just how to select, handle and combine foods. Green juicing is one of the simplest, most nourishing and least costly ways to enjoy deep flavours and rich nutrients in a liquid shot. Rather than pop pills and rely on synthetic supplements, it's so much more satisfying and healthy to select freshly grown vegetables, and some fruits, wash and chop them, and then make a juice that represents the bounty of the season – and in any combination that satisfies your craving.

Downing a small glass of freshly made vegetable juice before breakfast is an extraordinarily pleasurable and satiating routine. It is an ideal way to break the fast of the night. Resist the temptation to drink any more than about 100–150ml of such richly flavoursome and nutrient-dense juice; it's a tonic, not a refreshment. Make a green juice after you rise, and you will find that the simple act of handling fresh and living ingredients prepares your mind and your spirit for the new day and shows an appreciation and respect for food and its rightful place in our daily lives.

Order of juicing: every juicer or blender will have its own characteristics, and the ability either to spin fast or slowly compress the juices from the fruits. What works best is to alternate drier vegetables with wetter vegetables/fruits so that the machine doesn't clog up with coarse fibres.

–

Get all your ingredients prepared and start juicing... enjoy immediately.

Amazake
Fermented rice drink

Makes about 1.25 litres

400g shortgrain whole brown rice, or sweet black sticky rice

1 litre freshly filtered water

400g koji rice (see page 67)

Pinch of sea salt (optional)

For quick amazake
Makes about 175ml

150g Koji rice (see page 67)

165ml filtered water at 60°C

Amazake diluted with water, served hot and topped with a little grated fresh ginger is perfect for a cold winter's day and a soothing pick-me-up.

THIS TRADITIONAL, MOSTLY SWEET, slightly savoury fermented drink has been appreciated in Japan for over 1,500 years. The source of the fermentation for the amazake is koji rice, which has itself been inoculated and fermented with the locally occurring mould or fungus, *Aspergillus oryzae*. Amazake is enjoyed as a drink, which is more like a smoothie, as a pudding, a baby food, soup enhancer, a snack in itself, and to bring a sweet umami character to a vinaigrette. The Japanese also use it as a digestive tonic, as a gentle cure for a hangover and to bring a healthy glow to the skin. Street vendors sell amazake diluted with water, served hot and topped with a little grated fresh ginger – it's perfect for a cold winter's day and as a soothing pick-me-up.

There are many ways to make amazake, but in these two versions one is made with koji rice and brown rice, and the second, with koji rice only. The first will ferment faster and sweeter if you increase the proportion of koji rice. Two parts koji rice to one part brown rice is ideal, but equal proportions work well too. It is also important to maintain a temperature of 60°C – any hotter and you will destroy the enzymes; cooler than this and it will not be deliciously sweet. Don't allow it to ferment for too long because all the available sugars will be consumed, making it both acidic (sour) and alcoholic. You will be on your way to making sake...

Amazake with brown rice, 1:1 ratio
The evening before, rinse the brown rice and leave to soak overnight.

The following day, drain the rice and put it with the water either in a rice cooker or a large pan, and cook with the filtered water, with the lid on, for about 40 minutes. Meanwhile preheat the oven to 60°C/gas ¼.

Once cooked, transfer the rice to either a ceramic or glass bowl (not metal) and beat it vigorously with a large wooden spoon to cool the rice to about 60°C. When at 60°C, add the koji rice and mix it in well with your hands. Cover the bowl and place it in the warm oven. Leave the mixture to ferment for about 10–12 hours, stirring from time to time.

Taste after 8–10 hours, and by 12 hours you will find that the mixture will be very much liquefied, and also be fully and wonderfully sweet. Transfer your amazake to a pan, bring to the boil, and add a pinch of salt. Leave to cool and store in a covered container in the fridge. Enjoy as it is or whizz in a blender for a smoother consistency. Or, dilute it 1:1 with water, and warm, serving with a grating of fresh ginger.

Quick amazake
Combine the koji rice and water, pour into a wide-necked Thermos flask and seal securely. Leave to ferment for 8–12 hours. When ready, whizz in a blender to make a smooth paste. Store in a sealed container in the fridge. Enjoy as above.

Wine is natural, isn't it?

Enjoying wine is a pleasure founded in ancient times, and until very, very recently, wine was indeed made from fermented grape juice and nothing else. Making wine, in principle, is easy. Crush some grapes and let them ferment. However, making a fine wine from nothing but fermenting grapes is a real art.

Within the past 50 years, just like cow's milk and dairy foods, olive oil and bread production, wine-making has become a major industry for a small number of regional, national and often international conglomerations. All these foods and drinks, in their own way, have been commoditised, standardised and made predictably consistent. And yet we tend to live in hope, in a sort of nostalgic and sentimental trance, wanting to believe that these foods and drinks remain natural and original and unsullied by mass production.

The majority of wine-making is no longer a natural process. Wines made over the past 45 years, and especially the past 25–30, have followed the unsustainable path of intervention and manipulation, and the attempted control of nature, from growing the vines as a monoculture to the extreme levels of manipulation during vinification. True, wine, like olive oil, has been subject to adulteration throughout history, but not on this persistent and consistent scale. It's certainly been a boon for the agri-chemical, pharmaceutical and flavourings industries. Pesticides, inorganic fertilisers, yeasts and sulphites, micro-oxygenation, anti-foaming agents, sterile filtration and reverse osmosis, along with a host of additives, such as sugar, tannins, gelatine, phosphates, casein and albumen – these are just some of the many permitted tools and potions of the majority of the modern winemakers. None, of course, is declared on the label, aside from sulphites, and sometimes, the tannin. The result? Wine that is largely sterile, from a microorganism point of view, and wine that has been tainted by its method of production. Wines have been found to contain pesticide residues many more times greater than the permitted levels for drinking water, which is madness as wine is mostly water. Most modern wines are no longer so vital or, in reality, alive, and so no longer age gracefully. All in all, we've been witnessing, passively and unwittingly, the large-scale creation of exceedingly unnatural wines that have no soul, no natural variety and no heart.

In so many ways, however, wine production mirrors developments in the tastes and desires of the marketplace, from shipper, to retailer, to consumer. During the past 40 years, wine has become big business, and the majority of wine sales are driven by the demands of consumers purchasing single bottles in the supermarkets. Given the choice and variety of wines produced, the consumers have looked for guidance, and so wine has been made and sold to the popular requirements of very low prices, excellent consistency and easy to recognise tastes, especially when promoted to be matched with foods. For such a fast-growing market, producers have responded accordingly, creating brands that are easy to find, developing an awareness for selected grape varieties (think chardonnay) and making stronger, less subtle, more fruity wines at every price point.

Despite this overwhelming trend, there have always been wine producers who have sought to make wine in harmony with nature. Happily, their numbers are on the rise and some of their natural methods are being adopted by the major producers. As for artisan bread-making, raw milk production and raw cheese making, or small-scale olive oil production, there is a growing appreciation and market for what are loosely called 'natural wines' made on a small scale using ancestral methods and respecting traditional values. Measures for certification and traceability are being developed to create a bond of trust between the producer, middle man and consumer. Such producers farm with biodiversity and sustainability as their mantra, shun pesticides and inorganic fertilisers and make wines simply by fermenting grapes, without additives, including no or very low levels of sulphites.

So how do they taste, these natural wines? Well, they taste full of life, of character, of their diverse origins, of their terroir – an expression to sum up the climate, the terrain and the winemaking traditions that are used to grow the grapes. This is and will be a shock for the majority of consumers, and the craven following of the supposedly elite producers, some of whom have acquired celebrity and cult status. Many natural wines are, quite simply, delicious. Delicious in nature's way; they're fresh, alive and nourishing. Some natural wines, like nature itself, are a challenge. Others are very challenging – which is no bad thing. It's time to wake up the palate, to restore it to life, to reclaim an appreciation for originality and to be alive to the simple pleasures of naturally fermented grape juice.

Kaanji *Fermented carrot and mustard seed drink*

Makes about 1.5 litres

Freshly filtered water

250g black or purple carrots, or orange ones plus 1 small beetroot

Sea salt to taste, try 10g to begin with

2 tablespoons ground brown mustard seeds

Optional

Large pinch of cayenne pepper

¼ teaspoon asafoetida

¼ teaspoon turmeric

KAANJI IS A REFRESHING DRINK ideally made from dark-coloured varieties of carrots that range from purple to black. It's a traditional North Indian spicy drink enjoyed during the mad spring festival of Holi, when the vernal equinox is welcomed in a riot of irreverence, parties, special foods and drinks, and famously, spraying coloured water or throwing powdered dyes on friend and foe alike.

Carrots don't ferment readily, so you need to leave this drink to develop for at least a week. Black or purple carrots are preferred, as they contain more antioxidants and make a refreshing tonic, perfect for clearing away the heaviness of winter. Black carrots are indeed the original ones, as most carrots were dark coloured until the Dutch selectively bred them in the seventeenth century to be orange. If you can't find dark carrots use orange ones and add a beetroot to the ferment. Make sure you use brown mustard seeds (*rai* in Hindi) – they are rich in omega-3 fatty acids as well as magnesium.

–

Wash and peel the carrots and, if necessary, the small beetroot too. Slice thinly or cut into matchsticks (julienne).

Toss into a wide-mouth 2-litre glass jar, three-quarters fill with filtered water, and add the salt and ground mustard seeds, as well as your optional ingredients. Taste for salt.

Stir well, seal the jar and leave in a warm place for at least 5 days. This drink will not carbonate, so there's no need to burp it. After 5 days it will taste nicely spicy and sour. Serve over ice, with a slice of lemon or lime. The carrot sticks make the perfect fermented snack accompaniment.

Carrot juice and cream

Makes about 200ml

500g very very fresh carrots
(orange, purple or black), peeled

Raw cream, to taste, try
1–2 tablespoons

CARROTS HAVE WON MANY SUPPORTERS for their curative and protective properties. They are a tasty source of beta-carotenes, a provider of vitamin A. It's clear that the ideal way to increase the availability of this fat-soluble vitamin is to combine the food with good fatty acids, which we can get from butter or cream. Butter and cream have a natural, indulgent and healthy association with carrots; try cooking and glazing carrots with ghee or butter – so delicious (see page 234).

This recipe makes a rich tonic. It's not one for quenching a thirst, more for sipping, and contemplating just how marvellous raw dairy fat and fresh pulled raw carrots taste together.

–

Whizz the carrots in a juicer, or extract slowly in a raw juicer. Stir in the cream, clockwise... only joking.

It won't keep, so share this juice right away.

Carrot juice and vanilla ice cream – a carrot juice float

This is a Persian speciality. It's another brilliantly refreshing and cooling combination of dairy fats and carrot juice. Scoop some vanilla ice cream into a bowl or glass and pour over some freshly made carrot juice.

Butter and cream have a natural, indulgent and healthy association with carrots.

Kombucha

Black or green tea (bags or loose tea)

Rapadura sugar

Freshly filtered water

Some raw kombucha or apple cider vinegar (see page 62–66)

Kombucha SCOBY from a friend or purchased online, or grown from some raw kombucha. Growing your own may take about a week

Beware, this makes a fizzy drink (see page 298)

Equipment

Large wide-mouth glass jar (that holds about 3 litres)

Glass bottles with stoppers

Muslin

KOMBUCHA IS A SPARKLING FERMENTED TEA DRINK that is thought to have originated in Manchuria, before becoming popular in Russia by the early twentieth century. Known throughout Asia as tea fungus, tea mould or tea mushroom, kombucha – its ersatz Western name – sounds rather more attractive and healthy. Kombucha is indeed fermented by a colony of bacteria and yeasts, known as a SCOBY or mother, which floats as a rubbery disc on the surface of the fermenting drink. The drink, when raw, contains the organisms too, so a new SCOBY can be created from the liquid itself.

Well made, kombucha is extremely refreshing, especially in hot weather, being naturally fizzy and delivering a mysterious combination of sweet and sour; its complex grouping of flavours – and a very small amount of alcohol – tease our taste buds, so we yearn for more. All ancestral fermented drinks have complex, ever-evolving flavours, as well as a fizz, and so it seems that we are hard wired to appreciate carbonated refreshments. This fact has favoured the relatively recent, hopefully soon to be historic, success of the soft drinks industry.

Kombucha-making is now a thriving commercial venture in America, with some national brands, as well as an ever-multiplying selection of local breweries, creating their own imaginative flavours added to what is, after all, sweetened fermented green or black tea. A miracle drink? Raw kombucha, like all raw ferments, does contain unique and live colonies of symbiotic bacteria and yeasts, which may agree with and enhance your microbiome and your wellbeing, or they may not get on with your flora and fauna. It is wise, therefore, to try a little at first and see how you like kombucha. Every kombucha culture will be different, indeed unique, and every flavour requirement very personal. So, best of all, make it yourself, to the tartness you like and with the flavours you crave.

You can make plain kombucha by fermenting sweetened tea with a SCOBY, or you can bottle and enhance plain kombucha by adding flavours, whether herb, vegetable or fruit, or any combination of these, which will then undergo a secondary fermentation in the bottle.

Once you start making kombucha you will find that every time you make another batch your SCOBY will tend to spawn more plate-like clones of itself. Watch them grow and then peel them off and experiment with more wacky brews, or give these away to friends, or compost, or make a facial paste or create a fruit leather style snack. There's more inspiration, as ever, online.

A note on which tea to use
In principle use only plain black, green or white tea, not scented leaf or herbal teas. Some SCOBYs thrive on green tea only, some will need

a black tea fix from time to time, about once a month, some will only survive on black tea. Each SCOBY will have its own favourite sweet soup. When you have SCOBYs to spare, why not try a fruit or herbal infusion?

–

Primary fermentation

In a big wide-mouth glass jar, make up a strong tea with boiling water, using about 3 teabags per litre. Half-fill the glass jar. Note that kombucha fermentation is an aerobic process, meaning it needs to be in contact with air, which is why a wide-mouth jar or fermentation vessel is best.

Now add sugar to the strong tea, and you really must do this to taste, but you could begin with about 100g of sugar per litre. Stir well to dissolve.

Once brewed, remove the teabags or loose tea, and top up the glass jar to just over three-quarters full with cold water. The infusion should now be body temperature warm, which is cool enough for you to add the raw kombucha – about 50–100ml per litre – and the SCOBY. If you don't have any raw kombucha, use raw apple cider vinegar, but only about 30ml per litre.

The SCOBY will float happily to the top, sink or sit on its side. All are fine, as long as within a few days a SCOBY has settled or formed on the top of the sweet tea. If no SCOBY forms you will have to start again.

Cover your jar with a piece of muslin and secure with a rubber band. This will keep the fruit flies at bay and reduce the risk of mould.

Leave your kombucha to ferment in a warm, airy but not sun-drenched spot, at about 24–30°C. If it's cold, your ferment will take many weeks; when warm, between 10–14 days.

Insert a straw to the side and underneath the SCOBY every day or other day and taste your kombucha. When it's just the right level of sweet-sour, remove the SCOBY using your hands and place it in a bowl,

Kombucha is extremely refreshing, especially in hot weather, being naturally fizzy and delivering a mysterious combination of sweet and sour.

immersed in some of the newly made kombucha. This SCOBY and
the liquid are now ready to be added to a new batch of freshly made
sweetened tea. And so the cycle continues.

Before you bottle it's always good to stir the kombucha up in the brewing
vessel, that way you will mix in the yeast which usually sits at the
bottom. This yeast will help to create some successful fizziness when
you bottle the kombucha.

You can bottle this plain kombucha or you can flavour it. If you are
keeping it plain, fill bottles to about seven-eighths full, seal and
refrigerate; or if you want some fizz, leave out at room temperature in a
cardboard box for a few days to carbonate. Once pressurised, refrigerate.

Secondary fermentation

Fill your bottles to about three-quarters full, and then add whatever
flavours you like, although ginger does work powerfully well because
of its invigorating flavour profile and the fact that it contains a lively
selection of its own lactic acid bacteria and yeasts. So, how about:

- Grated or thinly sliced ginger
- Lemon juice and grated ginger
- Fresh pomegranate juice and some seeds
- Grated turmeric and ginger root
- Grated ginger root and finely chopped lemongrass
- Chopped mint and lime juice
- Crushed raspberries
- Fresh apple juice
- Crushed blueberries

Don't fill the bottles more than seven-eighths full. Seal the bottles, and then leave out at room temperature, in a cardboard box for safety, for 2–3 days until pressurised. Refrigerate.

Kombucha stock management

Always label your bottles with the date bottled and its flavour. If you don't you will soon lose control of your stock and won't know which to drink first.

In principle, for a good fizz, keep your bottled kombucha for about 2 weeks before opening. It doesn't last long once opened.

Kombucha and alcohol

Typically kombucha has less than 0.5 per cent alcohol by volume, and is classed as a soft drink. Enjoy irresponsibly.

Kombucha accessories

As kombucha has grown in popularity there has been a similar proliferation of kombucha suppliers, and brewing tools and accessories. These are derivatives of the home-brew industry and include warming plates and continuous brew kombucha vessels. If you drink a lot of kombucha, then the continuous brew is the easiest, safest and cleanest method. However, you will have to keep up with your SCOBY, or the kombucha will tend to go sour. From an 8-litre vessel, you will be making about 4 x 500ml bottles per week.

Water kefir

Makes 1.5 litres

1½–2 tablespoons water kefir grains (from a friend or purchase online)

1.5 litres freshly filtered water

150–200g rapadura sugar

2 tablespoons raisins or sultanas

For flavours, how about:

Lemon and ginger: some sliced or grated fresh ginger and a lemon, quartered, and thrown into the jar

Blood orange and lemon: a quartered blood orange and a lemon

Raspberries and strawberries: some crushed raspberries and sliced strawberries

Turmeric and ginger: some sliced fresh turmeric and sliced fresh ginger root

Beware, this makes a fizzy drink (see page 298)

Equipment

2-litre glass jar

Some muslin, an elastic band and some cooking twine if you're keeping your grains in a little sack

Flip-top or screw-top glass bottle

FORGET INDUSTRIAL SOFT DRINKS. It's time to make your own ancestral soft drinks with their naturally fermented nourishment and refreshing flavours. Water kefir is easy to make, very effervescent and thirst slaking, and can be created and flavoured in as many ways as you can imagine, from fermenting simple sugar water with seasonal fruits, to coconut water or fruit juices.

Alongside its fermentation relatives, dairy kefir and kombucha, water kefir is also made by the action of a SCOBY (symbiotic colony of bacteria and yeast) that thrives by digesting a carbohydrate-rich liquid, creating lactic acid, alcohol and carbon dioxide. The water kefir SCOBY is a collection of creamy-looking, part translucent granules, also known as tibicos, Japanese water crystals, Tibetan crystals and water kefir grains. They are found worldwide, and no two colonies are the same. Water kefir grains are not the same as dairy kefir; a dairy kefir colony is made up of a different collection of bacteria and a greater variety of yeasts.

Just like dairy kefir, though, water kefir grains are vigorous and productive, making a new batch of water kefir every 2 or 3 days. Unlike a kombucha SCOBY (see pages 302–5), you will need to attend to, refresh and feed your water kefir grains regularly, or they will literally pickle in their acidifying solution and die. Again just like dairy kefir, when well looked after, water kefir grains can multiply like crazy, and so you will be able to give some away freely to others, and to spread the water kefir word. On average you will only need about 1 tablespoon of water kefir grains per litre of water. Don't worry, it's not a relentless treadmill, as you can break the production cycle and give your grains a holiday, and also dry or freeze them. More on this below.

—

Rhythm

Making kefir is easy. Keeping the grains alive and thriving is all about establishing a rhythm and realising that you're the mother to a set of unique living creatures, a family of micro-pets. You can make and bottle 1.5 litres water kefir on a 2 or 3 day rotation, so that, assuming you drink about a glass or two a day, you will always have a stock of water kefir.

Loose grains or grains in a little sack?

You can let your grains float in the sugar water as they are, or you can tie them up into a little sack of muslin, and drop this in. From time to time you will need to open and remove some of the growing population of grains to keep your grains to water ratio at about 1 tablespoon per litre. When you do this, it will also be time to replace the muslin and the string tie. Do give them away or you can dehydrate them and keep them in a jar in the fridge, or pat them dry and freeze, just in case you need some spare grains in the future.

It's time to
make your own
ancestral soft
drinks with
their naturally
fermented
nourishment
and refreshing
flavours.

Coconut water and other sweet water kefirs

You can use your water kefir grains to ferment coconut water, fruit juices, coconut milk, other nut and seed drinks, such as almond milk, and also sweetened leaf and herbal. If the fruit juice is naturally rather acidic, dilute it before fermentation with some sugar water.

Make more water kefir

Wash out your jar and make up a fresh batch of sugar water and raisins, add your water kefir grains, and you're ready to start again... everlastingly. From time to time, rinse your grains or your mini sack of grains in fresh running water.

Water kefir-making holiday?

Your grains will thrive and multiply if you make kefir continuously, as they are feeding on the sugars in your water.

Longer term – no feeding

Rinse and dry the grains, carefully and thoroughly, and freeze them, or rinse and then dehydrate the grains and store them in a glass jar in the fridge.

Medium to longer term – feeding every 2 weeks

Rinse the grains and pop them into a sealed jar of very sugary water and store in the fridge. Every 12–14 days remove and rinse the grains, discard the sugar water and then return the grains to the fridge in a jar of fresh filtered water and sugar.

Make water kefir

Pour the water into the jar, add the rapadura and stir to dissolve. Add the water kefir grains or your little muslin pouch of grains, and the raisins. Now add your flavourings.

Cover the jar with a piece of muslin and secure with an elastic band. Leave out at room temperature, but not in direct sunlight. The warmer the ambient temperature, the faster the ferment.

After about 24–36 hours you will see little bubbles in the water, and also any fruits floating to the surface to join the kefir grains. Taste the water kefir for the sweetness you prefer. The longer you leave it, the less sweet and the more slightly sour it will become. Do not leave the brew to ferment for longer than 3–4 days or you may kill the water kefir grains.

Spoon out, or collect the grains in a coarse sieve. Or, if you are wise and use a little muslin bag, just lift it out.

Remove the fruits for compost (give any fleshy ones a squeeze before removing them from the jar) and then bottle the water kefir in a flip-top or screw-top bottle. Leave out at room temperature for a day or two, but place in a cardboard box for safety; this is your secondary ferment, and will usually ensure that your water kefir is delightfully effervescent. After one or two days, move the bottles to the fridge to slow down and more or less stop any further fermentation.

Be careful when you open the bottle, it may be very fizzy, so have a glass ready to hand. Enjoy over ice, with a slice of lemon, with some added sparkling water, and if you like, a dash of your own apple cider vinegar (see pages 62–66). Bottled water kefir will last for up to a month in the fridge.

Ginger ale or water, or switchel

Makes 1.5 litres

About 1.5 litres freshly filtered water

1½–2 tablespoons rapadura sugar or raw honey (to taste)

4–6cm fresh ginger, with skin on (to taste)

Beware, this makes a fizzy drink (see page 298)

TRADITIONALLY, this is a lightly fermented, slightly carbonated, non-alcoholic and extremely refreshing drink, made at home; in American colonial history it was popularly known as haymakers' punch, and served to thirsty farmworkers at harvest time.

–

Make up about 1.5 litres of sugar water solution. Mix well and bottle, so that the bottles are no more than three-quarters full.

Coarsely grate the ginger complete with skin, divide it into equal measures according to the number of bottles and add a measure to each of your bottles of sugar water. Seal and then shake thoroughly.

Leave out at room temperature in a cardboard box. The ferment will take between 2–5 days, depending on the ambient temperature and the sweetness of your sugar water.

Once ready to drink, refrigerate, and then pour through a tea strainer or small sieve, and enjoy over ice with a slice of lime or lemon.

Turmeric water?

Make as above, but replace ginger with fresh turmeric root. If you want to make the turmeric more bio-available, you will need to add some freshly ground pepper. Ginger water mixed with some turmeric water is very refreshing.

With vinegar?

Make as above, but add apple cider vinegar (see page 62–66), to taste, and some sea salt if you wish.

Traditional ginger beer

Makes about 8 litres

Fresh ginger root, with skin on

Freshly filtered water

About 650g rapadura sugar

4 lemons

Beware, this makes a fizzy drink (see page 298)

For ginger tea
Makes about 4 cups

1 tablespoon freshly grated ginger root

1 litre freshly filtered water

Raw honey, rapadura sugar or some slices of lemon

This is very much a British drink and was extremely popular throughout Victorian times until the Second World War. The original ginger beer is made with a SCOBY, known, curiously, as a ginger beer plant, although it is very similar in appearance and feel to water kefir grains. Households would have had their own ginger beer plant, and made their ginger beer more or less alcoholic as they pleased. The recipe is simple: ginger, sugar, water, lemon or lime juice, and the ginger beer plant. It is also possible to make ginger beer with other cultures and starters such as water kefir grains and baker's yeast. You can buy ginger beer plants online and then make ginger beer and nourish your own ginger beer plant, as for your water kefir grains. It is also possible to make ginger beer with a simple homemade culture, using ginger, sugar and water, known as a ginger bug.

Ginger beer with a ginger bug

Grate 2 teaspoons of ginger into a large jam jar, add 2 teaspoons of white sugar and 325ml of filtered water. Seal, shake, and leave out at room temperature for 24 hours.

Every day, feed the culture (your bug) with the same quantities of ginger and white sugar, for about 7 days, or until you see the ginger culture bubbling happily.

Make the ginger beer itself in a large ceramic bowl or stainless-steel jam pan.

Boil a full kettle of fresh filtered water and pour 2.5 litres into the bowl and dissolve the rapadura in this. Add the juice of the 4 lemons, and then 4.5 litres of cold fresh filtered water. Pour the liquid from your ginger bug into the bowl, but keep the sediment. Stir well, and then cover the bowl or pan. Leave out at room temperature for about a week, and then bottle and close the lids. Place in a cardboard box and leave out at room temperature for as long as necessary for this secondary fermentation to carbonate the drinks, but be careful about the pressure in the bottles. (See the advice on carbonation on page 296). When carbonated, refrigerate.

For your next production, keep half the ginger bug sediment, add this to your new bug and make as above.

Ginger tea

This is used for sore throats, coughs, colds and flu throughout Asia.

Steep the grated ginger in boiling water for a few minutes. Strain when you serve, adding honey, rapadura or some slices of lemon, as you wish.

Kvass

Makes about 4 litres

Some old rye or spelt bread (350–400g will usually be plenty), chopped or torn

Dried herbs (mint and/or thyme)

For the ferment

125ml refreshed sourdough mother (see page 270) or some water kefir grains (from a friend or purchase online)

Large pinch of salt

125ml raw honey or rapadura sugar

Juice of 1 lemon

Beware, this makes a fizzy drink (see page 298)

Equipment

Preserving pan or a large mixing bowl

Cheesecloth or old tea towel

Large, wide-neck jar (approx. 3 litres)

KVASS IS THE POPULAR FERMENTED SOFT DRINK OF EASTERN EUROPE, made with old bread. Sour and bubbly, very slightly alcoholic, it is thirst-quenching and extremely popular during the hot and dry summer months; small-scale producers continue to sell traditional kvass by the glass, jug or bottle dispensed from mobile kvass wagons or simple street stalls.

After the collapse of the Soviet Union, the arrival of sweet, inert and addictive industrial soft drinks from the West seemed, at first, to be a popular replacement for this local brew, but a combination of patriotic zeal, mistrust of the multinationals and a fatigue for the simple, one-dimensional false pleasure of colas and other flavoured carbonated sugar waters has ensured a recent kvass revival. A popular kvass brand in Russia is Nikola, (ne kola means 'not cola' in Russian) and they are fully engaged, as you might expect, in an anti-colanisation campaign. Good for them.

You can make kvass with more or less any sort of good old bread; the darker the bread, the darker the brew. Rye is the grain of choice in Russia and the Ukraine.

Pre-ferment

Dry the bread chunks in a warm oven for 15 minutes.

Throw the chunks into a large pan, such as a stainless-steel jam pan, or a large mixing bowl, and scatter over some dried herbs.

Pour boiled water over the bread and press the bread down so that it is submerged. Ideally, you want to add about 4 litres of water. Place a plate on top of the bread to keep it immersed in the water. Cover with a cloth and leave overnight.

Press, wring and squeeze

Next morning, your task is to strain and press the liquid from the soggy bread. Line a colander with an old tea towel or some cheesecloth and set it over a 5-litre bowl. Ladle some of the soggy bread and liquid into the lined colander, press the liquid through, and then draw together the corners of the cloth so you can wring out the remaining liquid into the bowl.

Sour and bubbly, very slightly alcoholic, it is thirst-quenching and extremely popular during the hot and dry summer months.

Throw away or compost the bread as you go, and continue to press, wring and squeeze all the liquid out of the bread.

Ferment

Transfer the liquid into a suitable large jar (it won't need to be sealed) and for every 4 litres you make, add the ingredients for the ferment. Stir thoroughly, leave out at room temperature, and then cover with a cloth for a day or two, stirring when you remember to do so, such as morning and evening. Once it starts to bubble vigorously, it's time for the secondary fermentation, in a sealed bottle.

Secondary fermentation

Bottle the kvass and seal. Place in a secure cardboard box (see the advice on carbonation on page 298) and check for pressure after 12, 18 and 24 hours – kvass is renowned for its fast fermentation and lively carbonation.

Once sufficiently fizzy, move the bottles to the refrigerator to stabilise fermentation and carbonation.

For your next batch, keep back some of the kvass to use as a starter – you won't need any sourdough starter or other culture.

Turmeric (golden) milk and tea

Golden milk
Makes 4 cups

350ml raw milk or almond, hazelnut or coconut milk

1 heaped teaspoon freshly grated turmeric root

1 heaped teaspoon freshly grated ginger

A twist of freshly ground black pepper

Pinch of ground cinnamon

Raw honey to taste (optional)

Rosehip powder (optional), to serve

Turmeric tea
Makes as much as your pot can manage

4 slices of fresh turmeric, with skin on

4 slices of fresh ginger, with skin on

1 star anise

1 crushed cardamom pod

Some flakes broken off a stick of cinnamon

A crack of freshly ground black pepper

All day turmeric and ginger tea
To make an all-day infusion, just for you

4 thin slices of fresh ginger, with skin on

4 thin slices of fresh turmeric root with skin on

A twist of black pepper

1 teaspoon coconut oil

ONE OF THE MOST SATISFYING and pleasurable ways to enjoy the considerable benefits of turmeric is by making a turmeric hot milk drink, known as golden milk, or by brewing an infusion of turmeric, to make turmeric tea. The Okinawans of southern Japan, in particular, are prodigious drinkers of turmeric tea and turmeric drinks; interestingly, they are also world leaders in longevity.

The powers of turmeric have been known for millennia, yet only now rediscovered and heralded as a new superfood. Turmeric contains curcumin, which possesses antioxidant and anti-inflammatory properties. We also know that to make the curcumin bio-available to us, we need to consume turmeric warm, with black pepper and with good fats.

Throughout Asia, turmeric has been long appreciated for its ability to ease digestion and digestive upsets, to ward off colds and sore throats, and also to fight depression. Golden milk is the perfect bedtime drink.

Golden milk

Combine, stir and warm the ingredients in a pan until the milk is nicely hot, but do not boil.

Serve in a warmed cup with a dusting of rosehip powder.

Turmeric tea

Boil the kettle and make a brew of these ingredients, and let it steep for 4–5 minutes.

Serve with coconut milk.

All day turmeric and ginger tea

Pour boiling or recently boiled water over the ginger and turmeric slices in your favourite mug. Crunch some pepper into the drink and add a teaspoon of coconut oil. The root slices and the pepper will settle on the bottom of the mug and the coconut oil will float on the surface.

Stir, sip and top up with fresh hot water throughout the day.

Sweet or salt lassi

Plain sweet lassi
Each makes about 4 glasses

500ml plain yogurt – soured style

100ml ice-cold water or, for a richer sweet lassi, 100ml raw milk

2–3 tablespoons rapadura sugar

Pinch of ground cardamom

Some pistachios or almonds, finely chopped

Mango lassi

500ml plain yogurt – soured style

300g puréed mango

1–2 tablespoons rapadura sugar, depending on the sweetness of the mango

Pinch of ground cardamom, to sprinkle on top of each glass

Salt lassi

500ml plain yogurt – soured style

100ml raw milk

Large pinch of sea salt

½ teaspoon rapadura sugar

¼ teaspoon ground cardamom

¼ teaspoon ground lightly roasted cumin

Some finely chopped or sliced fresh mint leaves – either whizz up in the mixture or sprinkle on each glass, or both

Turmeric lassi

500ml plain yogurt – soured style

100ml raw milk

Large pinch of sea salt

Generous grinding of black pepper

½ teaspoon rapadura sugar

1 teaspoon grated turmeric root

Some grated fresh ginger, to sprinkle on each glass

LASSI IS THE MILKSHAKE OF THE INDIAN SUBCONTINENT, popular from the foothills of the Himalaya to the beaches of Sri Lanka, in winter as well as summer. Creamily nourishing, it is also particularly thirst-quenching in hot weather, and typically one is offered a choice of sweet or salt plain lassi, usually served with a meal, the heat and spiciness of which will be tempered by the lassi.

Lassi is especially delicious when made with fresh raw milk (in India and Pakistan this could be buffalo milk) and homemade yogurt, which is more tart than sweet. Whereas street vendors might whip up a lassi with a wooden whisk, blitzing milk, yogurt and ice in a simple blender will more than suffice. Cardamom, with a touch of sugar, makes for a perfect harmony with the yogurt and milk.

–

Plain sweet lassi
Put the yogurt, water or milk, sugar and cardamom in the blender. Blitz for about 1 minute, add ice cubes and process for 1 minute more. Pour, and sprinkle some finely chopped pistachios or almonds on each glass.

Mango lassi
Make as for plain sweet lassi.

Salt lassi
Make as for plain sweet lassi.

Turmeric lassi
Make as for plain sweet lassi.

Super-creamy and rich lassi
To your yogurt base, add some cubes of very cold butter, some cream, or some homemade cardamom ice cream or all three.

Coconut milk

Milk from fresh coconut
Makes about 350ml

2 mature coconuts

250ml warm water

Milk from shredded coconut
Makes about 1 litre

150g unsweetened shredded coconut

1 litre hot, but not boiling, water

Coconut is also rich in iron, magnesium, phosphorus, potassium and iodine. It deserves to be respected as an authentic superfood.

COCONUT MILK IS TRADITIONALLY MADE by grating fresh coconut meat and squeezing out its milk, which you can easily do at home, or there's a somewhat more convenient solution, which is to process packaged shredded, unsweetened coconut with some hot water. You can't use desiccated coconut; it is too fine and too dry. Coconut milk is of course not the same as coconut water, which is the fluid found in immature green coconuts and often in older coconuts too.

Coconuts may have less protein than other nuts, but they more than make up for this with their superb balance of rich nutrients and in particular, fatty acids. The creamy rich texture, taste and satiety of coconut flesh and milk is mostly derived from its high fat content. Coconut is 60 per cent fat, of which 92 per cent is saturated fat. Of these fatty acids, perhaps the most important is lauric acid, an extremely powerful medium-chain fatty acid, which not only helps to strengthen the immune system, but also offers potent antiviral, antifungal and antimicrobial benefits, as well as providing a quick source of energy. Coconut is also rich in iron, magnesium, phosphorus, potassium and iodine. It deserves to be respected as an authentic superfood.

Milk from fresh coconut

Drain out the coconut water by piercing the two soft spots. Enjoy the coconut water just as it is.

Extract the meat

Either put the coconuts in the oven at 180°C/gas 4 for 10–15 minutes, which will crack the shells open and make them easier to split, or you can go at them with a hammer.

Separate the meat from the shell using a sharp knife, and then slice away the dark skin.

Extract the milk

Next, either coarsely dice or grate the coconut and put it in a food processor with 250ml warm water and whirl it up. Either way, you end up with a mess of coconut flesh that you need to press to extract the milk.

Line a sieve with a piece of cheesecloth or muslin, fill it with the coconut flesh, and then gather up the cloth and squeeze out the milk. This first pressing of the coconut is thick and rich, and typically would be used for puddings and sauces.

You can also extract a second pressing of the coconut flesh by letting it sit, wrapped in the muslin, in a bowl of warm water, for about 1 hour. Squeeze the milk from the muslin again. This time the milk is thinner, and much more of a drink. Store in the fridge for 4–5 days.

Refrigerate the coconut milks; they will keep for up to 4 days. If they separate, shake or stir before using.

Ferment the coconut milk

Naturally you can ferment coconut milk; use kefir grains for this. Drop the grains into a jar of coconut milk, cover with a piece of muslin secured by a rubber band, and leave out at room temperature. Taste every 6–8 hours or so and, once to your liking, remove the grains and chill the fermented coconut milk.

Milk from shredded coconut

Put the shredded coconut and the hot water in a food processor and whirl up until it is thick and creamy.

Now follow the steps on page 318 to extract the milk by squeezing the coconut mass in a piece of muslin.

Milkshakes

Milkshake vanilla ice cream
Enough to three-quarters
fill a 500ml tub

300ml Guernsey or Jersey cream, or other thick raw cream

50ml raw milk, otherwise Guernsey or Jersey

6–8 egg yolks from pastured hens, lightly whisked

1 tablespoon raw honey or rapadura sugar

2–3 teaspoons vanilla essence

Ultimate banana milkshake
Serves 4

2 ripe bananas

2 egg yolks (at least)

As much milkshake vanilla ice cream (see above) as you like – say 200g

50ml Guernsey or Jersey cream, or other thick raw cream

200ml raw milk, otherwise Guernsey or Jersey

1 tablespoon fermented cod liver oil (very much hardcore/optional as the oil does taint the drink somewhat, and not indulgently)

WHEN YOU WANT TO COMBINE DEEP NOURISHMENT WITH REAL PLEASURE in a convenient, quick and easy-to-prepare package, a milkshake is tops. It's also a family drink, loved by young and old, and there's no time of the day not appropriate for whizzing up a milkshake.

Milkshake is also the perfect moreish drink to bring really important nourishment to those who need it the most, particularly children, the infirm and the elderly. Made with raw dairy ingredients or cultured raw dairy (such as kefir), and raw egg yolks from pastured hens, it will provide a truly vital and bio-available source of the most important vitamins our diet lacks, especially during winter – the fat-soluble vitamins A, D, E and K. Vitamin D is a particularly difficult vitamin to acquire in winter in the more temperate regions, when the sun is low in the sky for half the year, and so vitamin D deficiency is common. All these vitamins are found in specific foods, particularly when very fresh and well grown or reared, such as raw eggs, raw dairy, leafy green vegetables, carrots, some fruits, offal, fish and their oils, such as krill and cod liver oil. Children tend to shun such ingredients and supplements. Now, with a milkshake a day you can make this deep nourishment delicious and moreish besides. What could be more satisfying?

The foundation of a good milkshake is homemade vanilla ice cream. This recipe is specifically designed for super vitamin milkshakes, as it is very firm when frozen and packed with delicious raw ingredients. It's perfect for smashing up in a blender with whatever seasonal and indulgent ingredients you find.

–

Milkshake vanilla ice cream
Combine all the ingredients in your ice-cream maker, taste for vanillariness and adjust, and then churn until as firm as possible. Enjoy a spoon or more of the scoopable ice cream before freezing. When frozen it does form a dense block, so you will need to carve it out with a bluntish knife when making milkshakes.

Ultimate banana milkshake
Place some glasses in the freezer for at least 15 minutes to frost them. Whizz up all the ingredients in the blender. Serve immediately in the super-chilled glasses.

Daily milkshakes
To ensure your milkshakes are popular every day, vary your repertoire of flavours, such as: chocolate, almond butter and banana, strawberries and raspberries (freeze-dried or fresh), blueberries and banana, forest fruits, mango, maple syrup.

And mix it up with the dairy too, with: plain yogurt, dairy kefir or soured cream.

Grain milk drinks

MAKING A DRINK FROM RICE IS NOT A NEW IDEA. There are ancestral recipes found from the Middle East and throughout Asia for rice drinks, often fermented. In China, a freshly made rice drink is renowned as a gentle form of nourishment during illness. Most recipes are unsweetened; fermented or cooked rice is naturally sweet, as its starch is broken down into simple sugars, including glucose. Although sweeter than cow's milk, rice drinks do not contain the complex selection of nutrients, minerals and good bacteria found in raw dairy milk; however, rice milk is of course gluten, lactose and cholesterol free.

Various grains can be made into drinks; the recent popularity of dairy alternatives has ensured that there's an increasing selection of grain drinks available, such as oats, barley and quinoa, as well as rice. If you are buying ready-made grain drinks, always check the list of ingredients; many are sweetened with refined sugars, most include unpronounceable or bizarre ingredients you wouldn't keep in your larder, let alone drink willingly.

A note or two on dairy alternative drinks: they do tend to separate when stored. Shake or stir to combine. They may also split in hot drinks, so let the drink cool a little before adding a grain milk. Can you froth them? Some will, some won't. Try. You may well find you need to steam them more intensely than cow's milk.

—

Brown rice drink

Brown rice drink
Makes about 2 litres

100g brown rice, ideally sprouted first (see pages 98–101)

2 litres water

1 teaspoon sea salt

60ml whey (see pages 41–43) or water kefir grains (optional, from a friend or purchase online)

Cook the rice in the water for about 2 hours; it must be very mushy. If you have sprouted your rice, this will take about 1–1½ hours.

Mash this mush through a food mill into a glass storage jar, stir in the salt and refrigerate if you are not adding whey or kefir grains.

If you use whey, seal the jar and leave at room temperature to ferment for 2–3 days before refrigerating. If you are fermenting with water kefir grains, leave the jar open, but cover with a piece of muslin and secure. Leave for 2–3 days before refrigerating.

Dilute your rice drink with more water if necessary. Store in the fridge for a couple of days.

Almond drink
Makes about 500ml

175g raw almonds, with skin on

500ml freshly filtered water, and more for soaking

Sea salt (optional)

Sweetness, such as date syrup, raw honey, rapadura sugar (optional)

Flavours, such as vanilla extract or paste (optional)

60ml whey (see pages 41–43) or water kefir grains (optional, from a friend or purchase online)

Quinoa or oat drink
Make as above, but first soak your oats or quinoa in warm water, drain, rinse and drain again before cooking.

Ideally use sprouted quinoa and oats. If you do, there's no need to soak overnight.

Nut and seed milk drinks
You can make a drink from pretty well any edible nut or seed. It's a simple process of preparing the nuts or seeds, usually by soaking, then

Equipment
Muslin, cheesecloth or a nut bag

milling, straining and diluting with water if necessary, or – taking it one or two steps further – to activate the nuts and seeds before grinding, and also to ferment your nut and seed drink with whey or water kefir grains.

Always select raw nuts and seeds. For more information about activating nuts and seeds, please see pages 102-5. As for adding salt or sweetener to your drinks – that's entirely your call. Many people like to add date syrup to almond drink, and others reach for the sea salt too. The walnut drink tastes good with vanilla. Finally, you always end up with some pulp or meal after straining nuts or seeds. What to do with this? You can add it wet to smoothies, porridge, biscuit recipes or you could spread it out on a baking sheet and dry at a low temperature in the oven, or a dehydrator. Once completely dried out, bag and store in the freezer, like breadcrumbs.

Almond drink

Soak the almonds so that they are immersed in warmish water overnight or for up to 2 days. By about the second day they will have swollen a little, indicating that they want to sprout. Catch them before they sprout, and you will make a creamy, flavoursome drink.

Drain, rinse and then slip off the skins by squeezing each nut between thumb and forefinger. This is a therapeutic process, and also a social one, so invite a friend to help. Removing the skins will make the drink less bitter. There's tannin in the skins, and it may not agree with your digestion. But if you don't mind the skins, leave them on.

Throw the almonds into your blender along with the water. Pulse and whizz at the highest speed for at least 2–3 minutes, so that you create a smooth, thick, whiteish paste.

Pour the paste through a sieve lined with muslin, cheesecloth or a nut bag and press the solids with a spoon, gather up the cloth or bag and squeeze the nut meal inside as hard as you can to extract all the liquid.

Taste your almond drink and dilute, salt, sweeten or flavour as you wish. Refrigerate in a glass jar or bottle and use within 2–3 days.

If you are up for fermenting, add the whey, seal the jar and leave at room temperature to ferment for 2–3 days before refrigerating. Or, if you are fermenting with water kefir grains, leave the jar open, but cover with a piece of muslin and secure.

Pecan drink

Follow the almond recipe, using the same weight of pecans, but soak them in salted warmish water for no more than 4 hours before making the drink.

Walnut drink

Follow the almond recipe, using the same weight of pecans, but soak them overnight.

Jamu kunyit
Turmeric tonic

Makes 1 litre

10cm fresh turmeric root
(no need to peel if fresh)

1 litre water

1 teaspoon fresh tamarind,
seeds removed

1 teaspoon raw honey

1 teaspoon lime juice

Twist of freshly ground
black pepper

Sea salt

JAMU KUNYIT IS A TRADITIONAL INDONESIAN TONIC valued by people of all ages for its power to heal ailments or enhance beauty, strength or stamina. This elixir is made from turmeric, tamarind, lemon and honey, and is similarly highly regarded in Ayurvedic (Indian) and Chinese medicine.

Turmeric is fast becoming recognised as yet another new (old) superfood, largely driven by the realisation that its primary ingredient, curcumin, is an extremely powerful antioxidant and immune system booster. To be fully bio-available, it needs to be heated or combined with good fats (animal or vegetable) or with freshly ground pepper, as in this tonic. Many Asian recipes combine all three turmeric activators.

If turmeric is the current newly rediscovered food, then tamarind will be the next ancestral food hero. Tamarind is truly nutrient dense, containing the antioxidant tartaric acid, protective phytochemicals and many essential minerals including potassium, iron and copper, and is also a rich source of vitamins.

Whizz up the turmeric, water and tamarind in a blender. Blend for a few minutes, and then strain through a sieve into a glass.

Add the honey, lime juice, pepper and a pinch of salt for added flavour. Be sure to include the pepper – it is essential to get the full benefit of the turmeric.

Store in the fridge for no longer than 3–4 days.

A note on fresh tamarind

It's best to buy fresh tamarind with the shells on. Peel, remove the seeds and scrunch the fruit into a ball. Seal the fruit in a container and leave somewhere warmish. It will ferment and taste sour (no longer sweet and sour) when ready.

If turmeric is the current newly rediscovered food, then tamarind will be the next ancestral food hero.

Index

Credits & Acknowledgements

I have been guided and inspired by so many enthusiastic friends whilst on my Eat Right journey; some have given recipes, advice and detailed information, all have given their time generously. Thank you.

Aline Mattli (Beetroot & Goat's Cheese Salad)

Ban Stewart (Sprouted Lavash, and Sprouted Buckwheat with Spelt Pancakes - Blinis)

Peggy Sutton of To Your Health Flours (Sprouted Flour Cornbread)

Christopher C Brookes, of Meadow View artisanal and organic culinary school, and bed and breakfast (Honey-Crust Sprouted Spelt Bagels)

James Swift of Trealy Farm (Slow-Cooked Pork Belly)

Bertel Haugen (Kombucha) and his mother *Machteld Haugen* (Porridge Fritters)

Tanita de Ruijt (Mak Kimchi, Bubur Ayam and Jamu Kunyit)

Betina Hette (Poached Wild Salmon with Traditional Norwegian Butter Sauce and Cucumber Salad)

Karlijn Audenaerde (Dutch-Style Gingerbread Loaf with Spelt and Honey)

Akiko Kimura (Tsukemono, Shio-Koji, Saba no Misoni, Amazake and Mishoshiru,)

Romi Chan (Mak Kimchi, Kimchi Omelette, Kimchi Jigae)

Per Brix Merlin (Roast Chicken, Danish Style)

Limpet Barron, of Tangerine Dream Café, Chelsea Physic Garden (Porcini and Potato Sprouted Wheat Tartlets, Sprouted Multigrain Soda Bread, and assistance with the Oatcakes)

Aidan Chapman and *Matt Jones* at Bread Ahead (Creating a Sourdough Mother in 5 days, Sprouted Sourdough Pizza, Sprouted Spelt Sourdough, the No-Knead Method, Sprouted Wholewheat Quick Loaf Baked in a Dutch Oven, Sourdough Rye Bread)

Magda Devaris, of One The Square, Forest Row (Quinoa and Aubergine Salad, Late Summer Garden Salad, Sprouted Oats and Activated Seed Flapjacks, Activated Seed and Nut Energy Balls)

Natalie Wheen (Raw Fresh Salted Sardines, and Other Fish, Guacamole)

Yasuko Fukuoka (Hatsuga Genmai)

Jennifer and *Jordan* at Fab Ferments.

Hannah Crum, The Kombucha Mamma.

Alison and *David Leo-Wilson* at Anglesey Sea Salt, Halen Mon.

Steve Meyerowitz, Sproutman.

Sandor Katz, Julian Woods, Jo & Alex Higgs, Peter Scandrett & Nicola Child, Sarah Batt, Annie Dru, Louise Brocklehurst and her father, *Neil Brocklehurst*.

All the farming photography took place at Tablehurst & Plaw Hatch Community Farms.

Liz Charnell, Nir Halfon, Tali Eichner and *Robin Hall* welcomed us to Plaw Hatch Farm, and at Tablehurst Farm it was *Rachel Hanney, Rob Tilsley, David Junghans* and *Oliver Fynes-Clinton* who enthusiastically organised our visits.

Author photography whilst shopping was made easy at Chegworth Valley Farm Shop, Borough Market.

Philipp Kauffmann of Original Beans gave me some of his truly inspiring chocolate wisdom, and his chocolate.

Natalie Wheen and *Deborah MacMillan*, Avlaki Olive Oils. Natalie wrote an olive oil rant for me, and I tempered it.

Isabelle Legeron and *Deborah Lambert*, RAW Wine Fair. Isabelle's book, Natural Wine, is essential reading. As Isabelle once said to me: 'Nick, you make wise food choices; you should do the same for wine.' Admittedly the language was more colourful than this.

Dr. Gerald Pollack of The University of Washington; his TED talk on water is wonderfully thought provoking.

Laura Ledas, of ellenutrition, read every recipe and essay, and provided thoughtful and nutritionally wise comments.

John Naunton Davies scrutinised the manuscript in Barra, Plockton and White Waltham, insightfully. *James Cowderoy* helped too.

An apology: some 200 recipes were assembled, and had to be cut back to fit – please accept my apologies if you did not make it this time.

This is the team that made this book with me:

Jenny Zarins, photographer. The evidence is here. So brilliant, so calm. Assisted by *Sam Harris*; *Nerissa Niva Nortje* was the assistant on the first shoot.

Julian Roberts, designer, and his team at Irving & Co, for effortless, superlative design and style.

Alison Roberts, stylist. Truly meticulous styling, an immaculate home as our location, generous hospitality, and more.

Alison would like to thank *Fiona* and *Emma* at David Mellor and *Natalie*, *Mark* and *Catherine* at New Craftsmen for the generous loan of the beautiful handmade tableware and accessories from their wonderful and inspiring shops which added soul to the styling of this book.

Tabitha Hawkins styled the first shoot.

Linda Tubby and *Annie Nichols*, the cooks; between them, on different shoot days, they prepared the food so brilliantly, and always with enthusiasm. And *Elisa Crestani* helped them. On the last day *Laura Urschel* found the fish we needed.

Araminta Whitely and *Alice Saunders* at LAW, as literary agents, are very good at teasing the best out of me.

You really are the dream team. Thank you one and all.

Assistance and inspiration:

BBC Radio 3 Late Junction. So many late nights. So much good music.

12 year old Glen Garioch. A very good whisky. Thank you for the introduction James.

Original Beans chocolate. Excellent with the above.

The Weston A. Price Foundation and the Price-Pottenger Foundation; for their thought-provoking and inspirational publications and conferences.

Peter Everington & *Romi Chan*. Thank you for welcoming me to your home in the mountains; it is the perfect venue for writing.

My publisher:

Kyle believed, and *Sophie Allen* delivered. *Stephanie Evans* edited with great sensitivity.